Praise for
Earthly Bodies

"In this triumphant and vibran[t] [ ] [ ] history, Vanessa Chakour grapples [ ] [ ] [ ] the
natural world—including in her [ ] [ ] that
inspires joy and courage. I loved i[ ]

— SY MONTGOMERY, BESTSELLIN[G] [ ] *Creature:
A Memoir in Thirteen Animals*

"Part memoir, part modern-day bestiary, *Earthly Bodies* is a must read for
humans who have become estranged from their animal selves. Vanessa
Chakour draws surprising connections that will make you look at the natural world around you with fresh eyes—whether you're coexisting with
wolves in the wild or bats in the city. A thoughtful reminder of all that is
wild within each of us."

— AMY SHEARN, AWARD-WINNING AUTHOR OF *Dear Edna Sloane, Animal
Instinct*, AND OTHER NOVELS

"Somewhere between a field guide about wild animals and an intimate
memoir about a woman's journey toward wildness and truth, Vanessa
Chakour's *Earthly Bodies* will make you think deeply about the relationship between your internal and external environments, and the way that
each is threatened by modern life. I left this book feeling much more attuned to animal life—my own included."

— ERICA BERRY, AUTHOR OF *Wolfish*

"The magic of Vanessa Chakour is that her words are both balm and flint,
encouraging us to reconsider how we are living our lives, where we are living them, and whether we are alive enough in these earthly bodies we are
given. I couldn't put this essential and sensual book down."

— COURTNEY MAUM, AUTHOR OF *The Year of the Horses*

"In a time when humans are taking over and literally killing our magnificent planet and at the same time killing ourselves, Vanessa Chakour's
Earthly Bodies, an inspiring journey into the intersection of our inner
landscapes and the wisdom of the wild, can lead the way. She clearly shows
that personal rewilding—connecting with nature from the inside out—is
the easiest way to embrace our animal nature, heal the fractured landscapes within and without, and, ultimately, learn to thrive alongside and

mutually coexist with all living beings on our shared planet. If *Earthly Bodies* doesn't change your head and heart and get you outside, little will."

—MARC BEKOFF, PHD, AUTHOR OF *Rewilding Our Hearts: Building Pathways of Compassion and Coexistence* AND *The Emotional Lives of Animals: A Leading Scientist Explores Animal Joy, Sorrow, and Empathy—and Why They Matter*

"An essential text for all those who feel a deep reverence and responsibility to the animal kingdom and their own personal growth, power, and service to the Earth."

—HEIDI SMITH, MA, RH (AHG), AUTHOR OF *The Uncommon Book of Prayer: A Guide to Co-Creating with the Universe*

"In this timely call to return to our animal bodies, Vanessa Chakour invites us to remember our embeddedness with other beings and the Earth we are fortunate to share. It is a beautiful book about healing, wonder, and belonging."

—DR. CHRISTINE WEBB, AUTHOR OF *The Arrogant Ape*

"Through poignant storytelling and keen observation, Chakour illuminates the lives of often misunderstood creatures, weaving their struggles with her own and our human journey. Her deep empathy and scientific rigor shine through, making *Earthly Bodies* an absorbing, transformative journey that reminds us of our responsibility to protect and cherish all life on Earth."

—CAMILLA FOX, FOUNDER AND EXECUTIVE DIRECTOR OF PROJECT COYOTE

"A page-turner that grapples with the questions of our time. In a technology-driven world where we're barraged by information about humans' impact on the globe, how can we look to our animal kin to reconnect to our natural rhythms and live as good stewards of the Earth? Chakour's personal narrative is interwoven with animal stories as she finds love, tenderness, and meaning as a human animal looking to fellow creatures for guidance and direction."

—MALLORY LANCE, EDITOR IN CHIEF OF *Ravenous Zine*

"*Earthly Bodies* is a fiercely compelling call to embrace our animal natures and rewild ourselves. . . . Equal parts profound and playful, *Earthly Bodies* urges us to listen closely to our bodies and our environments so we might one day learn to live in harmony with all of our kin, both wild and tamed."

—KRISTEN J. SOLLÉE, AUTHOR OF *Cat Call: Reclaiming the Feral Feminine*

PENGUIN LIFE

EARTHLY BODIES

VANESSA CHAKOUR is an author, naturalist, visual artist, former pro boxer, herbalist, and nature advocate. Drawing on a dynamic blend of her vast personal experiences over twenty-plus years, she facilitates rewilding retreats and courses, helping students access their inner wild while learning from the plants, fungi, and animals that share their ecosystems. She lives with her partner in Western Massachusetts, where they steward Mount Owen Forest Sanctuary, promoting ecosystem diversity and resilience through forest stewardship and propagation of native and endangered plants and fungi. Her previous book, *Awakening Artemis*, shares her journey of healing through the lens of twenty-four medicinal plants.

EARTHLY BODIES

Embracing Animal Nature

Vanessa Chakour

A Penguin Life Book

Excerpt from "To the Unseeable Animal" by Wendell Berry from *New Collected Poems*,
copyright © 1970, 2012 by Wendell Berry. Reprinted with the permission of The Permissions
Company, LLC on behalf of Counterpoint Press, counterpointpress.com.

Excerpt from "The Summer I Lived as a Wolf" by Pippa Little. Reprinted
with permission from Pippa Little.

LIBRARY OF CONGRESS CATALOGING-IN-PUBLICATION DATA
Names: Chakour, Vanessa, author.
Title: Earthly bodies: embracing animal nature / Vanessa Chakour.
Description: New York: Penguin Life, [2024] | "A Penguin Life book." |
Includes bibliographical references.
Identifiers: LCCN 2024006210 (print) | LCCN 2024006211 (ebook) |
ISBN 9780143137757 (trade paperback) | ISBN 9780593511879 (ebook)
Subjects: LCSH: Self-actualization (Psychology) | Animal behavior. |
Human behavior. | Human-animal relationships.
Classification: LCC BF637.S4 C4929 2024 (print) | LCC BF637.S4 (ebook) |
DDC 113/.8—dc23/eng/20240607
LC record available at https://lccn.loc.gov/2024006210
LC ebook record available at https://lccn.loc.gov/2024006211

Printed in the United States of America
1st Printing

Set in Tibere OT with Varius
Designed by Sabrina Bowers

For misunderstood creatures,
my beloved, and my beloved wild kin.

Remember the plants, trees, animal life who all have their tribes, their families, their histories, too. Talk to them, listen to them. They are alive poems.

—JOY HARJO, "REMEMBER"

Contents

HUMANS

PART FIVE
Helping

Author's Note

You only have to let the soft animal of your body
love what it loves.

—MARY OLIVER, "WILD GEESE"

When I was a child, foxes, birds, butterflies, bats, and all manner of creatures populated my storybooks, animated cartoons, and my imagination. My bedroom was piled high with stuffed animals and I read and reread books like *Winnie-the-Pooh*, *The Velveteen Rabbit*, *Horton Hatches the Egg*, and *Charlotte's Web*, where rabbits, elephants, and spiders were intelligent, complex, and feeling. I spent every moment I could in the woods behind our house on Summer Street in Western Massachusetts and imagined that, like Snow White, I could talk to woodland animals and befriend them. Dogs, wolves' ancestors, were my family members. We always had at least two large dogs living in our home; our patient and gentle Newfoundland named Daphne taught me how to walk. I would grab on to her thick black fur, slowly stand, and stumble as she led me around.

As I grew older and learned to stand on my own, a painful dissonance grew between my world—where more-than-human animals were family and friends with rich emotional lives—and the "civilized" world, where they were seen as intellectually and spiritually inferior, and in some cases devoid of emotion. Many of these contradictions were explored in the books I loved—in *Charlotte's Web* Fern eats bacon but is desperate to save beloved Wilbur—and made plain in Disney movies like *Dumbo* that portrayed the abuse of wild animals for "entertainment" and turned me off to circuses for good. Instead of understanding the relationship between animals and humans to be an interconnected ecological web, for much of recorded history the anthropocentric Western worldview arranged species into hierarchical pyramids like the Great Chain of Being, which places humans above the rest of nature. The top of a pyramid is a lonely, isolating place. Instinctually, I knew this arrangement was a lie.

Yet as I came of age I began to separate from my own animal body. As a teenager, I bypassed cries of hunger and learned to judge my body and her natural, primal urges as shameful, silencing howls within gilded cages of civilization. Wrestling with beauty myths and other cultural enclosures, I struggled internally. But human exceptionalism and the insatiable Big Bad Wolf were stories I could never fully believe in. Like Walt Whitman writes about more-than-human animals in "Song of Myself" (from the 1892 version), "Not one is dissatisfied, not one is demented with the mania of owning things, / Not one kneels to another, nor his kind that lived thousands of years ago, / Not one is respectable or unhappy over the whole earth." This was clear to me, too, and I remained fiercely devoted to wild creatures outside, even as I tamed my own animal body into womanhood.

When I was ten years old, I took my concerns straight to what I perceived as the "top" and wrote letters to the president about environmental injustice. I would later volunteer for Friends of Animals, intern at an animal rights magazine, protest circuses, and work on behalf of wolves. I studied our interconnection through ecology and confirmed my early instinct that the hierarchical pyramid was a lie. But something was missing. I adored animals and felt a sense of peace in nature, but like many humans, I had forgotten how to navigate my environment, and most of all—I had forgotten that I *am* nature. I was circling my own need to rewild. It wasn't until I studied herbalism and learned to forage food, becoming truly intimate with the land under my feet, that I began to feel like an animal aware of her ecosystem. A veil was lifted that had stood between me and the natural world. Home to countless plants, insects, birds, and fungi— whose health and well-being is inextricably connected to ours—the land around me came alive. It was then that I realized my work: to reconnect people to nature and, in my own way, remind humans that we, too, are animals. I began offering nature-connection experiences in collaboration with wildlife organizations like the Wolf Conservation Center in New York, where I finally met a wolf and truly learned to howl. At the Jaguar Rescue Center in Costa Rica, I learned about the emotional lives of howler monkeys firsthand and I had the honor of witnessing animal rescue, rehabilitation, and release.

When we forget that we are nature, we destroy the very home we and all other animals depend upon to survive and to thrive. Woven together in wild beauty, we belong here. We need not feel so lonely. This book is my invitation to you to embrace your animal nature.

Like gray wolves, black bears, howler monkeys, and other wild kin, our animal bodies offer us profound pleasure, love, wonder, healing, and connection. We thrive when we are at home in our skin, yet we often try to tame our bodies and deny our most basic primal needs. A human being detached from their bodily existence is not rational, yet it is rationality, our supreme intelligence, or in some cases the pious or spiritual part of us that we've been told makes humans different from fellow animals. Aggression toward animals and the animal aspects of ourselves is routine. This book is my own journey beyond the shame of pleasure, hunger, and the pressure to be "good," to embracing my earthly body and becoming whole.

The four parts of the book—enclosures, rehabilitation, soft release, and homing—follow the arc of an injured animal's return to nature and home. And, in our case, a more embodied, instinctual self. A self that heeds circadian rhythms, embraces pleasure, maintains necessary boundaries, and is able to express anger instead of bottling it up inside. In *Earthly Bodies*, I return to my childhood love of more-than-human animals as a lens through which I more clearly see myself and my animal body that works so hard to take care of me even when I've criticized her and tried to push her away. Celebrating the lives of twenty-three animal kin, I share aspects of our common ground while shedding misguided stories of separation.

For centuries, we've built walls—both literal and metaphorical—between ourselves and the "wild." We've built a world of comfort and control, and in doing so we've severed vital connections. Forgetting or denying that we are animals might also mean that we clear-cut forests and put our creature comforts above the well-being of the environment. Plants that at one point in time helped us heal have become scenery and, in some cases, weeds to eradicate. But land outside is much more than a resource to be exploited or scenery to be maintained. Framing nature as "other" alienates us from our planet, our home, leading us to lose touch with our interdependent roots. When we separate ourselves from the wild, we diminish our own wholeness, silencing howls that ache to be heard.

But something stirs beneath the surface—a yearning not just to observe the wild through our windows, smartphones, or screens but to embrace the wild as ourselves. The wild isn't just "out there," it is our flesh and bones.

This is a call not to abandon civilization but rather to rewild its misguided ideals and dangerous stories. It's about weaving the wisdom of the wild into the fabric of our human lives, transforming irrational fears of animals like bats and wolves into respect, and transforming feelings of isolation into the reality of interconnectedness. It's about learning to speak the language of Earth where howling is not a threat but a song of belonging. When we embrace our animal nature, we reclaim our wholeness, tear down walls, and truly come home.

Preface: Freedom

my muzzle carved air into four queendoms and I knew them all
as they knew me, tooth, soul, tatterdemalion heart,

and I flew, I think, in that time, when nobody needed
or shamed me and I was always hungry, bloody-tongued

but louche and free and supple, perfumed in pine and ashes.

—PIPPA LITTLE, "THE SUMMER I LIVED AS A WOLF"

It is dusk, the golden hour, and light outside is fading. Shadows stretch across the ground, adding depth and dimension to the landscape as the sun lowers in the sky. Safe inside, I am illuminated only by the glow of my computer screen. I hear other animals howling beyond my walls and I want to unplug and go out into the woods, too. But I know it isn't wise to walk alone—especially at night, especially as a woman—even though I'd like to linger beneath the moon and stars.

I close my computer and close my eyes. I imagine being wild and free with space to roam and no fear of predation. No traffic, no sirens, no leaf blowers nor the incessant hum of technology. Just crickets, melodic birdsong, and, if I'm lucky, the distant howl of wolves. There are no lawns, just rolling hills of dandelions, milkweed, yarrow, mugwort, and goldenrod alive with pollinators. I swim naked in fresh water with no shame of my animal body and as night falls, I wander in the moon's glow. I walk barefoot on beaches and look out at ocean, endless blue unmolested by cruise ships. In the salty air, with no backlog of digital messages or obligatory calls, my body and mind have space to breathe.

But when I open my eyes, I am tethered to technology. Technology is supposed to make life easier, but that supposed ease often feels like a trap. There are texts and emails that must be answered in order to keep the walls and the safety of my enclosure around me.

PART ONE

Enclosures

An enclosure is any structure or device used to restrict an animal to a limited amount of space, such as an aquarium, a pen, run, cage, pool, or New York City apartment. Some enclosures are necessary for safety, rehabilitation, or "soft," gradual release into the wild, while others are tragic, lonely spaces where animals will never learn crucial survival skills and will never be free.

Most of us are born into enclosures of some kind—social constraints and expectations, family dysfunction, religious beliefs, financial strain, or miseducation. Transitional life needs enclosures: an egg, a womb, a nest, a body. We outgrow these loving, protective spaces that nurture us for a period of time, and it can be painful to release our grip or open the gates to leave. But it's ultimately detrimental to stay.

We may have romantic ideas of being wild and free, but we are all injured animals. These are stories about finding freedom from and even within our enclosures.

May all beings everywhere be happy and free.

—SANSKRIT MANTRA

Gray Wolves

For centuries in Western and biblical lore, gray wolves have been portrayed as ravenous killers. Predatory villains in tales like *Little Red Riding Hood* and metaphors for evil in Christian literature, wolves have seeped into our consciousness as inherently bad, vicious, and violent. But this is not true. These majestic animals are essential ecological stewards that live in tight-knit, well-organized, loving families. When wolves hunt, they target sick, weak, and injured animals, and they support other species with their leftovers—coyotes, grizzly bears, black bears, and eagles have all been seen dining on wolf kills. Some historians believe that humans learned to hunt by watching and imitating wolves and that at some points in history we had a mutually beneficial relationship, helping each other survive. Our canine relatives roamed the Americas more than 700,000 years ago, long before humans set foot on the soil.

Ancestors of "man's best friend," wolves are often used as metaphors to describe the parts of us that are untamed and out of control—the lone wolf, werewolf, bloodthirsty stalker. Although loyal and loving to their own, wolves, unlike dogs, have no interest in doing what they are told. They might look a lot like our domesticated husky or German shepherd companions, but they aren't interested in pleasing us, nor should they be. One of the most maligned and misunderstood animals on Earth, the wolf has come to represent the parts of ourselves we fear.

Whenever and wherever men have engaged in the mindless slaughter of animals (including other men), they have often attempted to justify their acts by attributing the most vicious or revolting qualities to those they would destroy; and the less reason there is for the slaughter, the greater the campaign for vilification.

—FARLEY MOWAT, *Never Cry Wolf*

1

Predators and Prey

I clutch my walking sticks as the male hikers close the distance between us, ready to use their sharp metal tips for self-defense if necessary. *Maybe I should hike with a knife*, I think. A knife would serve a dual purpose, for wildcrafting and for self-defense. *Or finally get a dog.* I've been wanting to for so long, but it would mean I'd have to move. Dogs aren't allowed where I live.

It is autumn 2021 and I am hiking alone, far from home. Layers of rust-colored leaves feel like lush carpet beneath my feet. I can easily lose myself here, rooting around in the dirt, exploring creatures of the woodland floor. The act of wildcrafting—looking for and harvesting wild food and medicine—has reconnected me to my animal nature in a palpable way, making me intensely aware of my environment and the species in it. Wildcrafting connects me to my genetic memory, to my ancestors, and to the plants and fungi that have become invisible to so many of us. No longer able to notice or navigate the gifts of the wild, we can be surrounded by food and medicine and still die hungry.

I walk beyond the trail to explore a dark growth on a birch tree that looks like chaga mushroom, a medicinal mass of mycelium spiraling from the center of the trunk. Drawn in by the intricacies of the birch and fungi, I forget myself again, remaining as quiet and as still as possible so the woodland world can speak to me. Communing with the forest is bliss. But suddenly, I feel prickles down my spine. I hear faint, low voices carried on the wind. They are coming my way. Unfortunately, fear is part of my genetic memory, too. As a woman alone in the forest, there is always part of me that must be on alert. Not for wolves but for men.

There are no wolves here, but there should be. Gray wolves went extinct in Massachusetts in the mid-1800s during a time of all-out, brutal slaughter. After thousands of years of stewarding forests and coexisting with the Indigenous people of the Northeast, the animals were shot, poisoned, trapped, tortured, and burned by European bounty hunters until they were gone. The colonizers didn't just kill wolves; they killed them in incredibly sick and disturbing ways. In his 2004 book, *Vicious: Wolves and Men in America*, the author Jon T. Coleman describes the sadistic violence inflicted on wolves. He writes that the wolves in New England "died afraid, biting at steel contraptions and vomiting strychnine. Far from wistful, the deaths of the last wolves were spasms of terror that capped lifetimes of anxiety."

Analyzing folklore and historical anecdotes, Coleman explains how stories helped colonizers construct a reality to justify their expansion and cruelty; their stories and their desires meant demanding that nature be subdued and subservient. Unlike Native American tribes like the Ojibwe, whose word for wolf is *Ma'iingan*, "the one put here by that All-Loving Spirit to show us the way," European fairy tales and biblical stories fed cruelty and fear. The same animals respected as guides, protectors, and teachers by First Nations were villains wearing Grandma's nightie in European lore.

The engraved cover of the original *Little Red Riding Hood*, published in Paris in 1697, shows a naked girl lying beneath a wolf. In the story, she has just stripped off her clothes when she encounters the wolf. The story will end with her death in the wolf's jaws. The image and original tale, by Charles Perrault, were elaborations on French slang for when a girl lost her virginity, *elle avoit vû le loup*—"she'd seen the wolf."

Later in England, in 1875, a print by Walter Crane shows Little Red in her infamous cloak while a sinister wolf hovers close, wearing sheepskin—a biblical reference to the devil. Repeatedly mentioned in the scriptures as a stand-in for evil or Satan, wolves are also a symbol for men who prey on innocent, God-fearing Christians, unlike Jesus, the shepherd, who keeps his flock safe. In the Gospel according to Matthew, followers of Christ are told to be wary "of false prophets, which come to you in sheep's clothing, but inwardly they are ravening wolves." Amid a growing idea of a hostile wilderness, wolves were hunted to an extreme.

A human predator who believes they are ordained by God is much more dangerous than a predator who simply needs to eat.

I recently spoke with Regan Downey, the education director of the Wolf Conservation Center, about the misplaced fear of wolves. When I asked her about the danger of wolves, she just laughed and said, "Honestly, you're more likely to be killed by a vending machine." In North America, there have been only two fatal wild wolf attacks in the past century, and in the lower forty-eight, there have been none. Deer, on the other hand, cause 1.5 million roadway accidents per year, with 150 human fatalities and 10,000 personal injuries, not to mention that they are a vector for Lyme disease. The absence of wolves has created an imbalance that is far more dangerous than the mythical danger of their presence. Still, Regan told me, people regularly ask nervously what they should do if they encounter a wolf in the wild. She tells them, "Take a picture, you're so lucky!"

When I picked up *Wild: From Lost to Found on the Pacific Crest Trail* by Cheryl Strayed, I prepared myself for a tense reading experience. I know hiking alone on the Pacific Crest Trail—a 2,650-mile trail from Southern California to British Columbia—is a dangerous feat in and of itself, but I was more worried about Strayed's vulnerability as a young woman traveling and sleeping alone in a flimsy tent. She writes, "I knew that if I allowed fear to overtake me, my journey was doomed. Fear, to a great extent, is born of a story we tell ourselves, and so I chose to tell myself a different story from the one women are told. I decided I was safe. I was strong. I was brave. Nothing could vanquish me." I braced myself throughout the book, sure she would be preyed upon by men. I had no doubt that she was going to make it through the harrowing hike but was more astounded that she completed a 1,100-mile journey without being assaulted.

While it is unlikely that a depraved man is lurking in the woods, I remember when I became aware of the presence of that fear in my life. I must have been about nine years old. My friend and I walked almost a mile from the elementary school bus stop through the woods to home because Wildwood, our chosen school, was beyond our district. During one of our walks, my friend told me a story about a young girl who had been raped in the woods. "It happened along this very trail!" she said. *Rape? What is rape?* I wondered. I don't remember how she described it (she always seemed to be in the know), but I do remember that in that moment, I was robbed of my right to feel free in the forest. Like Little Red Riding Hood, who wandered off the trail to pick flowers, I had been innocent and naive. But after my friend's story, I was self-conscious and afraid. Every time I walked home afterward, I was skittish. I spoke with the forest, petitioning the animals and trees for protection.

Back in the present, the men come into view and my inner chatter dies down. They seem harmless. Sweet, even. As they pass, they smile. "Hello, beautiful day for a hike!" I smile and nod in agreement. Poor guys; if only they knew I was ready to attack. The dichotomy is as unfair to them as it is to me. Still, I remain vigilant in case my instinct about them is off. After living in New York City for over twenty years, I've become guarded.

In Brooklyn, I was repeatedly warned not to walk the woods of Prospect Park alone because "women have been raped there." But here in Western Massachusetts, hiking alone is a freedom I am unwilling to sacrifice. Every time I embark on a hike, I try to get a little more free from feeling like prey.

THE URBAN WILD

I began working on behalf of wolves from my Brooklyn apartment when federal district court judge Donald Molloy upheld the 2011 legislation removing Endangered Species Act protections for wolves in the Northern Rockies, the first time Congress legislatively delisted an endangered species. A restless boxing instructor and budding herbalist, I was preoccupied and became involved as much as I could in the fight to keep wolves a protected species, signing petitions, writing letters, and posting in the early days of social media. I felt ridiculous working on behalf of wolves—even plants—from my expensive little box in the city. More and more, I questioned what the hell I was doing in the urban wild. I have always felt more free in the woods, more "myself," more connected to my childhood sense of wonder. But I felt stuck. I didn't have enough money to leave, and even if I did, I worried, *How would I support myself and where would I go?* Also, a big problem: I was in love with a man deeply rooted in the urban landscape. I knew he would never leave, so I tried to contort myself into wanting what he wanted, too.

I moved to the city on a whim in the midnineties. I had an opportunity to assist a well-known photographer and thought I should experience the city, make connections while I was young, then pursue my dreams of living among more-than-human animals and working as a *National Geographic* photographer. But I fell in love fast. First with a man and then with New York City streets spilling over with art and subway cars, each with more diversity than the liberal academic enclave where I grew up could ever hope to contain. In New York City, there was freedom in being able to reinvent myself over and over and over again. I could be an artist, a boxer, an activist, an herbalist, anonymous. Whatever I chose, I could find my people and feed off of the pulsing, creative energy of the streets.

At the same time, there was the constant struggle to make ends meet, the overwhelming scent of garbage in summer instead of milkweed flowers and fecund earth, the sound of sirens at night instead of tree frogs and cricket songs, and—with the exception of resilient so-called weeds like dandelions—lifeless pavement and buildings everywhere echoing the haunting absence of wild animals. Beneath all the excitement and inspiration, I was hungry for nature and fell in and out of love with New York City all the time.

It was in October 2011, not long after wolves lost their protection as endangered species, that my relationship with the urban wild truly ruptured. On that particular day, dressed in my favorite miniskirt and comfy walking boots, I chose a purse handed down from my grandmother, one I rarely carried. It was a quilted brown leather bag with gold shoulder straps. I carried it only for special occasions and tonight was one of them. Between on-again portions of my on-again, off-again relationship with my longtime beloved, I had a date. I had just renewed my professional boxing license, hoping to fight for a championship so I might finally have something to show for all the years I spent in the orbit of the sport. I was training hard and felt capable of moving up the ranks and winning, and if I did, I would use

boxing as a platform for more important things like ecological awareness and wolves. Feeling confident and filled with possibility, I zipped
my new boxing license into my skirt pocket along with my key and
strolled through Brooklyn streets with my grandmother's purse on
my shoulder to meet my date. It was a beautiful, balmy autumn night.
I remember enjoying that walk so much.

My date and I had dinner, wandered around Fort Greene Park,
and when it was time, I insisted on walking home alone. I had lived in
New York City for almost twenty years, loved walking around at all
hours, and considered myself street smart. I'd lived in rough neighborhoods, so Fort Greene, in comparison, was milquetoast. Plus, I
didn't have money for a cab and didn't want to admit it.

On a dark residential street, as I gazed dreamily at texts from my
date, I suddenly got that feeling. I sensed I was being stalked and noticed three guys nearby giving off weird, nervous energy. I needed to
strategize, so I nonchalantly turned down a block alight with lamps
and they went the other way. Relieved, and nearly in a busy area, I
went back to reading my date's texts, but soon my goose bumps rose
again. I heard soft scuffling behind me, then hands grabbed me from
all sides. Fingers wrapped tightly around my waist and forced me to
the ground while two cold hands pressed over my eyes and mouth. I
didn't scream, I didn't howl; I couldn't. The assault was a smooth, silent operation. I became incredibly calm, as though sedated.

My shoulder was yanked until the chain of my purse gave way. I
felt a twinge of sadness. *My grandmother's purse!* I kept my phone in
my hand until I felt a jab in the left side of my gut, then a hot breath
and vicious whisper: *Bitch, give me your phone or I'll shoot you.* I released my grip. My next thought was, *They might rape me.* I left my
body and dissociated. That's when someone—my savior—came out
of her apartment to take out her trash and they ran. I wouldn't realize
the impact of the trauma until the next day.

That evening when I reported the assault at the nearest police precinct, I was stoic; in retrospect, I know I was in shock. *Why didn't you just punch them?* the police asked, laughing. The only thing left zipped in the pocket of my leather miniskirt, apart from my key, was my professional boxing license, and the cops found this hilarious. I had been afraid I might be raped. I was wearing a miniskirt, walking alone at night on the city streets like Little Red Riding Hood through the woods. I sensed that it would likely be suggested that I was foolish and that somehow the attack was my fault. Ridiculed by men who were paid to "protect and serve," I felt angry and increasingly vulnerable.

I didn't press charges because I didn't get a good look at the perpetrators. The police said I could go and they'd be in touch if anything turned up. *Go?* The precinct was even farther from my apartment than my date had been. It was around 11:00 p.m. at this point and I had no phone and no money for a cab. Did it not occur to them that I may not want to walk alone on city streets after being mugged? I had to ask for a ride. But when I got into an unmarked car with two male policemen I felt trapped and incredibly unsafe. Only when we arrived at my apartment door did my clenched body let go, and I breathed a deep sigh of relief.

Inside my apartment, I shrugged off the experience as a nuisance—canceling cards, replacing money and IDs. Mostly, I was embarrassed. I'd been careless. I was supposed to be street smart. I emailed my friend Morisha and a boxer I'd dated, now a friend, who grew up in Crown Heights. He made me feel better. *Everybody gets jumped*, he said, as though I had finally undergone a Brooklyn rite of passage. I told fighters at the gym the next day and they said I was lucky, that it was my boxing training that saved me. *If you hadn't had the fight training, known how to remain calm under stress*, they told me, *you might have been shot.* Maybe.

But fear was lurking inside my body, waiting. It emerged as the sky grew dark that night. As I got out of the subway on my way home, a person walking fast suddenly appeared behind me and adrenaline rushed through my body in a surge I'd never felt before. Panicked and skittish as people crowded at my heels, I grounded myself by taking a deep, deep breath. I kept walking. Eventually, the surge of commuters dispersed and I began to breathe normally. Until a skateboard swished by and my internal alarm went off again: *run, Run, RUN!* I had been training women to fight for years, helping them walk around the city with more confidence, and now here I was, afraid.

Craving safe space in nature more than ever, I walked the short distance between my apartment and my community garden as much as possible over the following months, spending as much free time as possible outdoors, behind the safety of the garden's locked gate. Inside my apartment, I continued to work on behalf of the environment and wolves. And it was there, amid my online activism, that I learned there was a Wolf Conservation Center just one hour away.

AMBASSADOR WOLVES

I began teaching workshops and facilitating nature-connection retreats with the Wolf Conservation Center when Zephyr, a resident wolf, was three years old. Named for Zephyros, the Greek deity of spring and warm summer winds, Zephyr was born in an Arizona zoo on April 20, 2011, not long before his wild relatives would be removed from the endangered species list. A playful, charismatic gray wolf, he arrived at the Wolf Conservation Center with his sibling, Alawa, on May 27. While most gray wolves have wheat- to gray-colored coats, evolved to blend into deserts, plains, and tundra, Zephyr's black coat would have been more common in dark forests, where he could weave through the woods unnoticed. Black coats occur in about 62 percent of wolves in the forested areas of the Canadian Arctic, compared with about 7 percent in the icy tundra. Geneticists have determined that the gene variant responsible for wolves' black fur comes from domestic dogs who bred with their wild ancestors thousands of years ago.

It was October 2013 when I arrived at the Wolf Conservation Center in Westchester for the first time. Like many New Yorkers, I didn't drive. But the Wolf Conservation Center was close, an accessible escape via Grand Central, just an hour's train ride away. I had been waiting impatiently for a meeting with Maggie Howell, the director. I wanted to work on behalf of wolves, in person, and be immersed in nature. I wanted to forage, eat from the ground, reconnect with my animal self, which had been in the city for way too long. I needed something from the wolves. Some vital part of me felt like it was missing.

Before we met, Maggie had instructed me to alert the wolves when we gathered on their land. So as we approached one another, Maggie and I howled to greet the wolves, letting them know we were there sharing their space. It's strange to think that as much as I'd always loved these animals, I had never really howled before. I grew up in a family of musicians and singers but never felt I could sing. I was quiet; my voice emerged only on the page. In order to howl, I had to reach down deep into my gut and draw from a well of emotion and embodied sound. I was a little embarrassed that first time, but after a few pathetic throat-howls, I surprised myself when a true wolf-song emerged from my body. Howling was cathartic, freeing. And when the fifty or so wolves replied, their songs stirred something deep inside of me, bringing me to tears. I didn't know it, but—like the suffering landscape—my body was hungry for their voice.

Zephyr and I bonded that day and with every howl afterward. At least I felt that way. I would gaze into his inquisitive amber eyes and we would howl together, and as we howled, some wild, wanting part of me came alive. Zephyr was gentle and there was a silliness to him; he seemed to have a sense of humor. He had a sweet relationship with his sister Alawa, who would regularly groom him—biting ticks and other debris from his fur—and who I also bonded with. But being the alpha of his enclosure, Zephyr got to me and my heart first.

The Wolf Conservation Center's mission is "to protect and preserve wolves in North America through science-based education, advocacy, and participation in the federal recovery and release programs for two critically endangered wolf species—the Mexican gray wolf and the red wolf." Hidden enclosures of red wolves and Mexican gray wolves are "off exhibit" so as to be kept as wild as possible, away from human interference, with the hope that one day the wolves sheltered there might return to the wild. Ambassador wolves like Zephyr and his two siblings are gray wolves. Their populations are slowly increasing in the wild (despite occupying just 10 percent of their historic geographic range), but since these two were born in captivity, they are ineligible for release. Instead, they are destined for a "safe" domesticated life in an acre enclosure. But thanks to the Wolf Conservation Center staff, the sacrifice of their freedom has not been in vain. Along with other ambassadors, like his siblings and the late, great Atka, a beloved Arctic wolf who passed away in 2018, Zephyr has moved millions to act on behalf of his species.

Still, the enclosures punctured me. I don't know what I was expecting. The center's accommodations are far from being a zoo. The enclosures are large and wild, and the wolves are in captivity in order to educate humans or, in the case of red wolves and Mexican gray wolves, to be saved from possible extinction and potentially released. Without cages and captive breeding programs, we would have no more red wolves. It's tragic that the key to their survival is to have these wild beautiful animals in captivity, and that to this date my only interaction with wolves—who should be roaming throughout the Northeast—has been watching them behind a fence. Safe. But sadly, not free.

Despite my complicated feelings, my ongoing partnership with the Wolf Conservation Center gave me a way to work on behalf of wolves, experience a slice of wildness while living in the city, and offer embodied, educational nature connection to others. I offered Reclaim the Wild Woman retreats, bringing small groups of women to unplug and camp among the wolves, most of whom were candidates for release whom we couldn't see but we felt and heard. Regan Downey, the education director of the WCC, taught us about the true nature of wolves while I reintroduced people to edible and healing plants under their feet. Students and I gathered bitter leaves of mugwort—a wild medicine whose botanical name, *Artemisia vulgaris*, honors the Greek moon goddess, Artemis, the protector and defender of women, Earth, and wild creatures—as Zephyr howled through the spring, summer, and fall.

Maggie and I wanted to reframe the word *predator* for the sake of wolves. Still teaching boxing in the city, I created a class called Tap Into Your Inner Predator, a movement practice for visitors that took place near the wolf enclosures. The experience blended boxing with environmental awareness to help humans, especially other women, tap into the part of themselves that already knew how to fight.

It was a true collaboration between the Wolf Conservation Center staff, the plants, and, above all, the wolves. I was in my element. When we howled with the wolves it invigorated a sense of deep connection and, at the same time, awakened a hollow place inside and out: their absence from the land. Knowing I am nature, that there is no separation between my body and the body of Earth, it makes sense that wolves—native to the land but absent—were a vital missing piece of my inner landscape. The ecosystem and my body were aching to rewild.

In some Brooklyn circles I became known as "the wolf woman." News about my retreats spread through word of mouth, and my desire to free the wolves began to free something within me. A lifelong activist, I felt I could never do enough for the Earth and other animals, but these experiences touched on so many things—ecology, seeing beyond plant blindness to notice the beautiful, fascinating flora all around us and under our feet, the true nature of wolves, sisterhood, reclaiming wildness within ourselves. But after my camping retreats at the Wolf Conservation Center, I returned to the noise and chaos of New York City, and every time, it was harder and harder to digest the transitions. For a long time I fed off the city's dynamic, creative energy, but my love for it all—the overstimulation, the struggle to make ends meet, even boxing—was fading fast. After the mugging, I was on edge, robbed of the pleasure of strolling through New York City streets at night and, for a while, even during the day. My already sensitive nervous system was on high alert. If someone walked close, a rush of adrenaline flooded my system. Each time, I took a deep breath, shook it off, and pushed through. Amid all the concrete, the world felt lonelier and lonelier. Away from nature, I felt like an increasingly raw nerve.

Back home, locked in my apartment, my expensive little box, I felt like a caged animal. I lay in bed swirling. I needed to untangle from it all. It was time to get out of my enclosure, get back to nature, break free. I needed a new story.

Bats

Though they fly as birds do, bats are mammals who nurse their babies with milk just like humans. The only mammal capable of true flight, bats belong to the order Chiroptera, meaning "hand-wing," since their wings feature four fingers and a thumb. They might use their wings to scoop fruit toward their mouths as we do with our hands.

Using sound, bats see everything but color, and in total darkness they are able to detect objects as thin as spiderwebs. They are critical pollinators for plants like agave and cacao and are seed dispersers and mosquito-eating allies (just one bat can eat more than 600 mosquitoes in a single hour!). But since they show up at night, bats rarely get the credit they deserve for their hard work. Like many creatures of the night, they are shrouded in misplaced fear.

Into the darkness they go, the wise and the lovely.

—EDNA ST. VINCENT MILLAY,
"DIRGE WITHOUT MUSIC"

2

Seeing in the Dark

Between retreats at the Wolf Conservation Center, I teach boxing in Brooklyn's Prospect Park at dusk. A pack of five women, we have safety in numbers. We meet at Grand Army Plaza and venture into Long Meadow, a huge area of the park that is filled with picnic blankets, dogs of all shapes and sizes, fitness classes, and people reading under the shade of trees during the day but becomes deserted as the sky grows dark. Long Meadow is just within the perimeter of the park, not far from the road, so the area feels safe, and the best part is that at dusk it feels and looks like another world. We enter via a small path and are soon surrounded by trees. Beyond them, all we see is lamplit green. When we arrive, this busy area of the park is a moody, magical realm where we encounter raccoons and, if we're lucky, bats. City parks and botanic gardens are my refuge and theirs.

The bats found in Brooklyn go mostly unnoticed, but on summer nights, they fly high above our heads to annihilate mosquitoes. New York City is home to tree bats like eastern red bats and hoary bats that migrate south each year and return mid-April. Adorable cave bats, including little brown bats, big brown bats, and tricolored bats, manage to live in the city year-round. In winter, they hibernate inside or under urban structures, in leaf piles or under the bark of trees. When the weather warms, they roost under bridges and in crevices in rocks, tree hollows, and branches. Bats can live long lives compared to other mammals their size. The oldest recorded bat found in New York was thirty-four years old.

Because they are most active at night, bats depend on echolocation to navigate and locate prey. To echolocate, a bat emits short,
high-pitched calls that are outside the range of human hearing.
When these calls bounce off an object, bats hear the echo and can
almost instantly analyze the sound to determine exactly how far away
an object is, how big it is, what it looks like, and even what texture it
might have. Contrary to popular belief, bats can actually see with
their eyes, too—echolocation just helps make their flying and hunting skills more precise.

I wondered about human noise and the impact on echolocation—
*How can bats adapt and survive in an increasingly bright city and noisy
planet?*—and I've found conflicting information and studies. Some
researchers say that bats are efficient hunters even when it's too loud
to hear their prey—they just ramp up echolocation or rely on other
senses—and others say the opposite. A study published in the journal *Functional Ecology* found that bats exposed to traffic noise produced calls that were up to ten decibels louder than those produced
by bats in quiet areas. But studies also show that bats exposed to sim-
ulated traffic noise had higher levels of the stress hormone cortisol in
their blood and were less likely to form breeding pairs, and their offspring were less likely to survive. I imagine the study itself was stressful for the bats, but there is no doubt that like me, they are sensitive to
light. Artificial lighting impacts their ability to forage, commute,
roost, and hibernate. Basically everything they need to survive.

Like wolves, bats have been associated with witchcraft and demons
in European art and fables for centuries. These nocturnal mammals
have gotten a bad reputation in everything from horror movies to
vampire lore and creepy Halloween decorations, and have been
blamed for being a vector of viruses. But by eating mosquitoes that

spread diseases like West Nile fever, Zika, and malaria, bats help more than they could possibly harm. In some areas where bat populations have collapsed, the number of mosquitoes has exploded, along with rates of diseases the insects carry. The vast majority of disease spillover from bats to humans is due to human behavior—from selling dead bats in wet markets to feeding pigs mangoes that have been partially eaten by Nipah virus–positive bats.

The truly scary (and absolutely tragic) thing is that today, nearly 40 percent of the bats living in the United States and Canada are endangered or are candidates for the endangered species list, and nearly one third of all bat species worldwide are vulnerable, endangered, critically endangered, or "data deficient." Their steep population decline is largely the result of our destructive and mythmaking species. Habitat loss, pesticide use, climate change, wind turbines, fungal diseases, spooky fables, and human ignorance have all led to the demise of the misunderstood and ecologically vital bat.

In the dark, we listen closely to sounds around us to know whether or not we are safe. If we feel threatened, we may choose to remain quiet and unseen, or to scream and make ourselves known. David George Haskell asserts in *Sounds Wild and Broken: Sonic Marvels, Evolution's Creativity, and the Crisis of Sensory Extinction* that wings— the ability to fly and escape—gave birds and insects the courage to sing and be heard. He writes, "Their wings, like musical instruments, transformed their bodies into resonating chambers, and their voices, honed by the pressure of predator and prey, became expressions of identity, territory, and courtship."

I once felt safe in the city surrounded by people. I loved to disappear and wander, anonymous, amid a sea of strangers. But after the mugging in 2011, I grew less comfortable going out. My sensitivity to sound heightened and I became hypervigilant. When I had to walk to and from work at night, I imagined owls and bats—skilled at navigating darkness—flying with me, surveying my environment, and two wolves protecting me, flanking my sides. With these invisible creatures beside me, I took up more space, walked with more confidence and awareness, as though channeling their gifts. These creatures became incredibly vivid to me and I could swear others sensed them too.

The more time I spent in New York City, the less I understood it when people said the view of the New York City skyline was beautiful. More and more, it looked like destruction; stars, planets, and constellations lost in the overwhelm of artificial light. Creatures that populated the fairy tales and forests of my childhood seemed to be vanishing, too. Every day I read about habitat loss due to the human desire for more hamburgers, more plastic packaging, golf courses, lifeless lawns, palm-oil-laden snacks, fast fashion, and grotesque McMansions. All empty calories to fill a vacuum inside. An incessant, destructive hunger caused in large part, I think, by a disconnection from Mother Earth.

If I was going to continue living in the city, even for a little while, I needed to find my nook, my tree crevice, my pile of leaves, my cave. My home had to be a soothing sanctuary; my nervous system needed to rest. Inside my apartment at night, as the bats flew through Brooklyn, I surrounded myself with art and lush potted plants and found the right soundtrack—"Crickets on a Summer Night," "Babbling Brook," or "Meadow in Spring"—and lulled myself to sleep. Recalibrating in my cave, I was healing, but my body craved more: the hypnotic sound of *real* crickets, cleansing water I could feel moving around my fingers, and rolling meadows I could walk upon barefoot, away from the overstimulation of the city.

SAFE AND SOUND

When I was young, growing up in Western Massachusetts, I called bats at dusk with intuitive clicks, squeaks, and claps. I didn't really know what I was doing, but it seemed they would gather and circle above me, so in my child mind I imagined they heard and responded to my call. There were so many, dozens and more. Like my love for wolves and so-called weeds, I've always had a special place in my heart for bats and other misunderstood creatures. Maybe I identified with them. Often absent from school due to debilitating asthma, I felt like an outsider among my peers and remained silent about my vulnerable body and lungs, embarrassed and ashamed by what I felt was weakness. With piles of schoolwork I couldn't ever catch up on, I never really felt comfortable in classes, either. My wild imagination felt constrained when I tried to rein her in to focus on where my academic brain was supposed to be. At home, I doodled and daydreamed, got lost in art and the magic of the forest while immersed in a house filled with music. My mom always said I have the hearing of a bat whose ears are freakishly huge for their head. I hear with my whole body.

I grew up in the realm of music, soul mostly, and people were in and out of the house constantly to learn, collaborate, and record. I overheard the faint hum of bass guitars, the vibration of drums, intricate compositions on keyboards, and the wail of guitars. It was a soothing soundscape and underneath it all was nature. Outside, our small garden and the surrounding woods were my playground, and inside, I played classical piano, saxophone, and, for a short time, guitar. I had a good ear—I was able to hear intervals, understand the emotional palette of different vibratos, emote through breath, intonation, and rhythm—and music moved me. But ultimately, I was compelled to get noise out of my body through words and images, and gravitated to writing and visual arts instead. Music was in me, though. When I began to date I would ask men about the music they listened to; I wanted to know something about the pulse of their inner rhythm, what moved them. I believed the sounds they were drawn to said something about their capacity to feel, and maybe even how they loved.

When relationships lasted, we made mix tapes for each other, carefully recording and curating the perfect song lists from a double tape deck, CD player, or turntable. Each song had meaning. I would carry my Walkman everywhere in the nineties, wearing headphones listening to mixes of Stevie Wonder, Charles Mingus, Debussy, A Tribe Called Quest, Chopin, Roy Ayers, Erykah Badu, Miles Davis, Lhasa de Sela, Teena Marie, and the Roots on city streets. Music made me oblivious to the world around me, but sometimes it heightened my experience of the city, and the music would carry me for miles. At home, John Coltrane played in the background. As though my life needed a soundtrack.

Now, more often than not, I choose quiet. Though true quiet is hard to find. It tends to be defined by what it isn't—no buzz of technology, no gas-powered leaf blowers, no cars rushing by, no chatter of social media—than what it is. Even so-called silence may be punctuated by noise—ambient beats, guided meditations, the ever-present hum of home appliances, my busy mind.

There are nine species of bats found throughout the state of Massachusetts, five of whom are endangered. Most offspring of my flying childhood friends didn't survive. Human pressures and white-nose syndrome (WNS), a disease that leaves powdery-looking fungal sores on the noses and wings of cave bats and eats away at their skin, have led to a heartbreaking population decline. Imagine being so intensely uncomfortable; it is no wonder bats become restless in winter when they need to be hibernating. And no wonder they become active during the day (perhaps the sun provides relief, drying up some of the damp cold?), burning up fat stores they need to survive. Tragically, most infected bats end up dying of exposure to cold weather or starvation.

Biologists first saw bats suffering from WNS in 2007 in caves near Albany, New York. But according to the U.S. Fish and Wildlife Service's official White-Nose Syndrome website, cave explorers in that area took a photo of bats with white powder on their noses the year before, so it seems white-nose syndrome has been in North America since at least 2006. Since its arrival, the deadly fungus has spread rapidly in cave bats and caused devastating mortality. The disease was "accidentally transported by humans" from Eurasia, according to Bat Conservation International. People can move the fungus on their clothing and caving gear and spread the disease into uninfected areas. So far, an estimated 6.7 million bats have died.

Some treatments for WNS are similar to the treatments we use if our digestive system is out of whack—probiotics and antifungals— and I can't help but wonder if the fungus flourished because delicate cave ecosystems, like the delicate mix of microbes in our own gut, have been disturbed by human-made chemicals or extraction. After the bats deposit their waste, known as guano, on a cave floor, it is processed once again by millions of beetles and billions of decomposing microbes. Bat guano has been used in agriculture in many regions for hundreds of years. In the 1600s in Peru, the Incas valued guano so highly that the punishment for harming the animals who produced it was death. One of the best organic fertilizers out there, in terms of how plants respond to it, is bat guano aged in an arid environment like a cave.

The guano cycle begins with plant matter that is eaten by insects. The insects in turn are eaten and digested by bats. What's left is perfectly preserved and protected inside the cave—a natural fertilizer warehouse. Caves provide the perfect environment for this to occur, and so that is where most bat guano comes from. But guano needs to be aged in special surroundings before it is used, and it is not a rapidly renewable resource. It takes decades for the raw material from which this fertilizer is made to develop into the magical stuff people use. Harvesting bat guano can damage the ecosystems present in the caves, and it should never be harvested when bats are present. Beginning the process while the bats are inside could jeopardize their survival.

I try to call to the bats now and none come; the night skies are virtually empty in Western Massachusetts. I'm lucky if I see one or two bats at dusk. I see more in New York City. It's disheartening. And while I'm happy to have them in the city, I know the bright, noisy landscape is an uncomfortable compromise.

STARRY NIGHTS

My escape from Gotham City felt underway. In the sanctuary of my New York City apartment, I hibernated and visioned, dreaming of the life I wanted to live. The Wolf Conservation Center had become a refuge that was helping others connect to nature, but I craved more. I saw friends flying south to places like Central and South America to offer retreats in winter. *Why can't I do that, too?* But I didn't want to be an outsider plopping down in another land amid another culture and ecosystem, no matter how drawn, called, or connected I felt. Yoga and so-called healing retreats that don't consider local landscapes are harmful—a form of modern-day colonization, in my opinion—and as areas like Costa Rica become more popular, the threat of gentrification, deforestation, and habitat loss becomes increasingly significant. If I was going to explore and offer retreats elsewhere, I knew it was important to humble myself, learn from local teachers and from the land, and, over time, develop community. We need to adapt to local cultures and landscapes instead of making them adapt to us.

I was drawn to Costa Rica by the incredible biodiversity there. One in twenty of all plant and animal species can be found in Costa Rica, and the 109 bat species recorded there represent about 12 percent of the world's bat species. This includes bulldog bats, who (along with howler monkeys) are among the loudest land mammals in the world. Bulldog bats produce calls that reach up to 140 decibels, louder than a jet engine taking off. But because they produce calls at ultrasonic frequencies, above the range of human hearing, we're oblivious to their calls. There is a whole world of sound beyond our field of perception.

My first trip to Costa Rica was in the summer of 2008 with my friend Angela, a gift to myself after working on the Stop the Violence Movement with the hip-hop artist KRS-One. I was burnt out, I had been working on other people's projects for so long, and I was in limbo, ready for a new beginning. Winging it, Angela and I had no plan for our trip. Luckily, we ran into my friend Morisha before we left and she told us where to go: the Caribbean coast. She wrote a set of directions down on a piece of paper and we followed. Taking a cab from the airport, we boarded a five-hour bus ride to Puerto Viejo de Talamanca, Limón. We arrived late, everything was dark, and we were nervous: *Where the hell are we?* We booked the closest room we could find, not great. But in the morning, we woke to a coastal paradise. At breakfast, we savored some of the most delicious coffee, papaya, pineapple, and avocado I'd ever had, and later, we hiked forests alive with sloths, monkeys, hummingbirds, tree frogs, blue morpho butterflies, and gorgeous flora. We lay on the beach, swam, screamed underwater, made friends at the farmers market, and spoke our best (but terrible) Spanish. Unplugged for two weeks, my nervous system rebooted. I conspired with new friends who lived in Puerto Viejo, already planning to return.

Finally, in 2014, after many back-and-forth emails from my Brooklyn cave, I went to study and stay at my friend Rachel's ethnobotany center in the lush jungle of Puerto Viejo de Talamanca. I would eventually facilitate retreats in collaboration with local herbalism teachers and get to know Encar Vila, a primatologist and the founder of the Jaguar Rescue Center. I would cabin-sit for Rachel while she was away. Alone in the jungle, far away from other humans, I felt safe.

At night, I loved to turn off all the lights, disappear, and become one with the jungle. Almost immediately, every sound was amplified and my senses were heightened. Relaxed at last, I could hear with my whole body. I no longer had to build walls of tension against traffic or sirens or mask noise with more noise that my body feels anyway. In the jungle, I could listen and feel a gecko moving across the wooden floor; my ears picked up the sound of a bat working her way through the wind. If I ventured deeper into the rainforest I might find translucent tree frogs and glow-in-the-dark mushrooms under the moonlight. Mysteries unseen in the light of day.

Sitting on the porch of the rustic cabin, I could turn my attention to the lightning bugs and constellations that were suddenly everywhere. In the morning, howler monkeys woke me at 5:00 a.m. with a crescendo of deep, ghostly howls. They are the sound of the jungle I have come to crave.

Howler Monkeys

The black howler monkey's cry can be heard for up to three miles, the loudest vocal sound of any land mammal. Male howlers call at dusk and dawn and throughout the day to create space in trees, come closer together, announce a nearby intruder, or warn another group member to stay away from their mate. Howler monkey troops may include up to fifteen adult males and females with a dominant male and dominant female who help lead the group and keep everyone in order. While a howler's voice can be intimidating, these primates are peaceful leaf eaters who spend most of their lives swinging between trees.

When young monkeys reach maturity, the troop makes them go out on their own. During this period, the lone monkey wanders the jungle until they find another group willing to take them in.

We find animals doing things that we, in our arrogance, used to think was "just human."

—JANE GOODALL

3

Fitting In

Whenever I return from the jungle, I am hardwired to hear, see, and look for howler monkeys. When I see movement or large, unusual shapes in trees, my body and mind register: *Monkey!* Sadly, in Brooklyn, the moving object is usually a plastic bag animated by the wind.

Back in the city, I craved the wild so much that all my social media posts were about plants and places in nature where I studied and eventually ran rewilding retreats. My soul was in the wilderness even though I was walking down city streets. But social media has always made me uneasy. It is lonely to be temporarily entertained by screens that cannot touch us or love us back. We are craving connection and belonging, and we are seeking it in a virtual world, exposing ourselves in the innocent hope and deep yearning of acceptance.

It was through plants and animals that I found many of my people. Herbalism, wolves, and wildlife conservation gave me a community as strong, supportive, and vibrant as the one I'd found in boxing. And for a while now, I have been trying to figure out how to engage in the space of social media in a similarly authentic way. Not just authentic; I want to add something of value without being yet another person offering unsolicited advice, no matter how useful. I am reluctant to add to the already excessive noise and worry about the phantoms of judgment. When a heartbreaking event like a shooting or an environmental disaster happens, my head spins, searching for the right words. But often, I just need to sit, process, and feel. Sometimes when I'm engaged in the realm of social media I am an observer in my own environment, detached in order to find a "good post" that will somehow please others. Other times I am genuinely excited and inspired to share. But like an animal in a zoo I am on display there and don't really want to be. I'd rather be in a nook or lush forest where no one can see me, where I know I'm not being watched. But unfortunately, for an entrepreneur social media feels like a necessity these days. At least for now.

I think back to the hardcover diary I had as a teenager, the one with the little lock that held my soft, vulnerable words; tender places inside me begging to be healed. Safe inside the locked cover, wounds, confusion, joy, and the mundane of everyday life spilled onto pages that were just for me. I shared secrets with the page that I would never say aloud, and it felt good to let go without worrying what others would think or say or do. Only I held the key.

Today, some, like me, still keep diaries for themselves, but others have replaced therapeutic diaries with curated Instagram posts. "Online" is a strange, self-conscious space when we share vulnerable words in the boundless realm of social media. Vulnerability connects us, it's true. But when we splay ourselves open and expose ourselves to the wrong people in the virtual world, we might find more pain instead of healing. As "Iron Mike" Tyson said, "Social media made y'all way too comfortable with disrespecting people and not getting punched in the face for it."

When primates groom one another, combing through fur to remove entangled bits and pieces of vegetation and bugs, the touching triggers their brain's endorphin system, which underpins the creation of friendships. The social interaction in which one monkey sits close to another to comb through their hair, remove dead skin or parasites, or just gently touch their friend is called allogrooming. Scientists originally thought allogrooming might be a simple form of reciprocity, but after years of studying many primate species, they discovered that grooming not only removes external parasites but fosters tolerance, social support, mating advantage, and bonding between members of a group. Grooming reduces tension by lowering the heart rate and releasing hormones that calm and reinforce male-female mate bonds as well as same-sex friendship bonds. Chimpanzees allogroom for hours when reunited with old acquaintances. They also groom to calm emotions following aggressive outbursts. Maybe in some ways social media makes us feel as though we are grooming—like our primate cousins do—at a distance, triggering the same endorphin system that gives us a sense of warmth and relaxation.

Howler monkey babies receive constant care in the wild, from food and love to the touch and education they need to survive on their own. Howler mothers have only one baby at a time and nurture their young with loving tenderness and care. Babies nurse and stay close for years, and their bond is so strong that when mothers are mortally wounded, babies rarely survive unless adopted by a new mom. "They are introverts," my friend Encar Vila, a primatologist and the founder of the Jaguar Rescue Center (JRC), told me. "More sensitive than the other monkeys. They need to be close all the time, they need nurturing, they need to belong." These introverted monkeys are sensitive in all aspects of the word, Encar told me: "Their stomachs, their gut flora, their emotions, and their social needs. They yearn to fit in and to be loved."

Monkeys who arrive at the JRC have been victims of interactions with humans. In Costa Rica, it is illegal to keep wild animals in captivity unless they are in sanctuary or being rehabilitated for release into the wild. But Costa Rica isn't an absolute paradise. Across much of the country, howlers are displaced by environmental destruction, and mothers holding babies die on live electric wires trying to reach their trees. Some arrive at the center after being hit by cars or stolen from their troops and kept as household pets. Gentle animals, howler monkeys do not put up much of a fight against humans, so, sadly, they make easy prey. Whatever the reason for their arrival, Encar offers orphaned babies love, nurturing, safety, and community until they are ready to venture into the jungle and find a troop of their own. When they're mature enough, orphaned howlers join a community of their peaceful kin in a large enclosure where they eat wild fruits like manzana de agua and leaves like guarumo from the Cecropia tree.

Conga, a howler monkey, was found alone and abandoned next to a property in the town of Cahuita with a chain around her neck when she was just a few months old. It is unclear how she wound up there or who tied her up, but thankfully, she was rescued by the police and brought to the JRC. Conga arrived deeply depressed but she was lovingly nurtured, rehabilitated, and eventually released back into the wild by Encar and the JRC staff. Now Conga often comes back to visit—especially when she has a new baby. A proud mom, Conga climbs through Encar's screenless window to introduce her new son or daughter. So far, Encar has met seven of Conga's children (Encar's adopted grandchildren), who are thriving in the wild.

But once, Conga brought a dead baby to Encar. Desperate to do anything to help her child, Conga brought the baby to Encar, convinced she must be able to do something, perhaps holding the memory of her own rescue and the rescue of so many other orphaned howlers she came to know. Encar knew she had to take the rest of the day off and sit with Conga, to show her that she was trying and had tried everything. After hours, when Conga realized that nothing could be done, she wailed, heaving like a human in deep grief. Encar held her and later told me that Conga taught her so much about the emotional lives of howlers. "They love deeply; they are very much like us," she told me. "They are the gorillas of the Americas."

Raised in Barcelona, Encar spent fifteen years working with primates and mammals in various habitats, including eight years at the Barcelona Zoo, where she cared for gorillas including Snowflake, a famous albino gorilla who called the zoo home for thirty-seven years. Now it's rare to see Encar without an orphaned baby howler (or four or five) close to her chest, clinging to her as Mom after losing their own mothers. When I met Encar, I was in awe of her work and we became fast friends. She was living my childhood dream.

I was about eight years old when I first saw photos of Jane Goodall with chimpanzees in *National Geographic* and learned about Dian Fossey. Something lit up in me. *That's what I want to do!* I thought. *I want to live in the wild, befriend gorillas or chimpanzees, and be accepted as one of them!* It was a secret dream I held close. When I lived in the Bronx with a partner in the midnineties, a short walk from the Bronx Zoo, I considered volunteering to work with the gorillas. Maybe, I thought, that would bring me closer to living with them and working on their behalf in their natural habitat. But when I went for a visit my heart shattered. I couldn't bear to see them in enclosures, behind glass. So instead of volunteering I tried to forget that they were there, which made me feel even worse. It haunted me to know that there were wild animals in cages so close.

During a recent visit to Costa Rica, I walked up the stairs to Encar's house after writing in the Jaguar Rescue Center café, and just ahead of me, a male howler named Saske was climbing up the stairs to hang out at her house, too. Saske was rescued by Encar when he was about four months old. He was found in the outskirts of the jungle alone, his hand cut off by a machete. It's unclear whether his injury was accidental or intentional. Whatever the reason, he was by himself, in incredible distress, and in need of care.

After being rushed to the JRC hospital, where his wounds were treated, Encar visited him as he healed to give him motherly love and attention. "A lot of rehabbers forget that love is everything when it comes to healing trauma," she told me. "Monkeys need to feel a sense of safety. They need living, breathing, loving contact. Physical contact is the key between survival and death."

As Saske healed at the hospital, he became friends with another howler monkey, and when he and his friend were well enough, they were moved to the spacious monkey tower at the JRC rehabilitation center. Once there, they continued to receive loving care, and after a year in the tower, they were ready to spend time in the main howler prerelease enclosure at the JRC. In the afternoon, the howlers enjoyed field trips to the jungle to climb trees, encounter their wild relatives, and remember how it feels to be free.

As the monkeys grow confident, they become more bold and venture farther, until one day they join a troop in the jungle and stay. Good for the jungle, because when howler monkeys live there, more birds do, too. Trees produce more leaves and fruit when howler monkeys feed on them, and with more leaves and fruit for each tree, more insects follow. The bounty of insects can feed more birds. Some doubt Encar's process, believing that once-captive monkeys will no longer be able to thrive in the wild. But Encar told me, "Unless they are injured or incapacitated, they will always want to be wild and free."

Doing relatively well despite his injury, Saske moved on to the next stage: from the prerelease enclosure at the JRC to a prerelease enclosure in La Ceiba primary-growth rainforest, named in homage to a magnificent Ceiba tree thought to be about 500 years old. La Ceiba Nature Reserve forms part of the Gandoca-Manzanillo

Wildlife Refuge, an ideal place to release many of the animals that arrive at the center. Saske was moved with his best friend, a female howler, and after a week and half, when they seemed ready, the JRC staff opened the door and released them. But it didn't go well for Saske. He was attacked by other monkeys, who chased him to the end of a branch and forced him to jump. He fractured his leg and was rushed to the JRC hospital once again. Marginalized by his injuries, Saske has found it difficult to find safety and community in a wild troop that would accept him.

"He is kind of a sad monkey," a volunteer at the JRC told me. "Sometimes it seems as though he connects and relates more to other animals—animals unlike him." I imagine there is an ache for belonging in Saske, but his disability has also opened doors and offered him a life as a helper to other rescued monkeys. Not accepted into a wild troop at La Ceiba (yet), he has opened himself up to friendship with animals beyond his monkey kin.

Many people are like this, too. Different or unable to fit in and more at ease around other species. Some volunteers come to the center for the same reasons Encar tells me: they are more comfortable around other animals than around humans. The problem is, to work effectively for the rescued animals, workers have to be able to relate to other humans, too.

Like howler monkeys, we all seek belonging and acceptance into a group. Almost every teen movie depicts the dreaded elementary school, junior high, or high school lunchroom, wandering around with our food or paper lunch bag hoping to find a group that will accept us. Those memories are palpable for me. I remember holding my E.T. or Yoda lunch box in elementary school, looking for a place to sit down, wondering, *Who will accept me as I am?*

I especially dreaded recess in elementary school. I didn't know what to do with myself during that unstructured playtime, when kids could be so mean and where I felt physically deficient. I desperately wanted to be an athlete like my closest friends and the "cool kids," but my asthmatic lungs didn't comply with my desire. So I usually reverted to the "uncool" activity of four square, biding my time until recess was finally over. Counting down the minutes until art class, I just wanted to get back inside to read. Apart from close one-on-one friendships and the woods behind my house on Summer Street, I didn't really know where I fit in.

As an adult, my health has improved and I've realized my seemingly impossible dream of becoming an athlete, but my social tendencies haven't changed much. In conversations that lead to deep sharing, I thrive. But unstructured social spaces can feel like elementary school recess and I just want to be home reading a book. I have a hard time skimming the surface enough to go along to get along, and sometimes my reserved disposition feels like a cage. In intimate relationships, I'm often drawn to more extroverted males, and for a while the match seems like a good balance, until they get frustrated that I don't want to "be social" or that when we do go out with large groups I'm "so quiet." And I get frustrated having to explain myself.

When I read the book *Quiet: The Power of Introverts in a World That Can't Stop Talking,* I finally felt seen. Its author, Susan Cain, writes that introverts "prefer to devote their social energies to close friends, colleagues, and family. They listen more than they talk, think before they speak, and often feel as if they express themselves better in writing than in conversation. They tend to dislike conflict. Many have a horror of small talk, but enjoy deep discussions." Yes! I always thought there was something wrong with me. Cain writes that at school I "might have been prodded to come 'out of your shell'— that noxious expression which fails to appreciate that some animals naturally carry shelter everywhere they go, and that some humans are just the same." I was one of those humans.

Unlike with other animals, the roles in human groups aren't so clear. In my twenties and thirties, I longingly read books about Indigenous cultures close to nature who seemed to have figured it out. While my ancestors in Scotland had their own problems, I imagine that I might have been—until the witch trials, at least—a medicine woman living on the fringes of a township. An empathetic observer connected to nature; a sick person who had learned to become well. If I were a howler, maybe I'd be the helper monkey foraging medicine and doing lots and lots of grooming.

Among humans, the qualities needed for acceptance can be arbitrary. Sometimes—in groups like fraternities, the military, gangs, or even cliques—cruelty is required to pledge allegiance, to prove we are tough enough to belong or that we are willing to relinquish our morals for the sake of the group. That they "have something on us" and we cannot turn away. Many humans want to be "on top" even if that's not where they shine. But the top can be a lonely, isolating place, and one animal competing and moving up the ladder does not help our species. In *Survival of the Friendliest: Understanding Our Origins and Rediscovering Our Common Humanity*, the scientists Brian Hare and Vanessa Woods suggest that kindness, not competition, among species has worked for centuries to ensure successful evolution. In the case of our close relatives, "the most successful bonobo males leave more offspring than even the most despotic chimpanzees. This suggests that kindness can be a more effective evolutionary strategy than aggression." They believe that animals truly thrive because of partnership and cooperation, not competition. The most effective "alpha males" are the ones who actually keep the peace.

I spoke with Dr. Christine Webb, a primatologist and fellow member of Interspecies Dialogues, a discussion group based at Harvard

Divinity School. Christine teaches a class at Harvard called The Arrogant Ape, which is also the name of her forthcoming book. Early on in her career as a primatologist, she found herself in a situation with which she was deeply uncomfortable: working with monkeys in cages; studies set in "horrible conditions, nothing like their actual lives in the wild." That early work haunts her to this day. She told me, "Science is skewed by human exceptionalism or speciesism, a systemic problem. It is a lens through which we justify incredible cruelty toward other species in the name of science. It normalizes harm and promotes emotional detachment."

Christine told me the story of Macduff, a rhesus macaque who was among a group of monkeys that were part of an academic research project when she was studying in New York City. Alone in a cage and desperate for connection, he pressed against the bars as soon as she walked in, communicating his need for touch. Christine, though trained in objectivity, was compelled to groom him, and as she did, her empathy grew. "He showed me that he was an individual with his own needs and desires. We don't think enough about individual animals and their lives, we think of monkeys plural. But each one is an *individual* with feelings and dreams. Like us, they feel pain and experience love."

Christine thought working in labs was a rite of passage. Something she had to go through, a means to an end in order to be accepted into the scientific world. But now she realizes that the lab settings are not only cruel, but they are also bad science. "How can we study other minds in environments that are so unnatural?" Objectification is not good science and doesn't bring out an animal's natural behavior at all. In a lab, you are not studying a healthy being, and there are unavoidable dynamics between the researched and researcher. "Until you are accepted in the monkey's natural environment, into their troop," Christine told me, "you cannot truly see who they are."

When she heeded her urge to study and spend time with monkeys in the wild, she could never go back to working with them in cages. The monkeys she spent time with were constantly problem-solving, adjusting their behavior, and foraging according to weather. When their needs were met and they could relax, she saw them experiencing moments of awe and reveling in wonder. "The more time you spend with other beings, the more empathy you have," she said. "When we feel more, we cannot engage in such cruelty."

ACCEPTANCE

When my long-time on-again, off-again partner and I split up, I was reeling. Our love was one of the last strands of attachment keeping me in the city at that point, so when we went our separate ways, I put my belongings in storage, let go of my Brooklyn apartment, and went to Costa Rica to regroup. I studied plant medicine and connected with my jungle community while my heart slowly healed.

It was early January 2014 when I arrived, and I had wolf retreats beginning in late April. The retreats felt like a long way away when I landed in Puerto Viejo, but after a few months, they snuck up on me. *Will I return?* I wasn't sure if I wanted to; I needed more time to heal but cherished the partnership with the Wolf Conservation Center and didn't want to flake out on them. Plus, the retreats were full and it had taken time to develop relationships with committed students and the center. In limbo, I reluctantly returned to the States and stayed with my mom in Western Massachusetts until I figured things out. The location meant I was close enough to commute and facilitate the retreats while I decided where to land. I felt like a failure being at my mom's, but I reminded myself that I was building a new way of life.

After a period of grieving, and with a lot of coaxing from my sister to "just see, for fun," I agreed to try online dating. My heart was still tender and I was not sure if I was going to move back to Brooklyn, return to the jungles of Costa Rica, heed the pull of rural Massachusetts, or find somewhere new. I figured it would be a good idea to see who was out there, so I was open to exploring; open to a new way of choosing a partner. While I heard online dating horror stories from other women, I realized that being online had its benefits. I wasn't pulled by chemistry or carnal attraction, so I was more discerning. I'm sure I would have scrolled right past some of the men I'd dated in the past if I'd been able to read their profiles.

It's surprisingly easy to weed guys out based on their initial photo: Posing with a car or a yacht? No thanks. The big fish you caught? Nope. A selfie in the mirror of the gym holding a dumbbell (aptly named)? Definitely no. Until I came upon Rafael. He was lying on a beach in the Galápagos Islands surrounded by sea lions. He didn't appear to take himself too seriously, wasn't trying to be sexy, and, most of all, had the sea lions in his favor. Plus, he was a good writer. We wrote back and forth for weeks. First, he told me about an all-night hike through the jungles of Mount Chirripó in Costa Rica. He hiked through the dense rainforest alone at night to make it to the top of the mountain at sunrise. I replied, writing about my own experiences in Costa Rica and my fascination with plant medicine, and while I didn't speak as many languages as he did, I described the ways I had been learning a new language of plants in the jungle.

We met in person, in Brooklyn, three weeks later. It was mid-August, a hot summer day in the city, and we planned to spend the day at Fort Tilden beach. Nervous and excited, I waited for him at the G train station on Lafayette Avenue. When he pulled up on his scooter, he made me laugh and I immediately felt at ease. Beach gear in my backpack, I put on a helmet, grabbed on to his sweaty body, and rode down Flatbush Ave. on the back of his scooter to the healing salt of the sea. We played in the sand and water all day.

We had a second date the next day and went to my community

garden to harvest nettles from my overgrown plot. He gazed at me sweetly as I worked with the plants. I invited him to join me and he bent down, carefully gathering stinging nettles. Our hands buzzing from the plants, we walked back to his apartment and made a tincture together. We would keep it on the kitchen shelf as a memento of that day for years. When we finally decanted it, it was a beautiful emerald green. His term of endearment for me would be "sweet monkey."

Spotted Hyenas

Hyena cubs emerge from their mother's womb with eyes open, muscles coordinated, and sharp teeth ready to tear into flesh. Spotted hyenas live in matriarchies ruled by alpha females, and everything they do is shaped by female dominance passed down the alpha female's line. Daughters inherit a social rank below their mothers and usually remain in their birth clan for life, building close relationships with their mother and sisters—bonds that reinforce social rank within the clan hierarchy and remain stable for many years. Hyenas gather in social groups larger than those of any other carnivore and have been observed defending territories up to 620 square miles. Though they may look like wild dogs, these feminist icons have a family all their own, Hyaenidae, and are more closely related to cats than to canines.

Women have served all these centuries as looking-glasses possessing the magic and delicious power of reflecting the figure of man at twice its natural size.

—VIRGINIA WOOLF, *A Room of One's Own*

4

Ravenous

I was possessed by a need to become strong, a skilled fighter, and yearned to trust myself in the ring; a place where someone—my opponent—was trained to expose and exploit my weaknesses. To dominate, I needed to revise my long-standing narrative of the physically deficient asthmatic kid, show myself I was capable, and disprove all the mean things I'd told myself over the years. When I began my journey to becoming a boxer, overcoming that narrative felt far more valuable than the risk of getting my face rearranged. In a world where women are told beauty is our currency, boxing was my little rebellion.

I remember riding the subway from Tribeca to Brooklyn with an ice pack on my face in 1998 after my first sparring session. Nursing a bloody nose with a serious shiner on its way, I noticed people staring at me with horrified expressions. I wasn't as skilled as I thought I was. My face and my ego bruised in the aftermath, I hid in my apartment as much as I could. It took a few weeks to take care of my physical wounds and, though my confidence was shaky, I eventually got back in the gym, laced up my gloves, opened wide for my mouth guard, and stepped into the ring again.

The defiance that got me into the boxing ring had always been a little weak when it came to being with a lover. When in bed with someone, I would suck my stomach in, turn my body, or inconspicuously move his palm when he draped an arm over my waist and rested his hand on my abdomen. I wanted to relax and enjoy our softening together, but I was soft in places I thought I was supposed to be taut, flat, or firm. I've internalized the story that if I am not sexy enough or pretty enough, my partner might look elsewhere, maybe even leave me. Many of us are afraid of this, I think. We spend so much money and energy grasping for our lovers' gaze.

To some degree, it's natural: we are driven by biology, and all animals preen to attract a mate. But when other animals fan their feathers or, like the bird-of-paradise, practice their dance routines to display their beauty, the performance is short lived, during mating rituals. But humans live with the anxiety of "ugliness" all the time and, in many cases, feel ashamed of our natural animal bodies.

I know a true lover is a man who wants realness, not inhuman perfection. And yet I'm worried I'll lose his interest if my skin wrinkles too much and begins to reveal my age. The lines we are conditioned to loathe are reminders of the impermanence of life and the inevitable passage of time. But they also tell tales and are a map of precious days. The creases around my cheeks tell stories of smiles. Many, many smiles. Love is etched into my body. I don't want to reject or fear my future self.

I've always been conscious of my looks. Growing up in a culture where youth and beauty are commercialized to an extreme, it would be hard not to be. Like most in the modern world, I was indoctrinated early. The Disney princesses of my era—Snow White, Sleeping Beauty, and Cinderella—were sweet, "good," beautiful damsels in distress. While they could talk to animals (a gift I was profoundly jealous of) and seemed to have a deep relationship with nature, they were otherwise helpless prizes to be won by rich men. Walt may have been an environmentalist, but he definitely wasn't a feminist. Ariel, Belle, and Elsa presented stronger characters in later years and Jasmine, Pocahontas, and Mulan added much needed diversity to the mix, but the image of beauty was still the same: tiny waist, delicate features, and Barbie-like proportions. In the wild it is feminine prowess, strength, and vigor that are rewarded, while human women are taught to contort our bodies and, in most cases these days (with the exception of butts and boobs), make themselves smaller.

Body image problems may seem like superficial issues with potentially harmful consequences, but they are indicative of a systemic problem, and with the speed of technology, capitalism has exported objectification and self-scrutiny all over the world. Beauty culture creates the illusion of lack and tells us we are not enough until, maybe, we buy the right cream, sculpt the right nose, breast, or even labia—an increasingly popular cosmetic surgery that can impact the clitoris and dull orgasm. Men may argue that they are also the victims of increasing pressures to be buff and beautiful, but historically, as far as political power goes, the pressure is not the same. For the most part, unattractive, greedy white men rule the world.

For most of my youth, I remember being free of worry, but steadily I absorbed and internalized beauty myths. I guess the self-consciousness hit me or maybe oozed to the surface when I was about thirteen, that threshold time when I should have had some kind of rite of passage to adulthood. I was insecure, even angry about my developing body. Angry at the unwanted attention from older men, at my physical and emotional discomfort. Around this time faint memories of sexual abuse began to invade my dreams. I also remember scouring *Seventeen* magazine, *Elle*, *Vogue*. The intensity of adolescence is a confusing, contradictory blur. My closest friends in elementary school were athletes—naturally thin and boyish—who made fun of girls like me who developed early. Maybe, I thought (hoped), somehow they wouldn't notice me.

When I was ten years old my mom caught me trying to shave my arms after my "friends" made fun of me for being hairy. I had peach

fuzz all over. I was not only horrified to be caught but even more horrified when she told me that if I followed through, my hair might
grow back thicker and darker. Years later, I tried Nair, with its sickening, chemical smell and promise of smooth, shiny beauty. It gave me
the creeps when I wiped my leg and hair, wilted from the root, gave
way. What else was it killing? At the age of eleven, I got my period,
and at fourteen, I began to fight hunger. Not because I didn't have
enough to eat or even because I was trying to lose weight, but to
strengthen my will, assert self-control, and distract myself from
memories of sexual assault. At fourteen I was forced to have sex without consent, and in the wake of that, memories of earlier assault became vivid, and I felt entirely out of control of my body. I hated what
my body attracted, so I needed to rein her in; I needed to control her.

My incredible restraint and denying myself food—a biological
imperative and once a pleasure I loved so much—helped me hold disturbing memories at bay, numbed my emotions, and made me feel
strong. If I could move beyond hunger, I reasoned, I had total control
of my body, and that was power.

Female spotted hyenas have a clitoris so large and long—a single
urogenital canal used to pee, have sex, and carry offspring—that it
looks like a penis. For a male to penetrate, a female must voluntarily
distend her clitoris to allow the male access. It is physiologically
impossible for a male to mate with a female if she isn't into him. In
other words, it is impossible for a male hyena to rape a female
hyena. She is completely in control of sex. And since females rule
reproduction and tend to choose lower-ranking males, there is no reproductive payoff for male aggression.

After working together to bring down a large prey, spotted hyenas
then enter what looks like a competitive eating contest, taking in as
many calories as possible. During feeding, higher-ranking females,

their cubs, and adult offspring have first dibs on the meal, showing where social dominance hierarchies are most important: access to food. Hyena daughters born to high-ranking mothers inherit their status and get the choice selection of fresh meat. Contrary to popular depictions of spotted hyenas as scavengers—like the hyenas in Disney's *The Lion King*, who sneak around and steal food from the noble "king of the jungle"—they get at least half their meals by hunting. Hyenas excel in collaborative hunting and are more successful in kills than lions. Hyenas' complex social lives and unique adaptations have long been underestimated. But thanks to dedicated field researchers like Dr. Kay Holecamp, our understanding of these fascinating creatures is finally evolving. Her decades-long study of spotted hyenas in Africa, spanning ten generations, has provided a new appreciation for this misunderstood and misrepresented species.

While a symptom of underlying problems that I would eventually address, my teenage food restriction was reinforced by images and messages of beauty. Previously a junior size seven, I could soon fit into the children's clothes at my mom's consignment store, and I was proud. I drowned my body's pleas for love and nourishment with busyness. I learned to vacate my body and watch her, self-consciously, from the outside, not present for the earthly, sensual experiences my body was capable of giving me. Then, at sixteen, I fractured my back and my neck in a car accident and was trapped inside my bedroom and body for months.

On the long road to recovery, talk therapy, therapeutic release through drawing and writing, time in nature, and, eventually, physical therapy, strength training, and sports training landed me back in my body. But still I policed my food intake under the guise of health. I read books that told me to eat only fruit until noon and that if my body was distressed, it meant she was "detoxing." I read other books that said to eat a big breakfast but no dinner. And others that said to eat small meals throughout the day. They all had one trait in common: restriction, control, and the notion that we cannot trust our bodies and our cravings.

Then, at nineteen years old, after endless hiking and physical training, I went on a three-week Outward Bound trip to the San Juan Islands. My backpack was filled with essentials only: practical clothing, food, tent, sleeping bag, and, at the time, my inhaler. I wasn't weighed down with creature comforts or a mirror—an object of unhealthy fixation and distortion—and my time away was liberating. In the wild, I was looking elsewhere, less self-conscious, available for the wonders that surrounded me. I forgot to judge my appearance. I was more self-aware. I was living in my body, *really living in it*.

Upon moving to New York City, I scrambled to make ends meet. I worked as an artist, painting occasional murals, drawing logos by hand, and assisting a photographer, running behind him in heels while he shot celebrities. I was always on the hunt for something sustainable, so soon, I became a personal trainer. It made sense; I'd learned a lot from the car accident rehabilitation and worked hard to dismantle my stories of the physically deficient asthmatic kid to become an athlete. But personal training wasn't what I thought it would be. A growing profession in the midnineties, it led me into a world of mirrors where fitness-obsessed humans flexed, posed, and gazed at their muscles while trainers everywhere counted reps: *One, two, three.* In locker rooms, trainers popped pills and drank chalky liquids made of "performance" powders. Beautiful women came to me fixated on having smaller, perfectly toned thighs, perfectly sculpted triceps, or washboard abs. If and when they reached those ephemeral goals, they became obsessed with maintaining them, even at the cost of their own health and pleasure. The atmosphere felt vacuous, but I understood their goals. It took a lot of therapy and constant inner work to embrace my own body. I did my best to steer clients toward health and strength instead of preoccupation with the surface.

To fill the empty soul-space, I worked part time at *Satya*, an animal rights and environmental magazine. It wasn't easy. Sitting at my desk, I read emails and alerts about abuse of our animal kin in circuses, "research" labs, and factory farms; a stream of horror that wouldn't stop. I had nightmares about those confined creatures, hearing them screaming in the night, haunting the space between waking and dreaming for the sake of waterproof mascara, academic curiosity, new pharmaceuticals, antiaging serum, thickening shampoo, and concealing foundation. Nothing I did could ever be enough.

Then one day at the gym, I met a professional boxer and was consumed by the beauty of shadowboxing, maybe because I desperately needed to get all the angst out of my system. Since I had grown up in a family of artists and physicians, boxing was never on my radar, but I was enthralled and convinced the boxer to train me. I was soon obsessed with the therapeutic power of the sport and began a daily regimen of reclaiming my body. Wearing sneakers and hoodies on my walk to the boxing gym in Brooklyn, I visualized sparring sessions— perfecting and landing the perfect hook—getting my mind ready to train. Ravenous afterward, I stopped counting calories and learned to heed my hunger. Food became fuel for performance, no longer a potential threat. Eventually, I developed enough skill to coach boxing and teach other women how to fight.

SISTERHOOD

Despite the obvious intrinsic advantages of physical prowess— sexual dominance, more aggressive behavior, larger size—a new study of hyena social behaviors suggests that social support, sisterhood, is more vital to the animals. Healthy relationships and good communication are the reasons females govern clans, which can grow up to one hundred members—more than any other carnivore. Spending much of their time in breakout groups that come together to fight, hunt, or feed, hyenas have a social arrangement known as a fission-fusion society, and maintaining it requires sophisticated communication. Some studies have shown that spotted hyenas have social cognition and recognition on a par with that of primates. Ultimately, the stronger the sisterhood and the better the communication, the more powerful they are.

I often do an exercise in my herbal apprenticeships I call writing as the body. I began doing it out of necessity when I was reeling and didn't know why. I would sit down, get quiet, tune in to areas of discomfort, and let my body speak. When words poured onto the page, it felt like I was writing from the ground up, not the head down. Emotions were communicated in ways my conscious mind wasn't aware of (or chose not to hear) and I was always astounded at the wisdom that emerged. Through practice, I developed deeper listening and released tension where I carried trauma or shame. I cultivated more compassion for the parts of myself I judged.

In a recent online session with students, I offered a guided meditation to explore a part of our bodies that needed to speak. After tuning in, it was time for stream-of-consciousness writing, and almost all of the women in that class wrote from the perspective of their soft bellies. Bellies that just wanted to be loved, nourished, listened to, and accepted. They cried as they read from their bellies' voice: "I am doing my best, working on your behalf, processing what you give me. I love you, I need you to love me back. We need to become whole." It was cathartic. We heard one another and our bodies were heard, too. Listening is healing. They had been so cruel to their soft bellies; to themselves.

What are we really hoping for when we obsess about our looks and buy promises of youth and ever-elusive beauty? At the core, isn't it to be loved, accepted, and seen? And if we have those things, then what else? Why waste time feeling bad about ourselves? I ask myself these questions when I find myself judging my body, which works so damn hard on my behalf. *What is it really that's bothering me?*

Monitoring every fluctuation of our body and every wrinkle or blemish on our skin is bondage, keeps us distracted, unable to be present for the depth of true beauty. I know countless beautiful women—inside and out, even by our society's standards—who feel ugly. Feeling beautiful and looking beautiful are very different things. And if we don't get to the root of why we feel ugly, ashamed, and unworthy and do our best together to dismantle systems of oppression, we will exhaust ourselves, trying to keep our heads above water with surface-level compliments.

Nature is filled with stunning diversity. There is no such thing as one right kind of wildflower, waist, or shade of skin. With the onslaught of confusing, harmful messages, comparisons, and body shaming, we need constant reminders of the animals we really are. We need to wonder at the miracle and mystery of our bodies, and the countless pleasures they are capable of giving us. To release longings to be a certain size, shape, or height and instead acknowledge our deeper longings to be respected, embraced, and accepted. To explore our bodies' strength, athleticism, and potential. Like the sisterhood of spotted hyenas, we are more powerful than we know, and we are more powerful together.

Cheetahs

Female cheetahs are nomadic. They hunt, live, and raise their cubs alone, socializing with males only when mating. No courtship behavior is observed when cheetahs copulate; their pairing is pure desire with no attachment. Unlike other cat species, female cheetahs ovulate rarely and at unusual times. They also lack a regular reproductive cycle, and now scientists suspect that the male's stutter bark, a series of high-pitched barks that are emitted rapidly in succession, may have something to do with it. Researchers found that increases in males' stutter barking steadily raised the female reproductive hormones responsible for ovulation. Using sound to jump-start reproduction is common among birds, but before observing it in cheetahs, researchers hadn't been aware that mammals are turned on by sound, too.

When it comes to mating in the wild, there are no dominant males within a coalition (usually made up of two to three littermates that have stayed together) that claim exclusive access to females during a mating period. Estrus lasts up to fourteen days and females will mate with multiple males during this time. When a lucky male secures hold of a female's nape, intercourse ensues. The pair then ignore each other apart from meeting and mating three to five times a day for the next two to three days before parting ways.

To burn with desire and keep quiet about it is the greatest punishment we can bring on ourselves.

—FEDERICO GARCÍA LORCA, *Blood Wedding and Yerma*

5

Wanting to Be Wanted

The orange harvest moon rose over the field in Queens. It was 2015, and as usual, we were the last ones left at the beach. Salty and satisfied after a long day, I folded our mat and packed our belongings into Rafael's scooter for the ride back to Brooklyn. I was seduced again, pulled back by the magnetic tide of the city, revisiting New York City with fresh eyes. My new approach to work and the excitement of my relationship with Rafael seemed to offer a balance between the urban and rural wild, solitude and intimacy. I could lose myself in the beating heart of the wilderness—Costa Rica, the forests of the Northeast, my ancestral home in Scotland, a place I'd just begun visiting—and come back to my vibrant community in Brooklyn. He traveled for work and so did I. We ebbed and flowed—separation and togetherness, solitude and partnership, city and forest. It felt romantic.

Walking hand in hand, we went to the farmers market at Grand Army Plaza on Saturdays. Back at our apartment with a beautiful bounty of veggies, we chose soundtracks to drown out the noise of city streets—Leonard Cohen, Roberto Carlos, the Pixies—as we cooked together. We held hands across the table and as we ate. As we spoke and with every meal, we learned something new about each other. In the summers, we played in the ocean and took long weekend camping trips. Scrambling up rocks and mountains, we kept pace with each other, holding hands while I foraged woodland greens for our picnics. He thought it was funny to take pictures of me every time I peed in the woods and thought it was sexy that I was so comfortable in my skin. We walked around our apartment naked all the time and it was freeing.

The movement of cats is sensual and the flexibility of the cheetah's spine is especially unique. A cheetah's shoulder blade does not attach to the collarbone, which allows the shoulders to slither freely. Their hips pivot so their rear legs can stretch far apart when the body is fully extended, allowing for a large range of extension during running for exceptional stride. Their long muscular tails work like rudders, stabilizing and acting as a counterbalance to their body weight. Swinging the tail back and forth, continually adjusting to the movement of prey, steadies sudden sharp turns during high-speed chases. Hunting in early morning and late afternoon, cheetahs climb trees or termite mounds to get optimal vantage points for spotting prey against the horizon.

Female cheetahs lead solitary lives unless they are accompanied by their cubs. Unlike male cheetahs, who prefer to live in set territories with their coalition, females travel within home ranges that encompass several male territories. The large territory provides females with access to many males. Because of this, a recent scientific study labeled female cheetahs as "promiscuous." An interesting choice of words. Mating with multiple males is likely a survival strategy that evolved to confuse paternity, which deters infanticide and reduces male harassment that can cause injury or death.

Like all felines, cheetahs have a tenacious hold on life. Even when they fall from high places, they can land lightly.

After a couple of years, passion seemed to wane and my comfort with my animal body began to rob Rafael of mystery. There was nothing to peel away, he said. *Maybe if you wear more clothes around the apartment, maybe that will help.* So I put on clothes, waiting for him to tear them off, and he didn't. *When it's beach season, when we go to the beach, when I can fully relax. Then.* We went to the beach, had fun, held hands, played in the water, and I peeled and ate delicious mangoes with my fingers, the sticky juice dripping all over. When I licked my fingers to clean them off, he thought it was messy. *You should use a knife*, he said.

We went out to a concert in Brooklyn and I wanted to dance but he didn't. Back at home I pulled him into me, and he turned me away and said, *I don't like it when women are aggressors.* I was stunned. Aggressors? I guess early on it wasn't clear who made the first move; our desire and wanting was mutual. When we walked into our apartment after our outing, he turned on the television and I turned inward. I hated television, always did, still do. I don't want to watch people live; I want to live.

I began to request dates, since they weren't happening naturally, and on nights when he watched TV, I went upstairs to read and journal: *I'm ripe, bearing fruit, but all the juices just spill on the floor here and I have to clean them up. A waste. They should be soaked up by the soil. Food for flora, fungi; food for the chaos of life. He wants to stare into a tiny little box when there is a massively magical and expansive world out there.* I directed pent-up, frustrated creative energy toward writing, work, and movement practice. Convinced that sex was the crux of a relationship, and that men were insatiable, I began to wonder, *Is there someone else? Is he no longer attracted to me? Is he gay?* I wrestled with insecurities. I know that as women age, we can become more invisible—catcalled less, stared at less, seen as less desirable. I wondered, was that happening to me? I felt alone, my sexuality stifled, my body confused. Confused because we were still playful, affectionate, and loving. He still held my hand everywhere we went—in bed, among friends, walking down the beach and down city streets. He loved me, everyone could see that. But tension was building. More and more, there were parts of me that he refused to see.

When I felt frustrated or claustrophobic in our Brooklyn apartment, I went out to our communal courtyard, where the building's elusive cat prowled. Almost invisible in the unkempt grass, she quietly stalked her prey, waited motionlessly for insects or rodents to draw closer, and pounced when they appeared. Though she "belonged" to a neighbor, she seemed to exist in a liminal space between wild and domesticated. While they have been bred and kept as companions for millennia, cats retain many of their ancestral instincts and behaviors, making them more independent and less reliant on humans than other domesticated species. The countless cats who survive on New York City streets are a testament to their resourceful independence and ability to rewild.

Wild and "domesticated" cats have come to represent the bold, more aggressive aspects of women who are unconcerned with what the world thinks of them. It is their aloofness and apparent lack of interest in others that connects felines with women who live beyond usual societal roles—witches, spinsters, and awkward "cat ladies" living on the fringes of society. Female and feline connections have existed since at least the times of ancient Egypt—shifting from goddesses such as Isis, Bastet, and Sekhmet and their associations with fertility, motherhood, the underworld, the hunt, and warding off evil spirits to current associations of sexually promiscuous cat-women or sexless cat ladies.

In medieval times, leaders of the spreading Christian faith saw pagan, non-Christian religions as barbaric and a direct threat to Christianity. Through their patriarchal propaganda, female-feline hybrids were no longer thought of as bringers of fertility, patrons of motherhood, or symbols of feminine strength but were maligned as

godless, carnal, and lacking restraint. Due to feline associations
with pagan goddesses, cats, like wolves and other wild creatures,
were thought to be agents of the devil. Like the male werewolf, rumor
had it that witches were able to transform into cats and use cats as
tools for harnessing and channeling magical powers. It was believed
that if a werewolf or cat-woman suffered an injury while transformed, the same injury would remain when they were back in
human form.

Once I accepted that Rafael wasn't expending his sexual energy
elsewhere, I hunted for couples therapists and online and in-person
workshops, and read everything by Esther Perel. In *Mating in Captivity: Unlocking Erotic Intelligence,* she writes, "Love enjoys knowing
everything about you; desire needs mystery." Maybe that was the
problem. Maybe we had become too close.

Ready to do the work, I was open to almost anything and everything that might help. He was open to it, too, at first, but always put it
off. I'd give a little nudge here and there, but the more I brought it up
and the more I sent him articles and links, the more annoyed and re-
sistant he became. The more I mentioned sex, the less it seemed he
wanted it. "Love and intimacy doesn't have to mean sex," he said, and
I was moved. It made me feel almost ashamed of my desire to be
wanted, to bond in a carnal way. It was true that there was profound
tenderness between us. I also knew that I couldn't make the first
move because it turned him off, but if he was in the mood for some
reason, even if I wasn't, I tried to be because I knew it might not happen again anytime soon.

Eventually, I stopped seeking solutions and the subject of sex became awkward, almost unspeakable. Profoundly strange in an intimate relationship. And like any unspeakable thing, its absence
became a presence, a ghost that took on a life of its own. I could feel it

lurking throughout our apartment, pressing against our bodies while
we tried to pretend it wasn't there.

Clear about her boundaries, the courtyard cat hissed and clawed
when people tried to touch her uninvited. While feisty and sometimes standoffish, cats simply have boundaries that will only infuri-
ate those who wish to disrespect them. So when she chose to climb
up on my lap one day, I knew that I'd better stay put and pet her.
Maybe she sensed I needed something. Maybe we both did. Whatever it was, I felt honored, and she became a companion. As I spent
more and more time with her, I began to learn about "domesticated"
cats and found a study by scientists at Oregon State University that
determined that when given the choice, cats actually prefer affection
from kind human companions to food. How sad to be so wholly misunderstood.

RESTRAINT

The captive cheetah used as a prop for Cardi B's "Bodak Yellow"
video, filmed in Dubai, snapped and attacked Cardi B. Instead of
raising awareness that an endangered animal was being used as a
prop or that cheetahs in eastern Africa could be at risk of dying out
within two years because cubs are illegally stolen and sold for narcis-
sistic posturing, the news reports said Cardi B was "brave." The naturally aggressive cheetah was quickly replaced with a sedated one. In
the video, Cardi B holds a drugged cheetah on a chain.

According to the Cheetah Conservation Fund (CCF), an organization that works to rescue stolen, abused animals and offer them
healing and sanctuary, approximately 300 cubs—between two
thirds and three quarters of all those born—are taken from the wild

every year. Around 75 percent of those cubs die in transit from malnutrition or as a result of broken bones suffered when they are packed into tiny crates and shipped abroad. After being sold, most of the cheetahs die within two years from metabolic and digestive disorders because people don't know what to feed them, as well as from stress-related diseases due to trauma, obesity, and confinement. A recent CCF study documented 1,367 cheetahs for sale on social media platforms between January 2012 and June 2018, largely from Arab Gulf states. In a recent interview, Dr. Laurie Marker, the founder of the CCF, explained, "They don't love these animals. When one dies they simply go back to the wild and get another." Traumatized and stolen at a young age, most have not developed the skills necessary to survive in the wild.

Built for speed, cheetahs require vast expanses of land with suitable prey, water, and cover sources to survive. But as wildlands are increasingly fragmented and altered by human expansion, the cheetah's habitat is degraded. Numerous landscapes across Africa that could once support thousands of cheetahs now struggle to support just a handful. Even as their habitats are constrained and they're unable to live their lives unfettered, people still see them as "sexy" status symbols. "If we do the math," Dr. Marker says, "it's only going to be a matter of a couple of years [before] we are not going to have any cheetahs."

As Rafael's desire waned, his sweetness grew. I knew that our affection didn't have to, and would rarely, lead to lovemaking, so my body could soften into his touch and rest in a new kind of way. Still, I worried, *Am I suppressing my own desire? Is my body physically changing from this new quiet?* I explored the question from every angle and was surprised to find that when I let go of the incessant questioning and my insecurities, my body seemed relieved. I began to wonder about all the times I worked myself into the mood and said yes when I didn't really want to: *When did I use my body for the sake of a relationship? Were there times I consented to avoid the fallout of saying no?* I remembered times my body clenched when a partner touched me because almost always he wanted it to lead to sex. I remembered when partners pouted, got angry, or turned inward when I said no. There were none of these tensions now. Rafael's growing freedom from his libido was freeing me. In a world where women are seen as sex objects, sex was no longer the glue that held our relationship together, and I marveled at that. My body and I had time to rest and reflect, and could just be.

I had so much to be grateful for. I wrote gratitude lists in my mind, taking stock of tender moments in each day before I fell asleep. Sometimes I shared them aloud when he was next to me, and we would exchange romantic moments: *When we walked through the Japanese maples at the Botanic Gardens holding hands, when we harvested cherry blossoms in Prospect Park, when we kissed in the aisle of the co-op.* It was sweet, but in retrospect, I think my gratitude lists worked against me, against my nature. They helped me appreciate what I had, which was a lot, but also romanticized and inflated each drop of sweetness, compelling me to ask for too little. If I woke with desire, I suppressed the energy and held it inside. I could be cute and cuddly but not ravenous and feline. I cherished our love and tenderness, but at times, it felt patronizing. My gratitude lists were subduing my animal desires.

There were other problems, too. We argued about stupid things more frequently: the lights, the sound of the radio and TV when I needed quiet darkness. When I woke at night I often saw the glow of his phone screen. At the farmers market, relishing the harvest, I would see him out of the corner of my eye, reading the news. I felt I was losing him to those bright boxes of entertainment. My therapist asked, *Can you deal with those behaviors?* I didn't know because I judged them, assuming people who want to be entertained all the time are avoiding themselves. I saw the constant craving for noise or external stimulation as some sort of character flaw, some sort of avoidance of being human. *But what does it mean to be human, anyway?* The lack of courtship salve from consensual carnal bonding, an emotional bond reportedly undetected in cheetahs, was undermining our bliss.

He began to wear headphones all the time to give me some space from the stimulation he preferred, and he didn't like it. For him, containing noise was an unwelcome restraint, so I tried to balance the burden by taking my turn wearing noise-canceling headphones when he needed freedom. But my headphones are designed to let audible frequencies of human speech pass through, so the voices and conversations around me still penetrated. I used more noise—white-noise machines, fans, sometimes John Coltrane, sometimes Chopin—to drown out the soundscape when I needed to concentrate. I could work and write when I listened to Nocturnes, but my body was overwhelmed. Rafael didn't seem to understand that the quiet was my bodily need, I wasn't trying to constrain him or be annoying. My nervous system was depleted. My body was in need of not only release but rest. I was overstimulated in all the wrong ways.

Then I thought maybe my desire was also waning. *Maybe I'm getting old, maybe I am okay with just cuddling. He still kisses me, still holds my hand, and is even more tender. I am going through perimenopause, after all, aren't I?* At least it seemed that way. Plus, I could be away for long stretches of time without worry, jealousy, or the magnetic pull of chemistry. Like a feline, I roamed and traveled without feeling pulled by desire or a partner's possessiveness. *But what about the feline hunter and aggressor? The part of me that was bold, thirsty, and hungry?*

Beneath the earnest rationalizing of my mind, my animal body expressed her needs. Night after night, in the dream realm, I'd hear distant stutter barks and have exciting relationships with other men. The vivid experiences moved through my body, waking me, bringing me back to my irrepressible thirst for passion, connection, sensation. I wanted to be wanted. Many times Rafael was there, on the periphery of the dream, and when he was, I asked permission. *As long as it is just sex*, he would say. But when I emerged from bliss in my dream, I felt guilty, as though I had cheated on him. Awake in the middle of the night, I thought about asking for an open relationship, but I didn't really want one. I wanted one partner to dive deep with, someone I trusted and who trusted me. Someone who had the desire to enter my deepest longings, not just my body. There were so many conversations and negotiations between dreaming and waking that in the mornings, I woke exhausted.

Orchestrating sexual restraint brought cheetahs into my subconscious realm. In one dream, I found an empty cage that was a barrier between worlds. An illusion. A cheetah-woman suddenly appeared in the cage and I told her that I often dreamed about cheetahs. I told her I carried orphaned cubs to safety and that each dream was so vivid that I could still feel the cubs' warmth and weight. I told her I thought the cages weren't really cages but entries to other realms. *Yes*, she said. *That is exactly what they are. Don't be afraid. Open the cage and walk through.*

PART TWO

Rehabilitation

Rehabilitation involves the treatment and care of sick, injured, or orphaned animals with the goal of releasing them, once healed, back to their natural habitats. These animals—whether wild or human—are not intended for a life of entrapment but are not free. For healing to happen, animals and their caregivers must acknowledge trauma and tend to wounds.

In the process of healing, animals may be isolated in a cage, hospital, or bedroom, away from their community so they can recover and, sometimes, so they can keep their community safe. This might mean nonnegotiable rest, carefully selected herbs or meals, medical intervention, various forms of therapy, or healing practices like stretching, meditation, or journaling. The process of healing can be complicated for both the animal and the caregiver. Inner wounds, especially those of the emotional body and mind, can be difficult to see and confusing to heal.

To be released into the wild or sent home, animals must demonstrate mental and physical health, the ability to fend for themselves, and the power to function as a normal, healthy member of their species.

Yesterday I was clever, so I wanted to change the world.
Today I am wise, so I am changing myself.

—RUMI

Vultures

While many animals scavenge, vultures are the only land vertebrates that rely almost entirely on dead animals for food. By removing carrion from roadsides, meadows, forests edges, and lawns, these peaceful birds reduce the spread of disease. A vulture's stomach acid is so strong that it kills most bacteria and viruses, including anthrax and rabies, while their speedy, efficient disposal of bodies does not allow deadly bacteria to develop and spread. This means that when a vulture eats a dead raccoon that had rabies, the disease dies in their stomach and can no longer infect other animals. But if a fox or dog were to eat the same dead raccoon, they could contract the disease and spread it. Thus, vulture conservation is a matter of ecological, human, and economic health. In areas where vultures are absent, contagious diseases run rampant.

it is a serious thing
just to be alive
on this fresh morning
in this broken world

—MARY OLIVER, "INVITATION"

6

Quarantine

I am wasting energy again today, circling dead things. Things I wish I'd done, wish I'd said, decisions I wish I'd made differently. I bring myself back, uselessly, to the moments I should have listened to my gut, moments when it was possible to avert what was to come. I know I need to learn the lesson and move on, but something in me is fixated and I can't get away. *What do I need to learn? What do I need to see?* My therapist suggests getting curious when repetitive thoughts arise. She says they could be unconscious distractions I'm using to avoid something else. So maybe the question is: *What is it I don't want to feel, don't want to see?* I wonder, can I dive down, pick at the flesh, and move on?

It's February 2020. I have just arrived in Glasgow, Scotland, and feel particularly out of it. My heart feels achy and I'm struggling with the noise outside. Glasgow doesn't seem to hold the same spell over me that it has in the past. I don't feel the same kind of magic. But it's not the city's fault. Instead of arriving in spring like I have before, I am arriving in winter, post–holiday frenzy, and it's gray and rainy. The world outside is stripped down, naked, and cold. Many animals are hibernating or, like North America's raptors, enjoying warmer places. But I have flown here in winter to write a memoir told through the lens of twenty-four medicinal plants and, in the process, to unearth memories. In two days, I head farther north to the Highlands. First to a writer's retreat with friends in Lochaber, then to Alladale Wilderness Reserve, a stunning 23,000-acre nature preserve where I've offered retreats. Alladale accommodations are closed to the public until spring, so my friend, the manager, offered me a month-long stay in one of their cottages to be alone with my thoughts while it's empty. It will be interesting to see which memories, long buried, are still squirming and want to be seen.

In stunning seasonal migrations, turkey vultures, hawks, and their raptor cousins use air currents to travel in flocks of hundreds. Some generous turkey vultures may return early from Central and South America to scavenge dead creatures of winter that weren't consumed by other animals, fungi, or frozen earth. Doing us a service, they clean putrid flesh that would reek as winter thaws into spring. Using their keen sense of smell, vultures can locate dead animals on the forest floor, even beneath dense canopies. I have always enjoyed seeing the large, heavy-bodied birds spiral above me. I recently read that if a turkey vulture sees a mortally ill or wounded animal, they wait for the animal's natural death before descending. Patient, they don't rush death along.

In the summer, I've seen vultures eating, their heads covered in blood, guts, and rotting flesh. Somehow, they've evolved to kill all the potential disease that comes from carcasses. Our own stomachs are like acid lakes, too, but we can't digest what vultures can. There is an elegance and nobility to these birds who perform the honorable task of dealing with our dead. I always marvel at the fact that animals evolved with such distinct roles. *What is ours?*

I'm listening to *Mother Earth's Plantasia.* "Music to Soothe a Savage Snake Plant" is playing as I scribble in my journal and look out over the Glasgow Botanic Gardens greenhouses. I booked this room in the West End of the city because it was close to the plants. I was looking forward to being here, to visiting the flora and other friends, but now that I'm here I am already yearning for home. *But where is home, really?* Even though I've lived in New York City for over twenty years, it has felt transient, never quite like home. My apartments in the East Village, Williamsburg, Crown Heights, and Prospect Heights were places to keep things for a while. Before coming here, I wrote and house-sat in Ashfield, Massachusetts, and it was a taste of what I'd like my life to be, I think. A quiet, safe woodland sanctuary. Land near my family that I can grow intimate with, where I can cultivate my own food and medicine and maybe be buried to become earth and feed plants, when I die.

ESSENTIAL WORKERS

I sit down to write and I ask myself: *Who am I writing for?* I journal: *I am writing for the plants, the misunderstood creatures, the young me who felt that she didn't have a voice.* Afraid of censoring myself, I ask, *Who am I writing to?* I imagine a best friend, a person I would share anything and everything with, even my shadows. I want to be as honest as I can. When I'm done, I'll edit and ask, *What is in service of the story?*

I'm in lockdown at Alladale Wilderness Reserve. COVID has spread—coming from somewhere, from a bat in China's wet markets or maybe a dead, endangered, and illegally poached pangolin. Some are convinced it was born in a lab and part of a massive conspiracy. Whatever the cause, humans are responsible. In *Spillover: Animal Infections and the Next Human Pandemic*, David Quammen explores the root cause of zoonotic diseases like Ebola and SARS and states that we humans "should recognize that they reflect things that we're doing, not just things that are happening to us." Now I am here in the Scottish Highlands indefinitely, staying in a suite at Alladale's Victorian lodge, where I've run retreats that I couldn't otherwise afford. Sometimes I feel as though I am hiding out, awkward, the only person amid Alladale's 23,000 acres apart from the owner, Paul Lister, his partner, and a small staff. But soon the creaks in the stairs become intimate and what seemed ornate now seems ordinary. Walking outside through the endless rolling hills, I feel safe, free, and incredibly fortunate. I'm even more uneasy about going back to the city now.

I first learned about Alladale through articles about Paul Lister's vision to reintroduce wolves—now extinct in Scotland—to the denuded, colonized landscape. The Highlands, famous for their dramatic, naked rolling hills, were once biodiverse temperate rainforests that thrived alongside small human settlements. Those native Scots—my ancestors among them—were subsistence farmers living humbly in relationship with the land. They were forced to flee their homes during the clearances—local shorthand for the violent mass eviction by the English in the eighteenth and nineteenth centuries that made way for the profitable introduction of domesticated sheep. After Indigenous people were cleared, the sheep were soon joined by thousands of red deer, who were moved to the Highlands for aristocratic shooting parties. Since then, the Highlands have become "a rich man's playground," my friend Àdhamh, a Gaelic cultural activist, explained begrudgingly. In the absence of natural predators and Indigenous stewards, Highland forests have been decimated.

To dispel the people's fear of wolf reintroduction, Paul suggested creating large fenced areas of land where wolves could roam. But people in Scotland have the "right to roam," a law that allows humans to walk all areas of land, and a fenced-off area would keep people from accessing Alladale. But wouldn't that be a small price to pay for revival of native flora and fauna?

"Just stay over there, finish your book," Rafael tells me, and I am grateful, relieved. As someone who grew up with debilitating asthma,

I'm afraid of COVID. But in some ways, I feel like I've been training my whole life for this moment—the solitude and intermittent isolation of quarantine—because of my illness as a child. Absent from school, I had piles of work I could never catch up on. Notes excused me but my absences gnawed at me. Simultaneously, I had unstructured time that kids my age didn't have, and those gaps became sacred space for self-reflection. When I could free myself from worrying about what peers or teachers thought of or wanted from me, I could enter into my own world. I had time to wonder, be creative, just be. I had time to be with my body, breathe with her, and grapple with our fraught relationship. Now, alone in Scotland, I can breathe easily, but I still harbor the feeling of being "too late."

I've never stopped craving the creative solitude I had as a child, but as I've grown older I've had a harder time reconciling the need for that time and space with the need to support myself financially and, especially, with the need for quality time with loved ones. Sometimes I feel guilty when I make the choice to be alone to recharge or create instead of spending time with family or a partner. And I have a morbid fear: *What if that is the last time I have to see my mom or my beloved?* But here, in lockdown, I don't have to negotiate. The decision has been made for me. I cannot leave even if I wanted to, and in many ways, that is a relief. My mind is feeling more free here. I'm no longer swirling; I can hear the thoughts of my whole body, not just my head.

It is late spring now and I need to move and connect with nature, so I go out to hunt for mushrooms—life nourished by death and decay. More closely related to animals than to plants, fungi consume dead wood, leaves, and bodies from the forest floor and then erupt into strange, beautiful shapes. During the pandemic, it is not easy for humans to get food, so in addition to foraging, I am eating venison. The overpopulated deer are regularly culled here, and though I am fortunate to get deliveries way out here in the Highlands, eating deer (though often emotionally charged for me) is more sustainable than getting lettuce and strawberries shipped from who knows where. I recently read that roughly 60 percent of our modern diseases have been linked to the agricultural revolution—the period of transition from hunting and gathering to settled agriculture that began around 10,000 years ago. Close contact with domestic animals, the storage of food, the development of new social structures, and changes in diet created opportunities for pathogens to spread and evolve, leading to the emergence of many of the diseases we know today.

I became a strict vegan as a teenager, a choice of ethics I was proud of, but when I trained as a professional boxer in my late twenties I began to crave meat again. Ordering brown rice, steamed veggies, and tofu, I bypassed my body's response to the smell of burgers on the grill. It was deeply disturbing to enjoy the scent of animals being cooked, but after a year of much angst, I gave in to my body's pleas and ate a free-range, grass-fed steak. I have to admit, my body felt better for it. When I stopped boxing competitively, I again struggled with eating meat. Sometimes I would crave a burger, and when I listened to my body on those rare occasions, even though I chose only free-range and humanely raised meat, seeing the gentle cows ground up into packages would make me cry. But I also knew that being vegan—amid monoculture, soy plantations, palm oil, and processed, packed GMO food—wasn't harmless, either. I read labels carefully to know what I was perpetuating or contributing to when selecting food, and I tried my best to listen to my body despite internalized and contradictory messaging of good versus bad, pure versus impure choices.

Spending time with wolves helped me make peace with eating meat again. I would watch the wolves tear into dead deer, roadkill brought to the Wolf Conservation Center, and carry around detached limbs. We are animals—predators, too, after all—and during my 2018 retreat at Alladale, two vegans in attendance also chose to eat deer. Sometimes it is the nature of the kill rather than the kill itself.

One of my favorite vegetarian restaurants in the West Village of New York City—with a cow sitting cross-legged in meditation as its logo—was Sacred Chow. This name was a nod to the Hindu tradition in India that observes a vegetarian diet and protects the cow as a sacred animal and source of prosperity. Krishna, a central Hindu deity, is often portrayed in stories recounting his life as a cowherd; tales refer to him as the child who protects cows. Mahatma Gandhi, born in the Hindu tradition, once said, "If anybody said that I should die if I did not take beef tea or mutton, even on medical advice, I would prefer death." India contains one of the world's largest cattle populations—roughly 33 percent of the world's source.

Because of religious and caste taboos, dead cows are left to the vultures, and the domesticated carrion has become their greatest food source. A wake of vultures are able to strip cattle down to the bone in about twenty minutes. But sadly many vultures feeding on the carcasses in India suffer renal failure, visceral gout, and death. Their deaths were a mystery until 2003, when the culprit—diclofenac, an anti-inflammatory drug initially developed for humans that livestock owners used on their cattle—was discovered by Dr. Lindsay Oaks and his team at the Peregrine Fund.

Perched on trees and electric poles, cliffs and housetops, Old World vultures—native to South and Southeast Asia—were once ubiquitous in cities and countryside. But since 2000, they have been listed as critically endangered on the IUCN Red List. In the 1980s, the global population of Old World vultures was estimated at several million individuals, and in just over a decade, they were gone, their numbers plummeting to near extinction. The absence of vultures created a vacuum, and millions of cattle carcasses were left rotting, increasing the possible spread in India of tuberculosis; anthrax; hand, foot, and mouth disease; and rabies. In the ecological gap, scavengers such as rats and feral dogs moved in and became carriers of pathogens, increasing the spread of disease.

With the near extinction of vultures, the Parsi community also found it difficult to sustain their traditional funeral rituals. In Mumbai, the dead of the Parsi community are brought to the Towers of Silence, where they are consumed by scavenger birds of prey, mainly vultures. Parsis hold land and water sacred, and burying or cremating the dead is seen as polluting nature. Similarly, in ancient Ireland and Scotland, a tradition called sky burials was performed. Excavations of a 4,000-year-old tomb in the Orkneys of Scotland revealed sea eagle bones along with the human bones. It is believed that the bodies of the dead were laid out for scavengers to pick clean before burial, and the scavengers, the sea eagles, were buried along with the remaining bones of the dead. In Tibet, where sky burials continue, corpses are carried to a high-altitude region by monks, where the *rogyapa*, the burial master, burns incense to attract vultures— sacred birds who are believed to carry the dead to the Other World.

In contrast, the Christian Bible calls the vulture an "impure" animal because they feed on carcasses and are linked to the realm of death. Leaving bodies in their care was a sign of exclusion from society and from God.

Despite biblical lore and a bad reputation in some cultures, the truth is that vultures are natural sanitary workers, essential for ecological balance. We may not like the sound or smell of garbage trucks, either, or respect janitors and sanitation workers as much as we should, but, like vultures, they are essential workers, necessary for reducing the spread of disease. During COVID and other outbreaks of disease, like the one that harmed Old World vultures in India, the necessity of workers (whether bird or human) that we demean or disregard becomes crystal clear.

As I walk the land in Scotland, I plan. It feels more vital than ever to steward land and grow food. Victory gardens are sprouting again, and I am hopeful. Maybe people will do away with useless toxic lawns to grow food and forage dandelions. Maybe we could start over and learn from those who live close to Earth instead of forgetting this pandemic time altogether and just going back to so-called normal. But Rafael still doesn't want to leave Brooklyn, even with the constant sirens, rising death tolls, and the ongoing fear of infection. If the pandemic doesn't make him want to move out of the city, I reason, nothing will. He worries that if we change our circumstances when I return, and leave the city for a rural area, he'll be isolated. Or if we try living in two places, life will be too expensive and emotionally exhausting. All I know is that right now, it is a huge comfort to have the anchor of our relationship, of our love, however far away, amid the uncertainty of the pandemic. But the truth is, we are both alone. At night, I reach for Rafael's hand out of habit, only to find my shadow.

It breaks my heart to know he is struggling through COVID quarantine alone in our Brooklyn apartment. We share in each other's lives less and less and it's painful. Sometimes the pain is a skin hunger, a desire for touch that I feel, and other times, it's a loneliness of spirit, unable to commiserate or share with him my deepest longings. Parallel lives worked for a while, us doing our separate things, but the more I go off on my own the less I feel he knows me.

Part of the problem is that he wants finished products—the finished book, practical, distilled information, the harvest without hands in the soil. He rarely asks about *me* lately, rarely asks about my writing, research, and work. He doesn't want to read my book until it's done. But for me, the process is the most thrilling part. It's raw and rich and real, it's where I'm healing and discovering myself, and I want to share that experience with him. Now I feel as though I am in the life-altering muck without my partner. I wonder, *Is this the relationship I'm meant to have in order to do my work in the world? Would I get swallowed up with someone who was always there in the ways I crave?* We love each other and maybe, for now, that is enough.

It has been six months. I feel different, my body is more at ease, and I feel grounded and at peace after being in the Highlands for so long. Now I am faced with the possibility of returning. Airports are open and I can fly back to Brooklyn, but I don't want to. I miss Rafael, though, and my heart aches from indecision. We want to live so differently. I ask myself over and over again: *Does it matter? Isn't love more important?* Alas, the circular conversations in my head have returned. I breathe and place my feet on Mother Earth.

I'm afraid to be back in New York City, but I also know I have to go back and confront life there in all its beauty and ugliness. I can't abandon it. Like a heavy-bodied bird, I must fly back to both life and death, and see if our love is still breathing.

Coyotes

The coyote is one of the world's most adaptable animals. Due to human alteration of the landscape and the extirpation of wolves, these canids, native to the Americas, traveled beyond the prairies and deserts where they evolved. As coyotes explored and expanded in their range and habitat, they mated with dogs and wolves, changing their body size and dietary menu. No longer limited by grassland fauna of rabbits, mice, and insects, coyotes now consume everything from small mammals and birds to livestock, lost pets, fruit, vegetables, garbage, and, in the case of the Eastern coyote, even deer.

Once confined to the Great Plains, coyotes can now be found throughout North and Central America, in forests, fields, scrublands, golf courses, suburban backyards, and the urban wild. Coyotes are represented by roughly twenty subspecies, including Eastern coyotes, often confusingly referred to as coywolves. These creative, intelligent canids can manage in the city or wherever they find themselves it seems, but their incredible resilience comes at a cost, and with great misunderstanding.

The greatest lie ever told about love is that it sets us free.

—ZADIE SMITH, *On Beauty*

7
Between Two Worlds

The ad on Craigslist described the space in Western Massachusetts as a "writer's studio" on a twenty-seven-acre wildlife sanctuary. It seemed ideal, and the photos were beautiful. I scheduled a call with the owner, a writer and photographer in her seventies who raises and releases monarch butterflies. I didn't last long in New York City after my extended quarantine in the Scottish Highlands. So once the photographer approved my residency, I headed north to Massachusetts to continue my writing.

After seven months apart, Rafael and I chose to stay together while continuing to live in different habitats. I migrated to the sort of rural environment I'd been longing for, at least for a while, and Rafael remained in our beloved Brooklyn. We planned to visit each other, find a rhythm, and spend time together with more intention. At least that's what I told myself and what we told each other. We didn't know how it would work, but the collective lesson of 2020 seemed to be: embrace uncertainty. We didn't know how long the pandemic would last, didn't know if was safe to see our loved ones, if kids could go to school, or where the next paycheck was coming from. We were all winging it, trying to get comfortable with discomfort. But as soon as I made the decision to leave, I felt the emotional push and pull: *When are you coming? Why aren't you staying?*

It is dusk, mid-October 2020, when I arrive in Western Massachusetts, and at first, I am disappointed. The house is close to the road and on the outside it is ordinary looking. I don't see the rolling hills, apple trees, and sanctuary that were promised. *Scotland ruined me*, I think. Still, I gather my belongings and look for the green door in the center of the house, the entry to my temporary writer's studio. As I walk, I hear the soothing, hopeful sound of crickets and soon find my door. It is unlocked and when I open it, all of my doubts dissolve. The space is magical. With one long sliding glass door as the back wall, it is a passageway to rolling mountains—the Seven Sisters—dressed in shades of red, orange, and yellow. Autumn colors of change. There is a clawfoot bathtub in the center of the small room where I can soak and watch the full moon rise, and lining the walls are photos of monarch butterflies in stages of metamorphosis. It feels symbolic, like I, too, am going into a cocoon.

I sleep deeply that first night, and in the morning I wake inspired and go straight to my desk positioned against the glass door, where all I see is nature. Listening to birdsong, I gaze out at an ocean of wildflowers, apple trees, hawthorn trees, and forest. Outside is vibrant and alive, and inside this small space, I can hear my own voice more clearly. At night, I soak in the tub and see the moon rise, and if I'm lucky, I might hear the distant howl of coyotes.

In the mythology of Native Americans from the Plains, California, and the Southwest, Coyote is a creator, lover, magician, glutton, and trickster who invents traps but, like Wile E. Coyote in the Roadrunner cartoons, often gets caught by his own tricks. When watching the cartoon as a kid, I always wanted Wile E. Coyote to win; to get his aim and timing right and smoosh the smug Roadrunner with a boulder or Acme anvil. I felt bad for Coyote, always getting hurt and absolutely exhausted. Usually a male figure in lore, Coyote is cunning but not so cunning as to avoid his own schemes. In many of the Native

American Coyote stories, through the chaos he brings with his scheming and transgression of social boundaries, Coyote gives humans fire, daylight, and the creative arts. Coyote's helpful contributions to humanity and to life in general are a vital part of the story missing from the violent, endless chase of the Roadrunner cartoons.

Love can cause us to act strangely, and sometimes, like the behavior of the mythical Coyote in lore, it leads us to make questionable choices. But in the end—in all its bliss and pain—love can also lead to incredible beauty and creation. Right now, love (or maybe attachment) and my animal body are at odds. I'm in limbo, not stuck just between the push and pull of me and Rafael, but the push and pull of the city and country, and the push and pull happening within myself. I'm here to finish my book, but my body is already planning to stay. Meanwhile, love is scheming, confusing me, and I am doing everything to make our relationship work. I want to be sure I've tried everything and that I'm listening to all parts of myself—my gut, my head, my heart. I've begun to think that love is its own entity with its own agenda. It wants to live like any other creature and needs certain habitats in order to thrive.

For the Miwok, members of four linguistically related Native American groups indigenous to what is now called Northern California, Coyote is an ancestor and a creator god. In the Creation of Man myth, Coyote creates all creatures—grizzly bear, silver fox, fish, lion, raven, buck, and so on—and calls them to a council to discuss the creation of humans. The lion, the bear, the buck, and all the others want humans to be gifted with their own best qualities, like sharp claws, a "terrible voice," and "ears like a spider's web, and eyes like fire"—as captured in a collection of stories by Katharine Berry Judson called *California and the Old Southwest*. Despite calling for the council, Coyote mocks their suggestions, proclaiming that humans should have his own wit and cunning. Even so, each animal creates a human figure in their own likeness. Overnight, Coyote destroys them. Only his vision of humans—a creature born of his own nature—comes to life.

Like humans, coyotes are so adaptable that they can be confusing. When living in close proximity to us, coyotes tend to be nocturnal but may also be active in the early morning and at sunset. Sometimes they cooperate to take down large prey like deer, but most often, they hunt small prey alone. When people kill coyotes, coyotes make up for the loss by having more pups and may use multiple dens—hidden under downed trees, on rocky ledges, or in abandoned fox or wood-chuck burrows that they alter and enlarge—to protect their pups from predators. Depending on the geographic area, coyotes can be solitary or form traveling pairs or packs. Urban coyotes tend to be transient and travel alone. Some people report that coyotes are small and others mistake large species like the Eastern coyote for wolves.

Yet these beautiful, intelligent canines are seen as second class, often referred to as varmints, and experience the same persecution— but not the reverence—as wolves, their canid cousins. It is because of humans, of course—who fractured landscapes and extirpated wolves—that coyotes have spread across cities and towns where they aren't wanted. In many ways, coyotes are an indicator species like some so-called weeds: indicating landscapes of violence, distur-bance, and absence. Away from their natural habitat, I imagine there is an ache in so-called weeds and coyotes, too. Not only are they out of place, but humans—who spray toxic herbicide where they grow and hunt them where they den—never cease to remind them that they are unwanted. In urban areas the threat to coyotes is usually au-tomobiles, while in rural areas the threat is hunting or trapping. Laws regarding hunting vary from state to state, but in many places it is always open season on coyotes.

Humans malign resilient species like dandelions, pigeons, raccoons, and coyotes, but aren't they like us? Emblems of resilience and survival? Or maybe *antifragile* is a better term, one coined by Nassim Nicholas Taleb in his book of the same name. Taleb calls things antifragile that not only gain from chaos and uncertainty but "benefit from shocks; they thrive and grow when exposed to volatility, randomness, disorder, and stressors and love adventure, risk, and uncertainty." According to Taleb, "the resilient resists shocks and stays the same; the antifragile gets better." Coyotes have much to teach us, providing inspiring examples of ingenuity and adaptability in an ever-changing world.

Like coyotes, I have always prided myself on being able to adapt to new environments. I lived in many different apartments and habitats after landing in New York City in the midnineties—from Park Slope to the East Village, then the Bronx, back to the East Village, and finally to a fifteen-year home base in Brooklyn. I lived with easy and difficult roommates, alone, and with beloveds and their quirks. In every living situation, I adjusted, shape-shifted, and leaned into the beauty of each new place and person. But I also lived with a persistent ache in the city that I tried to relieve—or maybe distract myself from—through the green spaces of city parks and community gardens, creative expression through art, the addictive allure of boxing, and the passionate hypnosis of love. I loved the mourning doves that nested on my fire escapes, the secret gardens and outdoor cafés where I could write and read and pretend I was somewhere else. Each time I moved within the bounds of New York City, I found my sanctuary and adapted. But something was always a little off. Now I wonder if I was good at adapting or at putting my animal needs aside. I wasn't unhappy but something was unfulfilled.

MAJOR

It's going to be complicated to get in and out of the city during the unending pandemic without a car. In all my years in the city I didn't need one, but I'll need one here in rural Massachusetts. A New Yorker for more than twenty years, I rarely drove. I created no carbon footprint in that respect. I wasn't building on land; I was living in tiny apartments stacked on top of hundreds of humans living adjacent to one another. Between composting and recycling, I hardly created waste, and that felt good to me. Sometimes I wished humans would congregate in the cities—not in rural or coastal areas—so other creatures could live without the stress of our sprawling, destructive species. But after a while, I could no longer neglect my needs. The overstimulation, a bodily need for true nature, the "hustle," and the overwhelming costs wore on me.

Now it is late October 2020, and I've finally got a car. A Subaru hybrid. But for me the trick is driving into the city and I'm terrified. I've been in three car accidents—one with my mom when I was six; another with my aunt, uncle, cousin, and their two dogs when I was ten years old; and another with my high school boyfriend and best friend when I was sixteen. The last one changed the course of my life. Nearly paralyzed, I fractured my back and neck and dropped out of high school to heal.

With months of stillness in bed, I had a lot of time to reflect. *Who am I? Where am I headed? Will I ever truly heal? If I do, how will I navigate the course of life diminished?* As I began the slow process of recovery—healing my body through physical therapy, and processing mental and emotional trauma through psychotherapy—I began to land back in a body I'd been trying to transcend because of physical limitations and avoid because of past traumas. I grew tired of my boring, limiting stories: the sick asthmatic kid, the woman who needed to shrink. I began to hear and listen to my gut. I was tired of feeling weak, of judging myself, of living to please. I decided that if I ever truly healed, I'd sooner take risks, explore what my body was capable of, and be willing to be broke than feel like I was living the wrong life.

Because of the accident, my bones are different now—my body overcompensated in the process of recovery, and some vertebrae jut out of my spine when I sit for too long. Despite much inner work, car-accident fears still reside there. My body is tense when I drive; muscles painfully cling to my bones trying to protect me even though I know the tension only makes things worse. But the accident obliterated other fears. In its aftermath, life felt more fragile and more precious. I felt I had no time to waste, which led me to take different kinds of risks.

Pulling off the highway on my way to Brooklyn, I found myself in Van Cortlandt Park in the Bronx. This is where I encountered Major, a bronze statue of a coyote. The statue commemorates a twenty-nine-pound female who was hit and killed on the Major Deegan Expressway on February 8, 1995. At the time, she was the first confirmed coyote sighting in New York City since 1946. The Bronx is the only mainland borough of New York City and is attached to suburban Westchester County to the north, so it's relatively easy for coyotes to get there. Another traffic victim who was found and taxidermied in 1995 became the reference for a sculpture by the husband-and-wife sculpting team Glenn and Diane Hines. They named the statue Major, after the expressway. A little disturbing to include the name of the highway that killed her, but I appreciate the gesture. Since Major, coyotes have been seen in Woodlawn Cemetery in the Bronx, in Central Park and on the Columbia University campus in Manhattan, and even in Tribeca near the West Side Highway.

I parked and tried to shake off tension from the drive as I walked to Van Cortlandt Park in the Bronx to talk on the phone. It was the second time I'd driven to New York City alone and I was only slightly less terrified than I'd been the first time, only a little less sure I might die. But I saw far too many dead animals on the road. Among them, in areas where road severed forest, was a gorgeous fox and a creature that looked eerily like a bear cub. Maybe the creature was a porcupine, I don't know. As I drove by, I just saw a small, adorable animal dead on the side of the highway, an image that still haunts me. A natural death feels different—whether a being is eaten by a predator or simply exhausted of their life energy. At least an animal who dies naturally is able to live their life the way they were meant to instead of being interrupted by a human rushing to work or just . . . rushing. What if it were a human on the side of the road? It seems wrong just to drive by, and to try to ignore and forget these deaths. Humans have fractured wild habitats and too many highways are devoid of migration corridors: tunnels, bridges, or other safe passages that enable more-than-human animals to travel, access resources for survival, and adapt to changing landscapes.

A child growing up in Western Massachusetts, I honored dead rabbits, birds, squirrels, and snakes by picking wildflowers to place on their still, cold bodies. In autumn, I covered them with leaves or put them in a nook, away from human traffic, and that felt right. Ritual and grieving were natural impulses; I felt these once-living animals needed to be honored and seen. A grandchild of physicians, I knew enough about germs not to touch these creatures. I used sticks, tree bark, and other found objects to move them. I wanted to acknowledge their individual lives, and observe the end of their lives, with ritual.

Usually, these small ceremonies were private affairs, just me, the woods, and the animal. But sometimes I came across a dead creature while playing with friends, and when I suggested such a ceremony, I was told it was gross or that I was a weirdo. But the urge to honor the animal was stronger than the temporary sting of being ridiculed. I picked flowers, gathered leaves, and persisted.

It is early afternoon when I arrive in Brooklyn and parallel park on my own. I feel proud for confronting my fear and surviving the trip but stressed when I think about trying to sleep amid the noise of the cars on Atlantic Avenue, the television on all the time. I worry that we won't make love, won't go out to dinner (something he refused to do last time I'd journeyed back; he hated having waiters hover over him and thought eating out was a waste of money), that on some level we'll always do what he wants to do.

But our first day together is sweet—we walk, hand in hand, to the park and the grocery store, easily getting back into a routine. That's part of what scares me. I worry that if I go back to Brooklyn as often as he wants me to, love will confuse me even more. That I'll try to squeeze into a version of myself that no longer fits. Like other wild creatures, love can transform and become tame in the coziness of domestication. Love can convince us to stay in the comfy enclosure of the bedroom, the apartment, or the places we've outgrown.

Unable to shake the image of the dead fox on the road, I describe the fox to Rafael and ask him to say a prayer for the animal with me in bed that night. He starts, and we go back and forth, sentence by sentence:

Dear fox, I'm sorry you didn't make it to where you were going.

I hope you didn't suffer too much. I'm sure that it was very scary seeing cars coming toward you so fast.

I hope you didn't leave a family behind. If you did, I hope they are able to move on without you.

I wish we could bury you and honor you in the way that you deserve. I could tell, even in that brief moment, that you were cared for.

Yes, you were beautiful, a gorgeous coat, lush tail, beautiful black boots.

I know there are those who miss you now.

I'm sorry that humans have set the world up this way, making it harder for you. I hope that you are free and fulfilled wherever you are now.

We love you.

In the morning, we work quietly together, and I hear Rafael's breath behind me. Sometimes he blows me kisses. I always say that I focus better alone, but with him here, there is part of me that is also at ease. I'm soothed by the sound of his weight as he walks up the stairs at night to our familiar loft bed. I'm reassured by the creak of each step as he, a tall, lovely man, tries to sneak upstairs to kiss me while I read. In the warmth of his morning greetings, I don't wonder if our relationship is right or if we will last.

It's strange because when we see each other it's even sweeter; we seem closer in many ways. Yet between those reunions we seem to be moving in different directions. More and more he says, *We're so lucky*, and in many ways, it's true. He tells me he loves me all the time and I say it back because I love him, too. It softens my heart and makes me want to stay. But it doesn't take long for my gut to nudge me. I feel the familiar but uncomfortable pull: *You need to get back to nature, you need to go*. More and more, my body is expressing her needs, and more and more, Rafael and I are arguing about the back-and-forth.

MY OWN DEN

I pull into my gravel parking space in Western Massachusetts, alive, after another harrowing drive. I've driven back and forth three times now, and each time, I am a little less tense and a little less terrified. Fear is still there, but it is more manageable now. In *The Body Keeps the Score: Brain, Mind, and Body in the Healing of Trauma*, Bessel A. van der Kolk writes that in our bodies, beneath the protective parts of trauma, "there exists an undamaged essence, a Self that is confident, curious, and calm, a Self that has been sheltered from destruction by the various protectors that have emerged in their efforts to ensure survival." I like to think that I am revealing a little more of that Self now.

There are other changes, too: I have signed a year lease and moved upstairs into the largest of the three apartments at the wildlife sanctuary. My animal body won, after all. I am staying.

Now I have my own den, my own space, kept the way I like it. I like the low ceilings in the bedroom, the pale yellow sunshine color of the walls. This apartment feels like a tree house filled with embroidered pillows, mustard-colored linens, and my beloved weighted blanket and waffle bedspread. There are books and more books I've yet to read in stacks and on shelves, plants on every windowsill, many of them now-rehabilitated plants I found abandoned on Brooklyn sidewalks. I have pieces of art in progress, pieces that are finished, and some I may never finish or return to but can't bring myself to throw away. But the space is not cluttered. Twenty-plus years of living in New York City has helped me pare down. Every time I move, I let go of things I can live without.

I bring more back to Massachusetts with me, though, every time I leave Brooklyn—but my large pieces of artwork are still in the apartment with Rafael. My favorites still hang on the walls. Somehow I'm afraid if I take them, he'll forget me while I'm gone. Or worse, that I'll never come back. That they will be the last thing, the final peeling away. Empty walls, a stark reminder of my absence. The thought of that absence makes me ache. I remember when we rescued my art from my expensive storage unit and put it on the walls: four-foot pieces I showed in galleries but never sold. They were perfect for our loft. He told me he loved looking at my art while he worked and that meant so much to me. Now, in our own separate dens, arranged the way we like them, we have reverted to our natural habitats and are having an even harder time with landings and transitions.

In the beginning, I showed him medicinal plants and strange fungi that led us off trodden wood-chip trails. He seemed fascinated with me and my fascinations. I thought he loved going where we could get lost, but after a few years, he would walk way ahead of me. He seemed impatient when I meandered too much. I always thought of him as being deeply connected to the wild. I thought he'd come around and realize how beautiful it is in Western Massachusetts, or agree to get a place close to nature. But he's more and more plugged into the city and technology and it saddens me, bothers me, and maybe that isn't fair. It isn't fair to him if that's how he wants to live. I know the conveniences and community of the city make him feel safe. Maybe I just need to accept that. But I worry that somewhere inside, he is lonely.

Neither of us wants to deal with the pain of heartbreak, of losing the other. But I am hurting and I know he is, too. I also have the feeling that I am being selfish, that I am hanging on to him just to try, just to see, because when it feels good, it is oh so sweet. But he is not getting what he wants or what he needs and neither am I. We're hanging on by a thread, and I don't know if it's a thread of a metamorphosis that will bring us closer or if we are clinging to something that is changing, transforming, ready to rip and let me fly.

More and more, we are like separate landscapes with no connecting corridor. I thought I would get a city guy to move to the country, but it seems I was trying to convert someone into a different species.

I sit outside on the balcony of my new den and look out at the field of wildflowers and the rolling mountains and listen to a symphony of wildlife. It is a relief to know that within these twenty-seven acres and much of the land beyond, my animal neighbors—coyotes, bobcats, songbirds, black bears, deer, and so on—have plenty of uninterrupted forest. More and more, I replace worry with wonder. I feel grateful, full, in awe of the beauty around me. Being here feels like love. We are taught that romantic love with a partner is the "happily ever after" end of the story, but what if it is only one fleeting part of it?

I was in love with Brooklyn, too, for a while, with my apartment and my life with Rafael that nurtured my growth in so many ways. But now just being in the city breaks my heart. The city breaks my heart over and over again. When I think about the overstimulation and stress of the back-and-forth, my back clenches. My muscles feel like claws around my rib cage. My toes curl under, trying to clutch the ground involuntarily, trying to dig in, stay put. I need them to let go and let me ground.

I have been living outside my natural habitat for too long. I don't want to go back and forth anymore.

White-Tailed Deer

The white-tailed deer is a medium-size herbivore native to North, Central, and South America. In the heat of summer they typically inhabit fields and meadows, using broad-leaved or evergreen forests for shade. During the winter white-tailed deer keep to forests, preferring coniferous tree stands that provide shelter from the harsh elements. They follow well-used trails to their feeding areas and usually eat in the early morning hours and in the late afternoon. Their diet changes depending on the habitat and season, eating green plants in the spring and summer and corn, acorns, and other nuts in fall. In the winter, they eat buds and twigs of woody plants. If they have enough food, water, and shelter (and especially if there is an absence of predators), their population can grow quickly.

Now in many places, like humans, there are too many for the environment to handle.

Maybe that's all bravery is: when your hunger is greater than your fear. I resist the implication that bravery is noble. I must face the things that scare me in order to survive. And survival is not noble. It is not a sacrifice of self but in service to the self.

—MELISSA FEBOS, *Abandon Me*

8

Fight, Flight, Freeze, Fawn

I t is Sunday in December, a day off from hunting in Massachusetts. Snow has just fallen and all is quiet as I wander through the woods. I can wear black again today, able to blend into darkness without the fear of being shot. Young white pines bow toward the ground, heavy with white crystals. I shake the weight off their branches to release their burden. White-tailed deer tracks are scattered on the ground around me. Their hoofprints look like broken hearts. Aimless and wandering, going nowhere and everywhere. I can't help but wonder if the deer lost a mother, father, or child. I think of the chilling lines in Disney's *Bambi* seared in my mind since childhood. A young, innocent Bambi asks, "Why did we all run?" when a gunshot sounds. "Man was in the forest," his mother replies.

There are no wolves here, but there should be. In their absence, deer have overpopulated and are overbrowsing. Apart from occasional ambitious coyotes, we are the only predator other than disease. In places like these, where natural predators are missing, we are often confronted with a choice between saving deer and saving the environment. But unlike wolves, who cull the weak and injured prey, humans—unless intentionally culling deer—tend to go for the strongest, most robust animals. This air, which was once filled with beautiful, soul-stirring howls, is too silent. Especially in winter.

Back inside, I hear gunshots. My heart beats fast and my palms sweat. I know it is illegal to hunt on Sundays, so I start doing research, and it is disturbing. I can't help but imagine the terror and pain of the animals in pursuit—bears, migratory birds, coyotes, foxes, bobcats, and other small game people are allowed to hunt here in Massachusetts. When I describe my physical reaction to a friend, she says my body is experiencing a trauma response. *Maybe you were an animal in a past life*, she offers. *I am an animal now*, I remind her. *And so are you.*

When we are exposed to a real or perceived threat or danger, stress hormones are released that enact physiological changes to protect us. These changes keep us alert and enable us to react in an instant when we are in life-threatening or traumatic situations. Some people become aggressive (fight), while others panic and run away (flight), and others dissociate or are immobilized (freeze), unable to make a decision. Pete Walker, a psychotherapist, recently coined the term *fawn* in his book *Complex PTSD* and added it as the fourth *f* to describe instinctual responses to trauma. Someone using the fawn response may use people-pleasing to avoid conflict, often at the expense of their own needs. People who use fawning as a survival instinct look to others to find how they should feel. They might have a hard time saying no and attempt to make themselves as helpful and useful as possible, granting every wish and demand. They may feel guilty when they're unable to fulfill others' wants and needs. The fawning response may continue out of habit to avoid threats or because of an internalized belief that they are lovable only if they are being useful to someone else. Fawning can result in the neglect of personal boundaries, hypervigilance, and awareness of others' moods and emotions above one's own.

————

Deer are certainly hypervigilant, but given the choice of fight, flight, freeze, or fawn, white-tailed deer prefer to use flight as their survival strategy. Although they may seem to freeze when they encounter someone or when suddenly hit by headlights at night, it is simply because their vision is momentarily blinded, and they freeze until their eyes adjust. Then they do what they're programmed to do: flee.

Deer use their whole body—ears, eyes, nose, hair, tail, body position, vocalizations, and scent markings—to communicate threat, identify family members, convey hierarchies, express mood, and convey intent. Whitetails that see or hear a disturbance but cannot smell the source may use low snorts, head bobbing, tail flipping, and foot stomping to communicate danger. To activate the interdigital glands located between their hooves, they may stamp their front feet when alarmed. The scent left behind lets their kin know they felt unsafe there. Each deer has their own scent that is left each time he or she takes a step.

It is my first time living in the foothills of the Berkshires. When I came here to write, my body breathed a massive sigh of relief amid the beautiful, wild landscape, and writing flowed. But then the gunshots began.

I have always worried about other animals. When geese leave in autumn, I feel a tinge of melancholy as they fly above, determined, sending out calls in their V-shaped formations. I send them well wishes to arrive safe, without harm. It makes me feel better, however useless it might be. My friend Heidi offers me a prayer she says on behalf of wild creatures: *I pray for the turkey, the deer, the coyote, telling them where to hide when the hunters come. I pray that if it isn't for the highest good, the hunters leave. And if it was for the highest good for the animals to be hunted, then I pray that they meet swift and painless deaths.*

I've spoken to people on both sides of the hunting debate and many
point out that hunting is a vital part of conservation efforts, arguing
that fees and other expenses paid by hunters ultimately contribute to
wildlife. If that's true and money is the main argument for hunting,
we desperately need a new model of conservation. In this era of mass
extinction, animals—especially predators hunted for sport—are
worth more alive than dead. At the same time, I realize deer hunting
can be a sustainable and even beneficial practice when managed re-
sponsibly. I have eaten venison from the Scottish Highlands, culled
"humanely," after all. I know deer populations can grow rapidly if left
unchecked, which can lead to overbrowsing and damaged ecosystems. Yet deer are not mere pests to be eradicated, "harvested," or
"bagged," as the hunting vernacular goes; they are threads in the delicate tapestry of living ecosystems. Deer are intelligent, sensitive creatures, each an individual who experiences pain and fear.

It seems unfair to talk about culling other species, suggesting they
are the problem and not us. Deer are simply eating and existing, not
cutting down forest to build strip malls or buying food from across the
globe. What if instead of attacking other species we went inward to do
the culling? *What belief systems need to change? Why are we consuming
so much that forests—homes of other animals—are disappearing?*
Wolves, deer, and invasive species aren't the problem, we are. It is our
insatiable hunger for comfort and convenience (and, for some, a taste
for cruelty I'll never understand) that is fragmenting landscapes and
suffocating Mother Earth. *And if culling is the primary issue and a
need, wouldn't the truly humane action be to reintroduce wolves?*

Breaking with the conventions of his time, the author and hunter-
turned-conservationist Aldo Leopold evolved to see lands as interconnected systems where all living beings play a critical role. Born in
1887 in Burlington, Iowa, Leopold was raised believing that preda-

tors needed to be eradicated, but over the years he observed what happens when wolves are absent from the wilderness. He wrote, "I have watched the face of many a newly wolfless mountain, and seen the south-facing slopes wrinkle with a maze of new deer trails. I have seen every edible bush and seedling browsed, first to anemic desuetude, and then to death . . . In the end the starved bones of the hoped-for deer herd, dead of its own too-much, bleach with the bones of the dead sage, or molder under the high-lined junipers." For Leopold, "the individual is a member of a community of interdependent parts," and those parts include all elements of the natural environment, from soil and plants to wolves. A graduate of the Yale forestry school, Leopold studied evolutionary biology, promoted wildlife management, and supported regulated hunting to foster diverse ecology, including shooting a limited number of deer with the aim of keeping herd sizes smaller.

I find the number for the environmental police and call. Soon, I hear loud knocks at my door. A cop. "Someone is probably just practicing," he says with an exasperated tone. "But I'll drive around." The general message is, I need to chill. I'm not in Brooklyn anymore.

THE BAMBI FACTOR

A mother deer will leave her fawn hidden for hours at a time while she feeds. While they are waiting for their mother to return, a fawn will lie on the earth, quietly, with their head and neck stretched flat on the ground, making it harder for predators to find them. If a doe has more than one fawn, she will hide them in separate places, twitching her ears side to side and backward to listen for her babies in case they call. Fawns may use a low sound called a mew when they want attention from their mom or are responding to her, bleat when they want immediate attention, are hungry, or need urgent care, or bawl when they are in intense distress. A doe often runs toward the calls out of maternal instinct. *But what if the mother never returns?*

I saw *Bambi* in a movie theater when I was about five years old. It was my first movie in a theater and I was so excited. Like the adorable talking animals in my favorite children's books and the stuffed animals in my bedroom who were animate to me, Bambi and his loving mother, his precocious friends Thumper the rabbit and Flower the skunk, the wise old owl, and all the other creatures enchanted me. I watched as Bambi's sweet mother nurtured him and helped him explore the world. Playing in meadows and foraging food through the seasons, she taught him to survive, explaining dangers, such as man, that lurked in the forest. In the harsh winter, Bambi and his mother walked through harrowing blizzards, barely subsisting on tree bark they stripped from high on trees. When they were fed, safe, and exhausted, they curled up sweetly together under the cover of brambles.

I remember being on edge, worried about their struggle through the winter when they could no longer find tree bark within reach. "I'm awfully hungry," Bambi tells his mother. "Yes," she replies, "I know." They were starving, it was gut-wrenching, and I felt such relief when Bambi and his sweet mother encounter the first signs of spring. Finally able to emerge from their shelter, they walk out into the open to enjoy the sun. But the peace and feeling of ease didn't last long. What came next was a cinematic moment that will haunt me forever. Frozen in my seat with my heart beating fast, I saw Bambi's mother's sudden alarm and felt her panic as she anxiously attempts to get him to safety. She successfully hides Bambi, but soon gunshots sound, and after the violent bang, it is far too quiet. Snow begins to fall again and Bambi is alone, bawling for his mother. He is still searching and calling out for his beloved mother when his distant father, the stag, appears to confirm my greatest fear: "Your mother can't be with us anymore."

Growth is painful. At some point, we learn to accept the painful facts of reality: that death is an inescapable part of life and we will lose people, more-than-human animals, even land that we love. We learn that there is tremendous suffering in the world, and that all too often, humans are the cause. When I learned that movies like *Snow White* were a lie and it was better for wild animals to be afraid of me, I was gutted. I wanted so badly to be their friend.

Before seeing Bambi, I don't remember being aware of the fact that animals were hunted, or that people could be so cruel to other creatures. I was upset for days, weeks, months, years afterward and have worried about innocent creatures forced to remain vigilant under constant threat ever since. And I'm not the only one. The emotional charge of the film on some of us viewers has come to be referred to as the Bambi Factor, a sentimental, protective attitude toward "innocent" wildlife, especially deer.

When Disney released the animated film in 1942, *Bambi* was controversial. While some, like the *New York Times* reviewer Theodore Strauss, said that Bambi inspired conservation awareness and "laid the emotional groundwork for environmental activism," many others, like the *Outdoor Life* editor Raymond J. Brown, called the film "the worst insult ever offered in any form to American sportsmen."

Disney's Bambi was inspired by the book *Bambi: A Forest Life*, written in 1928 by an Austrian Jewish author whose pen name was Felix Salten. Salten rejected his given name, Siegmund Salzmann, in an attempt to integrate into Viennese society. As in the animated film, hunters are villains stalking innocent deer, killing them for their pleasure, and most of Bambi's relatives and friends are killed.

Ironically, Salten was a hunter himself, intimate with forests and wildlife, and in his book, unlike the Disney movie, wild animals are threats, too. When a mouse is violently devoured by a polecat, Bambi is disturbed. He asks his mother if one day he, too, will kill a mouse. "Never ever," his mother assures him. "Because we never kill anybody."

Salten wrote *Bambi* as a political, ecological, and existential meditation and a parable of the way persecuted people of his time were treated as inferior or dangerous beings and—like deer—hunted. Calling someone an animal has long been a derogatory term meant to "other" and dehumanize. But we humans are animals, of course. We are mammals related to every plant, fungus, and four-legged creature on this incredible Earth. Solidarity lies in the reality of our interdependence and our shared vulnerability. No other animal causes harm like humans do. I am proud to be an animal.

I just spent the day with my mom. Though I live closer to her now, just forty minutes away, I don't see her as much as I hoped before moving, or as much as I imagined I would if I lived nearby. When she drove to see me, I worried about her driving from Amherst along the winding country roads. She mentioned precarious tree branches that were looming above the road when she arrived, saying, "Someone should really tend to those, they're dangerous." I suggested she drive home the other way and a what-if flashed through my mind: *What if I suggest that she drive the other way and she gets into an accident?*

When I was young, she was my primary caregiver, and, like Bambi and his mom, it felt like the two of us against the elements. A sick kid with terrible asthma and allergies, I was in and out of the hospital all the time and my mom was there for me, ready to take me to the emergency room at a moment's notice, pick me up from a sleepover when I broke out in hives, or pound my back at night when I woke and couldn't breathe. I needed my mother and was terrified that anything might happen to her, so somewhere along the line I decided to be not only her daughter but also her protector. She divorced my distant father when I was two years old. After she fled the painful relationship, I often watched her put her needs last. Selfless and kind to everyone, she depleted herself over and over again, caring for others with a smile. As I've grown older and our family has grown, she has become a little more assertive, but for most of her life, like many women of her era and beyond, it seems fawning has been her principal survival strategy.

Unlike the Disney movie, in the original *Bambi* there is no happy ending. Bambi's father's ability to be ever watchful and wise, to live a solitary life, to appear only when needed and otherwise vanish into the forest—those are the keys to his survival. The message is: to be visible is to be vulnerable.

In the book's final pages, Bambi disappears alone in the forest with no notion of his happiness and no reassurance that the murder of innocent animals will ever end.

Octopuses

An octopus is incredibly in tune with her environment. She relies on the acoustics of water to communicate and navigate and maintains her shape with hydrostatic pressure, sometimes called a hydrostatic skeleton. She may crawl over the bottom of the ocean, pushing and pulling with suckers on her eight arms, or jet backward through the water. All movements are accomplished by muscles that squeeze and bend her fluid-filled limbs and form. An intensely sensitive creature, she can taste, feel, and perceive with every part of her being. Her skin can taste as well as touch. When she senses danger, an octopus can morph her body, changing the pigmentation and texture of her skin to mimic undersea objects and other sea creatures.

We writers are the raw nerve of the universe. Our job is to go out and feel things for people, then to come back and tell them how it feels to be alive.

—URSULA LE GUIN

9

Too Sensitive

One of the few gifts of the pandemic was the pause of human noise. I relished the quiet and I'm sure other animals did, too. While humans were sequestered under lockdown, mountain goats wandered in the streets of Wales, dolphins swam in the waters of Istanbul, pumas prowled empty streets of Santiago, Chile, and there were even the mythical sightings of dolphins in the Venice canals. The silence and lack of human presence provided creatures with an opportunity to explore their surroundings, offering a glimpse into a world where humans were no longer the dominant species. With no traffic and few cars on the road, smog lifted and mountaintops like the Himalayas that had been obscured for decades were visible. Cruise ships were docked and the ocean and her creatures were finally at peace. I was hopeful. Maybe, just maybe, the pandemic and its ecological implications would inspire people to go inward, to change.

It is spring 2021 in Brooklyn, and outside, delicate, ephemeral cherry blossoms are blooming. But inside, our apartment feels strange. I've moved almost everything to Massachusetts now, and apart from a few pieces of art on the walls, my creature comforts are no longer here.

After a long day of playing amid pink blossoms at the Botanic Gardens and getting reacquainted with each other, Rafael suggested we watch a nature show about creatures of the sea. Nature shows tend to depress me, so I hesitated. But he assured me that this one was supposed to be "inspiring and different," so I agreed. The cinematography was beautiful and we watched in our urban living room as a huge, ancient sea turtle laid her eggs in the sand and swam away, trusting that when her baby turtles hatched, they would know what to do and where to go. Guided by moonlight reflected on the water, sea turtles have evolved to venture toward the ocean, the source of life, when they're born. Yet this time as people filmed, many of the babies, confused by artificial light, waddled toward traffic instead, only to be crushed by cars. I was horrified. I felt sick and intensely sad all at once. *Why did they just film the tragedy and not help them?!* When I see an animal suffering, I feel it in my own body. Frustrated and teary eyed, I went upstairs to bed and had terrible dreams. I was haunted by the images for months and will always be.

When Rafael is watching something violent on television I turn my back to it, look away, or use my hand to shield my eyes from the screen. I have to ask him over and over again to lower the lights when I'm trying to sleep and to reduce the noise (I can't concentrate with the radio or TV on), and I will never, ever watch a horror movie with him. "You're too sensitive," he often tells me. He is sensitive, too, only in a different way. A sweet man, he is easily hurt and recoils quickly. When he touched me in a way that didn't feel right (and I tried to gently redirect) or cooked a meal I was grateful for but not hungry for, he took it personally. I don't mean to constrain him with my sensory boundaries or to wound him with my bodily responses; I'm just trying to express and honor my needs. But mostly, I am just worn out and worn through with no insulation.

A couple of months before watching the sea turtle trauma, we watched *My Octopus Teacher,* an intimate portrait of a common octopus and her relationship with the nature documentary filmmaker, naturalist, and founder of the Sea Change Project Craig Foster. We watched as Foster spent a year free-diving and visiting the octopus every day, gradually earning her trust as his feelings (and possibly hers) moved from curiosity to care. At first she was wary and shy, pulling shells over her spineless body for protection. But over time, she learned that Foster was not going to hurt her, so she ventured out of her shells to explore. "She seemed to be incredibly curious about me, and she would often come out of her den to inspect me. I think she was just as interested in getting to know me as I was in getting to know her," Foster said. He was not just observing her; he was connecting with her, allowed into her world. As I watched, I reflected on how a relationship with one animal, or even one plant or tree, can change the way we interact with other members of their species and the environments they live in.

Members of a class of marine animals including squid and cuttlefish called cephalopods, octopuses are capable of moving through spaces as small as a bumblebee, constrained only by their inflexible beaks. They have been seen opening jars, untying knots, and sneaking through tiny holes on boats. Food for many animals in the ocean, octopuses have become intensely creative. Their intelligence is partly an evolutionary response to living in environments such as coral reefs, in which they need to hide from predators and sneak up on their prey. Strategies for defending themselves range from shedding limbs to changing color, spraying an ink that lingers in the water and acts as cover, and even throwing rocks at potential predators or unsavory suitors.

In 2015, researchers from Australia, Canada, and the United States found that females hurled materials like silt, shells, and rocks at annoying males attempting to mate with them. In one instance, a female was seen throwing silt at a male octopus who was harassing her, at least ten times. The female held her chosen weapon under her body and placed it over a siphon used to push water out of a jet with force, propelling the object toward her target. The research team noted a clear difference between propulsion meant to clear out material in the way of their caves and the projectiles launched between the first and second tentacles for better aim. Male octopuses avoided getting clocked by shells approximately half the time.

While I enjoy and appreciate films like *My Octopus Teacher* that can change the way we interact with the world around us, I have a low tolerance for television. I think too much time in front of the boob tube can numb us, cause our brains to atrophy, and desensitize us to violence. I have been to too many houses where the television is on in the background and I can barely focus on what people are saying. Between murders on crime shows and sensationalized news repeating global tragedies or analyzing the latest horrible thing a politician said, there are previews for movies that are enough to give me nightmares. Some people, like Rafael, have suggested that I'm "too sensitive," and others that I have "auditory processing issues." But I believe that when we relax or zone out, what we see and hear slips into our subconscious more easily, creating excess static and noise to contend with. I have always felt that our health and well-being is a result of what we take in—food, imagery, words, conversations—and our ability to digest it. Maybe I lack the enzyme to digest violence, especially violence as entertainment.

And yes, I am a former competitive boxer. A contradiction to some but not for me. Participating in sports feels very different from passively watching them. In fact, boxing helped me cultivate the inner strength needed to support my sensitivity. As I grew stronger on the inside, I needed less of an outer shell.

A storytelling species, humans seem to be moved more by films like *My Octopus Teacher*, the true story of one octopus, or even by fictional characters like Bambi than by nature shows about octopuses or deer in general or by seeing images of disembodied abuse. In *The Soul of an Octopus*, the author and naturalist Sy Montgomery shares the story of her unexpected relationships with Athena, Octavia, and Kali, octopuses she came to know "as exquisitely intelligent, curious, emotional, and playful. Each is as individual as you or I." Even their arms have personalities all their own. "They may have some shy arms and some bold arms," Montgomery writes. An octopus arm is not just an arm but an extended brain packed with neurons. When an octopus loses an arm, they lose part of themselves.

In *My Octopus Teacher*, the octopus loses an arm due to a shark attack and retreats to her den to recover. We see her weakness as she turns pale, slowly regenerating her arm over three months. When an octopus rebuilds her body, she rebuilds her nervous system as well. And it is not without energetic cost. Even so, experiments have been done in the name of science, like one in which researchers cut off an octopus's arm and then discovered that the arm recoiled when they pinched it, even after an hour detached from the rest of the octopus. Or another, mentioned in a 2021 *Nautilus* magazine interview with Craig Foster, in which electrodes were put into an octopus's brain to see how they moved. When asked about this seeming lack of empathy, Foster replied that the problem is "disconnection from the personal lives of wild animals. It's what I call a cooling of the heart toward wild nature." He went on to say, "that disconnection from the wild, I think, is in some ways the most dangerous thing on the planet at the moment. If you have that feeling and that disconnection, you can do anything and feel okay. And I think that's why we're in a very precarious position as a species."

When I'm overwhelmed by emotions, news, or the rush of cars at night when there should be cricket calls or cicada songs, I like to take a bath, turn off the lights, and plunge underwater. The descent into water brings me back to Earth, calms me, until eventually all I hear is the sea inside. I've been reading *The Hidden Life of Trees*, and in the Brooklyn bathtub, I doze off thinking about the incredible network of microbes, mycelium, and other microscopic creatures communicating beneath me. Soon, in the liminal space of dreaming, I am welcomed underground by Hawthorn—a medicinal tree in the rose family—through an opening in her trunk. I descend into her roots that undulate and extend like octopus limbs and walk down deep toward the warmth of the Earth's core. It is a warm, nurturing hearth. When I begin to wake, I am in my grandmother's pink bathroom. I see the patterns on her perfectly placed towels, the fancy barrettes on the counter, rose-shaped soaps, the flowery rugs. Melting into the warm water, I feel safe and secure. When I wake, I wonder, *How far back can I trace my mothers?*

Like plants and all other animals, humans evolved in the sea. Scientists have determined that we—in our earliest, unrecognizable life forms—were confined to the ocean for at least 600 million years because the land was bathed in lethal levels of UV radiation. But thanks to plants who gradually ventured onto land, photosynthesis raised atmospheric oxygen levels high enough for Earth's protective ozone layer to form, making it possible for us to crawl onto the land from our vast oceanic womb.

Whales also made it to land, but they decided to return to the ocean. These ancient beasts—believed to have evolved from terrestrial hoofed mammals some 45 million years ago—made a choice and their limbs became fins. The mammal in them still has to come up for air. An octopus can walk on land, too, but can survive outside the water only for about twenty to thirty minutes. Typically, they travel along the ocean floor using all or many of their eight arms in a sort of crawl.

We might think of the deep sea as a peaceful environment resonating with haunting calls of whale songs and the signature whistles
of dolphins. But more and more, the ocean is polluted not just
with plastics and discarded pandemic face masks but with noise—
oil exploration, military sonar, Jet Skis, and cruise ships—that causes
severe damage to sensitive sea creatures. Studies have shown that
even relatively low-intensity, short exposure to sound causes severe
acoustic trauma. The impact of noise pollution in the ocean is considerable to creatures like humpback whales and octopuses—affecting
their ability to hunt, evade predators, communicate with each other,
even reproduce.

My heart sank when I read that cruise ships were out on the ocean
again. On August 16, 2020, news headlines touted their reemergence
as a "win," a sign that we were back on track. But the floating cities of
up to 9,000 people are a catastrophe for the environment, and everything that cruise ships come in contact with—air, water, fragile
habitats, coastal communities, and wildlife—is harmed along their
journey. Carnival Corporation, the biggest cruise company in the
world, has paid millions of dollars in fines, charged with dumping
food mixed with plastic waste in Bahamian waters, falsifying records
of environmental compliance plans, illegally releasing over 500,000
gallons of sewage and 11,000 gallons of food waste globally, dis-
charging oily waste off the coast of England, and dumping thousands
of gallons of wastewater into Glacier Bay National Park in Alaska.
The list goes on.

Once again, humans were partying and drinking on the surface of
the ocean while below our relatives were suffering because of it. How
do we so easily forget that we *are* the ocean, that we have an ocean inside us, that we come from the ocean of our mothers? That we sweat
and cry saltwater tears? How, as sensitive creatures of the sea, do we
navigate the pain and unjust circumstances of capitalism, racism,

and colonialism? Why do we exploit nature, separating us from each other and ourselves? In Alexis Pauline Gumbs's moving book *Undrowned: Black Feminist Lessons from Marine Mammals*, she centers questions like these. She writes that "meditations inspired by encounters with marine mammals are an offering towards the possibility that instead of continuing the trajectory of slavery, entrapment, separation and domination, and making our atmosphere unbreathable, we might instead practice another way to breathe." She writes that her "first marine mammal lesson was that if I breathe I can still speak even while crying. I can breathe through saltwater. I can live through this mess." Like the emotional charge of watching nature shows, Gumbs's book hits me in those tender places. Every time I read passages from her lyrical book, I cry.

LOSING A LIMB

I've learned, since watching that gut-wrenching sea turtle documentary, that in Nicaragua and many places where sea turtles are born, people have built walls to prevent babies from heading into traffic. A boundary against their confusion. Sometimes that's what we need, too. Our own personal boundaries. We need to know what we can tolerate and take in and what we can't. Like octopuses and other underwater relatives, when our sensory inputs are overwhelmed, it takes a toll on our bodies. We are made of water and are also creatures from the sea.

As long as we can cope in our ever-changing environments, sensitivity is not something to be fixed. It isn't a weakness. It takes courage to feel, to lay down our armor and experience the emotional ebbs and flows of life in all its depths. Like the octopus who feels, tastes, and knows with every touch, those of us who feel sensitive or are healing and going through a new period of growth may need more time to retreat under shells or in caves to recharge. We need dark, protected spaces to let the most tender parts of ourselves form. Rest and retreat are just as necessary for rehabilitation as the warmth and illumination of light.

We may also need to strengthen the muscle of our "no" in order to honor our needs. In the process of saying no to what depletes us, we say yes to a more nourishing life. And right now, attached to Rafael, I am afraid to admit what I might need. When I consider leaving him, I wound myself with our sweetest memories. I replay romantic moments in my head and ask why, *Why would you want to do this? Look, you're hurting yourself, you're hurting him!* All the moments when I thought he was my person swell to the surface. My heart feels like it's bleeding. Do we all do this? Is this flood of beautiful memories a last fight of love to be kept alive? Leaving him would feel like the amputation of a limb—severing myself from our future, and from years of memory embedded in my body.

Back in Massachusetts it is summer and it is raining hard. It seems as though the Earth wants to become ocean again. And I wouldn't blame her for wanting to start over, to wash all the pain away. In the midst of the storm, the hum of the refrigerator, the buzz of lights, and other mysterious sounds of electricity suddenly go quiet, and nature enters inside. With the power out, I feel the rumble and crackle of thunder, the intense pounding rain. The sounds soothe me, let me know that even amid human violence, nature is alive.

I look outside at the undulations in the land, the rise and fall of mountains and hills who offer shade and direct the movement of air and affect the flow of rivers and streams. I look at trees branching, I look at the veins in their leaves as I feel my own pulse. When the drama of the storm subsides, sweet, beautiful birdsong emerges. I am learning from and about the animals around me; beginning to recognize individual birds and their songs. I've come to know a squirrel who lives in the maple tree beside my balcony, a fox who ventures from the woods at dusk.

Quiet now, I'm thinking about my next book, about the next phase of my life, about the words that want to crawl onto shore.

Seagulls

Seagulls are monogamous birds who mate for life and rarely divorce. They have a strong social structure that works effectively against predators to their breeding colonies. Up to one hundred gulls may even gang up on intruders to scare them away, on occasion even driving them out to sea to drown. One of the few species of seabirds that can survive drinking saltwater—made possible by a special pair of glands just above the eyes that flush the salt from their system out through their nostrils—they can venture far out to sea in search of food. Seagulls have excellent vision and are one of the few birds with eyes that can move in their sockets. Expert fliers, they have mastered control of wind and thermals to ascend and dive through the air, using winds for sharp changes of direction.

We exchange dreams and desires, he and I. But not the same ones.

—ANNIE ERNAUX, *Getting Lost*

10

Lost at Sea

The beach was our special place. We were often the only ones there or the last ones left. We would pack food and drinks to last an entire day of play, drift off to sleep in the sand under the sun and sometimes wake as the moon was rising. We waited out rainstorms under our little beach umbrellas until the storms became rainbows and folded our trusty beach mat in the dark of new moons.

We swam off the Caribbean coast of Costa Rica, closed our eyes under a palm tree, and, when we opened them, found a sloth over our heads grinning at us. We swam off Cape Cod, in the water of my childhood memories, where we walked among seals and heard stories of sharks. But for him, nothing compared to Fort Tilden in New York City, a national seashore with protected nests of plovers and countless seagulls. Locking food in our bags so the seagulls wouldn't steal our bounty, he would take my hand to walk along the tide or the grassy ledge where I gathered rose and mugwort in summer and goldenrod in autumn.

Sometimes Rafael swam out to sea so far that I couldn't see him. I knew swimming in the ocean was where he felt most free, but the force, power, and pull of the ocean scared me. The sea could just swallow him up and render me helpless. My tense body would relax in relief when I saw his head bobbing in the water as he returned, growing closer and closer. Eventually his whole body would emerge, smiling. Satisfied and spent, he'd walk the beach back to me. He would get annoyed if I told him I was worried, so I tried to keep my worry to myself most of the time.

I knew beach-going was tied to the most precious parts of his child-hood; to the deep ache of wanting to grab time and get it back. And at first, I shared this need. It was such a joy to play in the water and sand and a relief to live in the city and yet have a national seashore close by. We could work for half of the day and then hop on his scooter and go, or vice versa. But sometimes I had other things to do. He was further along with work and career than I was and I needed to stay on top of the vision for work I was building. Whenever I stayed home he was disappointed and I felt guilty. There was a push and pull between work and play, and after a while, play became woven together with ex-pectation, need, and anxiety. I wasn't always the most fun person to be there with, either. Living in the city made me feel like all the wildlife in the world was being strangled by our mess. I picked up trash—plastic tampon applicators, straws, wrappers. I confronted a fisherman who brought a stingray out of the water, making the creature suffer for "show-and-tell" and selfies on a burning hot summer day, while Ra-fael and his friends were chilling and laughing on their beach blan-kets. A stingray cannot survive out of water for long, so I watched and waited while the fisherman brought her back out to the ocean. The allure of our special place was truly polluted for me after I watched the permaculture documentary *Inhabit*, which showed the overflow of sewage into New York City oceans after heavy rains.

And there was the drive. On the way to Fort Tilden, we drove by nursing homes on Flatbush Avenue where lonely seniors sat outside on the sidewalk concrete. Maybe I was projecting, maybe they weren't lonely, maybe they were perfectly content. But to me, the scene was deeply depressing. The prospect of growing old in the city terrified me. My intention had always been to experience it while I was young, then get out. Every time we rode by the nursing homes, I had less and less armor against them. Rafael didn't reassure me that it wouldn't be us. And now I hope it won't be him.

Gulls communicate with their mates during summer breeding season, using choking displays as part of (often) contentious discussions over where to nest. Although two patches of ground may be indistinguishable to us, gull couples spend a considerable amount of time debating the attributes of the exact spot where their priceless eggs will be laid. Choking displays involve repetitive, delicate murmurs given by one member of the pair who thinks they have found the ideal spot for the nest. Leaning forward, the gull will point to the place on the ground where he believes the nest should be built while producing the murmuring choke call. His partner will then walk in a circle around the point, considering it, joining in the choke display only if she agrees. This is an important decision, and one that is not always made. Like me and Rafael, some gulls spend their entire summer placing sticks in different areas of their territory and debating where to nest, never reaching a final agreement.

Weigh the pros and cons, my friends tell me. But can love be tallied with a list? I'm terrified of us not being together, I'm afraid that I won't find the same level of reliability, affection, honesty, trustworthiness, and companionship if I leave. I worry about regretting it, about making him sad.

But maybe he'd thrive with someone and something new, maybe we both would, maybe we could still be friends.

I will try to make a list. Although some things on that list are intangible—reaching for my hand at night as we drift off the sleep, lying sweetly on my chest in such a way that it seems that area was carved as a cradle for his head, the soothing way he kisses my eyelids, our simple walks around the park, along the beach, his morning greetings of happiness. Then there is his irritation about my fear of

driving, his impatience with my sensitivities, the lack of physical intimacy, and the overall lack of depth. Lately even when we are next to
each other we are drifting apart.

We smiled at each other a lot this week in Massachusetts. We
kissed with more passion than we had in a while and I thought we
might even make love . . . but as usual, we didn't. At night, we sat outside marveling at the fireflies, their love notes twinkling as the sky
grew dark outside my new home. Sitting on my balcony, he reached
for my hand and squeezed as if to say, *I am here*. My hand squeezed
back to say, *I love you*. And in that brief wordless moment, we were
revived. If only his hand were always there to anchor me, to anchor us.

He wanted me to go back to Brooklyn with him and I could have
gone. It is beach season, after all. But I knew I needed time alone. *It is
hard but good saying goodbye while wanting you to stay*, I said. It is
healthier to say goodbye while things are good. And we both know,
somewhere deep down (or maybe not so deep) that if I go to Brooklyn, we will start arguing before too long. And whether or not I want
to admit it, I know the truth: I have found my nest. We have been
back and forth and back and forth like a quarrelsome pair of seagulls
and I know I need to be here and not in the city anymore. I want to
slow down, go deeper, grow roots, and settle into a rural life he
doesn't want to live. We are trying to hold on, but if I listen closely
enough, even love says: *Let go while your hearts are still tender, before
bitterness sets in*. I no longer have my bags perpetually packed, and
today, I put my suitcase in the closet. I keep thinking about what he
admitted on our first date about his previous relationships: "I always
stay too long."

I have a package arriving in Brooklyn tomorrow, a benign but cruel
fact. Saturday would have been our anniversary. I didn't know that

after those nights among the fireflies, I would drop him off at the train station and it would be the last time I saw him as my partner. But I woke up recently and knew I needed to initiate the hard conversation. Within my body and mind, there was no more back-and-forth. I must have been coming to grips with the possibility of leaving as I slept.

I recently listened to Michelle Obama say in an interview that if she and Barack hadn't made the commitment of marriage, they wouldn't have made it through their hard times, and she is glad they did. I've heard others say that before, too. I wonder sometimes if I'm leaving too early. If in my yearning to grow, I can't just stick it out a little longer. When I look into Rafael's eyes, his compassion and warmth are endless, but there are places he won't go anymore. We've been moving in circles, treading water for too long now. There was so much of me, of my inner world, he didn't share—my writing, my dreams, our intimacy. I held my breath for a while, waiting . . . and I grew lonely in the deep end.

Shortly after I arrived in Western Massachusetts six months ago, he needed "to know." The ultimate non-planner, always attuned to the uncertainty of life, he asked to know. That night I was up with an aching heart to write him what I knew:

> I am here to finish my book and to write. As you know, I've always needed time in solitude to create, and being in nature is what fulfills me. More and more, I crave it; my body yearns for wild expanse. I'm able to pore through material without distraction here and it has been only about a week and a half. At the same time, I miss you. I miss your hands, your morning greetings, your tenderness, your silliness, your love.
>
> I am trying to allow time and space for creativity without making grand plans, which is why I didn't know how to answer

you yesterday. But I also know that the way we've been living is not something I can tolerate daily anymore; it wears away at me. The overstimulation of the city, the television on all the time, arguing about it. The television and noise are not conducive to my writing, which I'm investing in now, and will be doing even more of in the coming months and years.

I don't love the word "practical" and I know it's your favorite word. Sometimes it seems dissonant with your lack of planning and your open emotional experience of life. I have strong inner pulls that may not be practical. Practical can feel like a cage, like rules, like abstinence. Here is the closest thing to a plan I have:

Be here, be open to my creativity, and finish the book as best I can without constraint. It is and has been so much work and is both an exhilarating and terrifying thing to put out into the world.

I wonder if the healthiest thing right now might be to open the relationship up to see other people. That might make it clear that we want to be together or make us realize that as much as we love each other, we have helped each other grow and now it's time to go our separate ways.

I never sent the letter. Now I wish I had. I waited too long, waited until I backed myself into a corner with compromises and my body decided for me. My animal body couldn't tolerate the back-and-forth anymore and our departure from each other was not how we pictured it. We thought that if it ever ended, we would have a beautiful, tear-filled celebration of our time together. Maybe at the beach, our special place, where our tears could become ocean. But we never got the chance.

I introduced the conversation on the phone, badly—for him at least—and the memory pains me. It seemed that we could no longer avoid the fact that we were causing each other more stress than joy, that we were holding each other back, that we had become friends instead of lovers. But he didn't see it that way. He said I "pulled the rug out from under him," but for me, it was as though he were swimming farther and farther away, unable to see me. When I tried to address the distance, he could no longer hear me. We have different interpretations of our ending.

We had so many things we wanted to do together, but no plans. I think the tension in my back is trying to brace my body from being overcome in an ocean of tears.

THE SEA INSIDE

I've started crying in the grocery store, in the car. Everything I do reminds me of him. *Did I make a mistake? Really, did I?* I wrote a list of the reasons we parted in order to remember when I am reeling. I put it on the refrigerator and lately I've read it at least twenty times a day. I wish he were here holding my hand the way he does, marveling at nature, listening to birds, trying to figure out if the songs we hear are cardinals or robins. But I know I have a tendency to romanticize, and I know these memories are highlights. When I talk to people about our separation, I'm reassured that it's the right thing, but alone, I miss him terribly. My heart feels exhausted, and when my heart is exhausted, so am I. There is no "reboot." I must endure the ache and ride the waves of grief until they calm or fade away. Summer is a difficult time to feel sad. There is a heightened sense of vacancy; a hole illuminated.

Summer days move on and sounds around me change. Many of the migratory songbirds have flown and have been replaced by symphonies of crickets, cicadas, and katydids. I think of my favorite

quote from E. B. White's *Charlotte's Web*: "The crickets felt it was
their duty to warn everybody that summertime cannot last forever.
Even on the most beautiful days in the whole year—the days when
summer is changing into autumn—the crickets spread the rumor
of sadness and change." The insects are incredibly loud, but I call
their song silence; they are sounds my body longs for. Their mating
calls serenade me through the night and it is the mourning dove
whose sorrowful call wakes me instead of him. I will miss his morning wake-up calls, his smile as he looked at me and said, "Good morning, sunshine." Every single day we were together. That is painful to
leave behind.

Parking spaces at popular hiking destinations are empty now. I always dreaded the crowds, but now that I am the only one on the trail,
it feels lonely. I'm reminded of all the times we would go hiking in
autumn: Cold Spring, Breakneck Ridge, Minnewaska State Park,
Holyoke Range; of the late summer days at the beach, watching monarch butterflies dance around the beloved weeds. I even miss Brooklyn today. I am so sad about making both of us sad. I often dream he
is crying and I wake up with a sore heart. I don't call because he said
he needs space to heal and seems more upset when he hears from me.
He became upset when I said I still loved him. *It's confusing*, he said.
Now I don't know what to say. I thought we could be friends. Friends
can and do love each other, but we are still raw, still healing.

The peep of plovers, the sound of waves, and the call of seagulls will
always remind me of him. Scientists say that scent is most closely related to emotion, but in this case, for me, emotion seems most connected to sound. Ironic, since noise—television, radio, silence—is
one of the things we argued about most. For him, silence was deafening, and for me, the incessant noise of media dampened my instinct
and drowned the voice of my inner wild. The sounds of nature, in

nature, are what I crave, and when we shared those, it was beautiful. We loved hearing the gulls and the baby plovers as they ran on the sand chasing waves. Their little legs seemed so inefficient. They used to make me laugh; now they make me cry.

Birds form bonds with each other, yet sometimes, like us, they will get into fights or just drift apart. Naturalists have observed birds mourning losses just as I am mourning us. But we heal, we grow, move forward. While gull species are described as monogamous, it turns out that more than a quarter of paired gulls split up after their first attempt at raising a family. When too much energy is wasted on arguments, it interferes with reproduction—the purpose of mating for gulls in the first place. Rafael and I may not have been raising chicks, but our nesting choice did have a lot to do with our respective feelings of safety and, as artists, our ability to create. We needed different things to feel inspired, to give birth to new ideas, new creations, new projects. Looking back, we probably should have let each other go after one season of arguing, as gulls do.

After they let go, some gulls remain alone, but most find new partners. One day someone is the center of your universe, and the next they are gone. That may be the saddest part of all. Love is not always the glue we imagine it to be. But sometimes love means knowing when to let go. It might mean mourning death; not keeping a struggling relationship or attachment alive and on life support indefinitely. Sometimes, in order to heal, we have to find the courage to peel away, say goodbye, and endure an ocean of tears.

Spiders

A spider's funnel web resembles a cave opening—narrow in the middle and wide on the sides—and is usually found close to the ground in the woods or in areas with dense plant coverage. The familiar tangled webs, or cobwebs, found in dark corners of human homes and in attics and basements are abstract works of art with no definable pattern. Sheet webs are used by small spiders like the aptly named bowl and doily spider, and are woven together horizontally with threads that are usually very dense. They might look like linens hanging between trees, in bushes, or on top of grass, or like a bowl, with the middle curving downward. Orbs are the famous circular webs that resemble a wheel with a spiral that leads from the center to the outer edge. Often suspended between trees, orbs are most visible on misty days or in the morning dew.

A spider's web is stronger than it looks. Although it is made of thin, delicate strands, the web is not easily broken.

—E. B. WHITE, *Charlotte's Web*

11

Weaving My Web

With the exception of plants and insects, I now live alone. Though I have been alone a lot over the past two years, this feels different. Without a partner, even a partner who is far away, there is a heightened sense of solitude. At times I feel lonely and at times it feels liberating to be alone, away from a man, even a man I love. I have time to rest, decompress, and just be. I can be alone in my thoughts and reflections without being crowded by his. I have time and space to fall apart. It can be exhausting to hold myself together. My body can be civilized for only so long.

A spider, alone in her web, watches me from the far corner of the kitchen as I write. Poised, waiting for prey to appear, she seems patient and still. Trusting that in time, her creation will give her what she needs.

I just taught an online herbalism course and came outside for a stroll in the meadow. It's a misty summer day, and outside spiderwebs have turned into jeweled wonders. Small webs hover between grasses with tight woven threads, and large, impressive orbs stretch between fence posts and tree branches. Yesterday as the sun set, the same webs glistened in the fading light. Their beauty was hypnotic. As light traveled back and forth between silken strands, it looked as though a huge invisible weaver was hard at work.

Under normal circumstances, I would walk outside with my students and share the experience as we learned from local medicinal plants and the land. But things have changed because of the pandemic and I've been forced to create nature-connection experiences for a virtual world. It seemed like a contradiction. How could online experiences hold or even convey the palpable feeling of gathering in person amid plants that we can touch, taste, smell, and feel? With trees that offer us breath? Teaching from my sanctuary in nature, I'm doing my best to speak on behalf of the land and get others outside to connect with and care for land where they are. And I've been moved and humbled by the intimate conversations and closeness felt in (the much more accessible) virtual spaces—even with those far away.

Every one of my workshops and retreats—whether virtual or in person—begins and ends in a circle, a container for authentic connection and communal growth. When we gather in intimate circles, we can hold space for one another without hierarchy as we listen, heal, and learn from the cycles of nature. In today's class we spoke about relationships and webs of connection and how relationships with nature, with loved ones, and with one another have brought us through this difficult year. We spoke about the ways in which going inward and, in many cases, being isolated illuminated what and who is most precious to us, especially when seeing loved ones requires much more effort and energy. We also spoke about our inner knowing. The mysterious, instinctual place inside each of us that knows which webs to weave, what spaces to trust, and which circles to cast.

For me, accessing that inner space often means unloading excess noise through creative expression. Without a regular creative release, I feel like I am drowning in noise, trapped behind walls, or living in dead skins that I have to wrestle out of. I feel distracted, and my body feels stuffed, with less and less space to receive. Heeding the need to create means listening to the urges of my body. When I write regularly, beyond the noise of daily life, beyond self-doubt, and beyond the voices of social conditioning, cobwebs clear and I can see— even for a moment—into my vast interior worlds.

The creative process may ask me to wander in the woods, create personal space, and endure boredom or emotional discomfort before I break through. In the beginning of many projects, I feel like I'm melting, shedding, overflowing. Sometimes words or images rise to the surface like waves, then evaporate like scenes from a dream. Sometimes the creative urge comes at opportune times and sometimes, it seems, I have to carve out days, even weeks of nothingness before it appears. Sometimes the creative urge is a propulsion, a rare wave I have to catch and ride. Sometimes it's "the big one" and it appears from out of nowhere, and when it does, I am at its service and do not want to be interrupted. Sometimes I feel embarrassed that this is such an intense need because I don't know if my writing or art is "good enough." But good or not, something needs to be birthed, to have its own life in the world. Whatever the urge, my mysterious animal body is the source, the container, the vessel for it all. Maybe the nonmaterial is dependent on the material. Maybe what we call soul is really flesh.

Nearly every corner of my apartment is home to a spider. I clear spiderwebs only if they're spiderless. I have about eight in my bathroom and four in the corners of my bedroom. I refuse to kill the spiders or even relocate them. Some have beautiful, intricate webs and it doesn't feel right to destroy their work before they're done using them. A large female in the left corner of my bedroom by the window with a stunning web reminds me of Charlotte, the wise, kind, and self-described "pretty" spider from E. B. White's *Charlotte's Web*. I like having her, my own Charlotte, here. She seems to know we have an agreement. She is out of the way, catches bugs, and has a safe place to live. I believe that animals and insects can sense the difference between a threat and a benign or friendly presence. I say hello to Charlotte when I wake and see bug husks—the shells of her victims—dangling in her web.

The complex webs—both fragile and incredibly strong—are

made by the females. Male spiders are nomadic and tend to construct quick, sloppy cobwebs they abandon when seeking mates who are usually at least four times their size. After mating, a male spider quickly runs away to avoid being eaten. Sometimes he will bring gifts of bugs wrapped in silk, hoping to please his potential mate while filling her stomach. Most spiders are unable to digest food internally and instead inject their prey with digestive fluids and suck out the liquefied remains.

I have an entire room devoted to art here, something I've been hungry for but haven't had in years. My artwork—old, new, and in process—lines the walls. Knowing I had this new creative space, my mom brought me a stack of pieces I drew when I was young, from about five years old on. One created when I was about eight is a bizarre drawing of E.T. holding a bottle of purple soda that boasts "zero calories!"; another, created when I was about six, is a self-portrait of a young me leaning down from a second-story window of a house smiling at a line of animals outside my door. A bunny, a dinosaur, a fox, a squirrel, a bear, a cat, a dog, a bird, and some unknown creatures look up and smile back at me, holding what look like housewarming gifts.

I pin the housewarming drawing to the wall and try to recall the feeling of creation in that moment, at that age. Back then, with fewer distractions, no notion that "time is money," and little care as to whether my work was deemed good, I was immersed in the pleasure of creation and easily swept away. I remember feeling swollen with emotion as a child with so much love for more-than-human animals, even fictional aliens like E.T., that I ached. The characters in books like *The Velveteen Rabbit* and *Charlotte's Web* and in movies like *Bambi* and *E.T.* spoke to something true, something I felt but couldn't name in the busy human-centric world I was born into. I cried when

I read *Charlotte's Web* and fell in love with Wilbur, the pig who was destined for death, and with Charlotte, the spider who saved him but couldn't avoid her own. When Charlotte dies a natural death in the book, her spiderlings send out their fine silk and allow themselves to become airborne at the mercy of the wind and electric fields. Thankfully, some remain in the barn to keep Wilbur company.

Ballooning is a process in which spiders move through the air by releasing one or more gossamer threads. Ballooning for a tiny spider would be the equivalent of traveling across a galaxy. Some travel by chance across ponds, cities, even oceans. Commonly found in northern continents, on buildings and bridges, flying spiders are not a threat to humans. Their ballooning activity lasts only a short time, and once they arrive at their unknown destination, they build their web, a home from within. From epic travel to stillness, they weave and wait.

SPIDER WOMEN

People always talk about how time speeds up as we grow older, but maybe it's just how we're spending it. Ten minutes of meditation can feel like an eternity, while hours can be devoured binge-watching a favorite television show. There are times I feel distracted and restless, but I know if I endure an inevitable period of boredom and resist the desire to be entertained, I'll crack open into stillness and receptivity, where my senses are more awake and alive. When I unplug and step back to tune in to my body and surroundings, whether through meditation, a long sensuous bath, a walk in nature, or curling into a beloved and listening to the rain, time expands and I move beyond the drone of surface-level noise. Whether it's an external or internal storm, I've learned to sit quietly and tend to discomfort when it arises. It is after moments like these that some of my best writing emerges. In these moments, I encounter solutions to problems that were gnawing at me in the busyness of a workday. This is where I stop swirling around the perimeter of my mind and arrive, more embodied, at my center. Nature has her own rhythm. We can water and nurture a flower, but we cannot rush a flower into bloom.

The author and Jungian analyst Jean Shinoda Bolen writes that the Greeks had two words for time: *chronos* and *kairos*. Chronos is the time with which we mark our days and kairos is "timeless time; moments at which the clocks seem to stop; feeding, renewing, more motherly time. It's the time with which we feel one." Kairos is the sort of time that lengthens life and stretches days so that we inhabit them fully, without the sense that we weren't really there. Time is a strange thing. Moments of presence and a few words from a person we love can shape us for better or for worse, and linger through an entire life.

While researching spiders for this chapter, I came across a pest control website that said: "Spiders are creepy. No one wants them crawling around their home or covering their porch with spiderwebs." (Speak for yourselves.) "We love making sure your home is free of pests, and we can provide excellent spider treatments as well as spiderweb removal at each visit . . . You may not see any spiders, but webs are everywhere!" While clearly written to drum up business and freak people out, it's true. Webs *are* everywhere. We can try and get rid of spiders and their webs, but like it or not, everything is interconnected.

Our pain becomes others' pain when it isn't processed. When land and her wild creatures aren't treated well the trauma and imbalance ripples through waterways and travels in the wind to haunt neighbors near and far. When harmful fables separate us from each other and from nature, our social, cultural, and ecological fabric tears and in some cases is ripped to shreds. Land, waterways, eyes, ears, and even skin know no boundaries. We are woven together in this tapestry of life.

Cultures around the globe have stories of spider women and spinning goddesses helping humans and weaving our interconnected world. The Welsh goddess Arianrhod, known as the Goddess of the Silver Wheel, rules the arts and is associated with spinning, weaving, and rebirth. With her magical wheel she weaves the interconnected web of life. The wolf is among the animals sacred to the Arianrhod. To the Celts, the wolf was associated with the power and cyclical nature of the moon. Habetrot, another Celtic goddess, is connected to spinning and healing and was worshipped by the border groups in Northern England and Lowland Scotland. Often depicted as an old woman with rosy cheeks and black eyes who is disfigured from constant weaving, she lives underground in a flowery knoll. Her home is protected by winding vines of wild roses and concealed by the roots of an ancient tree. It was believed that those who encountered the good-natured Habetrot could perhaps convince her to weave them a magical garment. If she agreed, those who wore the garment would never suffer from sickness. Her gift was a protective, immunomodulating shield.

But the truth is, we are porous and healing is complicated. It is ongoing work; we're never really done. I often describe healing as a spiral toward our center and into subterranean caves of darkness where we might confront the unknown, reveal our innate wisdom, or unearth root causes of imbalance. We might resist dark spaces inside us, but the truth is, most of our healing and growth happens underground and under our skin. And it is often from (or because of) that deep, mysterious place that art emerges to pour both pain and joy onto paper. Sometimes it is only writing, movement, music, or visual art that can peel back layers, dislodge ideas and insights, and reach into emotions that cannot be accessed any other way.

Many humans find it difficult to engage in the creative process. They may hesitate, harboring a belief that they are not artistic, thinking that creativity is something special rather than something inherent in all animals—spiders and their webs, birds and their nests, coyotes and their dens. Maybe there is a constraint about revealing parts of ourselves that don't match our social identity; vulnerabilities might emerge. But the notion of everyday creativity involves the basic capacity of all living beings to adapt flexibly to changing environments. Creativity is the ability to express being itself.

After months of creative wandering and emotional release, I feel my energy returning. I'm healing. I know that preventative medicine means listening closely to my animal body, heeding the wisdom of my gut, anticipating the dark and light of seasonal changes, and being receptive to life's mysteries and pleasures. I feel ecstasy as I walk in nature and have even contemplated whether I need a lover or if I can simply soften enough to receive other kinds of deep pleasure. I have hiked, meditated, and woken at 5:00 a.m., and I feel more attuned. I explore the local woods and swim in a nearby swimming hole before anyone else arrives. My body feels satisfied and satiated and my mind is less scattered and less circuitous. There are fewer repetitive tape loops. I'm wasting less energy and am awake to the sensuality of nature. I feel desire clawing from within me. Hunger is stirring, my animal body is waking up.

PART THREE

Soft Release

Soft release acclimates an animal to a new, safe environment before fully releasing them into it. It is an in-between space—almost wild but not yet free—before the animal leaves the comfort of an enclosure or the protection of a caregiver and finds home. In some cases, animals are placed in prerelease cages close to the location where they'll be freed. In other cases—like those of brave howler monkeys and humans—they may be taken on field trips to a jungle, a university, or an unfamiliar town until they feel accepted and safe enough to let go.

All the "not readies," all the "I need time," are understandable, but only for a short while. The truth is that there is never a "completely ready," there is never a really "right time."

—CLARISSA PINKOLA ESTÉS,
Women Who Run with the Wolves

Yellowstone Wolves

Known as the Crystal Creek pack, the Rose Creek pack, and the Soda Butte pack, these celebrated wolves would be the first to live in Yellowstone Park after the species' seventy-year absence. Their politically fraught reintroduction began in 1995, when wolves from separate packs were captured in Alberta, Canada, radio collared, and flown 700 miles to Yellowstone National Park. While the wolves were in the air, the American Farm Bureau—with the misguided belief the wild wolves would destroy domesticated livestock—filed a motion that led to a court stay, during which the wolves could not be removed from their crates. At the same time, poisoning threats streamed in and Wyoming Republicans passed a measure offering a $500 bounty to anyone who killed one of the wolves outside the park.

Biologists kept the traumatized wolves hydrated by pushing ice cubes through breathing holes in the crate while thirty-eight hours passed. Finally, the stay was lifted, the small cages opened, and wolves entered one-acre acclimation enclosures with the protection of armed guards hiding in hunting blinds nearby. Using the "soft release" method, the enclosures contained natural habitat, with views of Yellowstone, to help the wolves adjust to their new environment and prevent them from trying to head home upon full release.

Dominant males were placed in enclosures with dominant females, along with several subordinate wolves, and within a day or so, the wolves in each of three enclosures had their pack structures figured out. Then, in late March 1995, after six months of captivity, the gates of their enclosures opened but the wolves didn't run. They avoided the gate, the area associated with humans, the strange primates that had separated them from their original packs. Eventually, an area was cut from the back of the fence—their safety zone—and the wolves ran.

It is your task to walk back from the woods with an animal, not a pelt, not a corpse, but something alive. Curate that energy, feed it, don't domesticate it, make culture from it. It should be walking alongside you, not slung over your shoulder. You build your structures from its growls.

—DR. MARTIN SHAW

12

Out of Bounds

It was a slow fade from Brooklyn, a place so intricately woven into my sense of identity. A soft release, I gradually peeled away from Brooklyn's densely populated, vibrant community to more spacious rural environments. Many of my close friends left Brooklyn during the pandemic, too, and those still there—still attached to Brooklyn's charm—are thinking about escaping the familiar congestion for bucolic lands. Friends' announcements, goodbyes, and going away parties make me wish I'd made a more dramatic exit or had some sort of ceremonial farewell, but for a while, I had one foot in and one foot out. I moved and acclimated slowly, steadily grieving and letting go.

Growing up, I was itching to get out of my bedroom, my house, my small town. I spent more time in my bedroom than most young people due to asthma attacks and a compromised immune system. The car accident I experienced as a teenager left me immobile for months and led me to drop out of high school. I learned how to escape to boundless inner landscapes in that small space by going within through writing, reading, and art. A wild imagination is necessary in captivity.

When my body healed and I was ready to be released into adulthood and from my convalescence, I was incredibly restless. The college town where I grew up felt much too small. So I ventured out hiking, went on camping trips, took college classes, and explored nearby cities. I dipped my toe into an accelerated school—Bard College at Simon's Rock—so I didn't have to repeat high school and could skip to college, but that environment felt stifling, too. I just wanted to be free, even though I knew venturing out of enclosures, on my own, could be dangerous. I knew the easy and "safe" path toward an exit could mean walking into a trap—an economic trap, a marriage trap, or the trap of a secure but soul-sucking job.

With righteous indignation, I refused to be groomed for conventional gates where I didn't see a healthy future. I didn't want to go through gates created by racism and capitalism—ways to make money that exploited others and the Earth—and was leery of conventional gates monitored by patriarchy, representing submission. So like the Yellowstone wolves, I waited, listened to my body, and watched. And when the powers that be weren't looking, I dug under their fences to find my way. A lone wolf, I ventured out into the unknown urban wilderness of New York City, but of course, I was never really by myself. Both tethered and buoyed by friends and family, I went searching for my place and my pack.

Now, when I think back to what my survival skills were, they had little to do with being an animal of Earth. I had a deep emotional connection to nature but like most humans these days, I didn't really know how to navigate the natural world. If I had been released into the forest in the ways I imagined, I would have died hungry. So I found ways to scrape by financially, trying to heal and make my voice heard in an anthropocentric culture I resented.

One month after a hole was cut out of the back of the wolves' enclosures and they ran free, the clunky radio collar on the Rose Creek pack's alpha sent a mortality signal. He had followed his pregnant mate into Montana, outside the safety of Yellowstone's borders, and was killed illegally by the hunter Chad McKittrick, who took his head. His pack mates—two young females—had fled in fear.

McKittrick would be charged with three misdemeanor counts—killing, possessing, and transporting an endangered species. His sentence included three months in jail, three months in a halfway house, and $10,000 in restitution. But McKittrick had many supporters. He gave autographs in the local saloons while his fans printed T-shirts and bumper stickers encouraging people to "smoke a pack a day." In the run-up to his trial, McKittrick rode his horse through town in an Independence Day parade, wearing a pistol on his hip and a T-shirt that read, "Northern Rockies Wolf Reduction Project."

In his 2010 memoir, *Wolfer*, Carter Niemeyer, a former federal trapper who spent decades as the top wolf official at Wildlife Services in the Northern Rockies, described his old job, at an arm of the Department of Agriculture that investigates claims of wolf predation on livestock, as being a "hired gun of the livestock industry." Now a sharp critic of his former employer, Niemeyer describes how he watched wolves take the hit for a broader set of anti-government, anti-regulation, anti-science, right-wing politics in the West.

When the Endangered Species Act passed in 1973, it imposed strict prohibitions on hunting and trapping animals that the federal government listed as threatened or endangered. Where imperiled species and habitats were concerned, the feds ranked above state authorities and wolves were among the first species to be protected. In response, the National Park Service initiated a decades-long process that featured the largest and most divisive wildlife management debate in modern US history and ultimately led to the reintroduction of wolves in Yellowstone and Idaho's Frank Church–River of No Return Wilderness. Conservative ranchers, lawmakers with an eye to resource extraction, and right-wing anti-government militants alike saw the law as an attack on their way of life. Extremism in the region further exploded under Bill Clinton, the president whose administration would oversee the wolf reintroduction.

Just days after her mate was murdered, the alpha female gave birth to eight pups. Under normal circumstances, all members of the pack would assist the alpha female in caring for the pups until they were weaned at about six to ten weeks of age. But since her mate had been killed and she had no other wolves to support her, biologists supplied her with food. Eventually, it was clear that the she-wolf and her eight pups needed the safety of the original Rose Creek enclosure. At the time, the she-wolf and her pups were almost half of the total wolf population in Yellowstone park, so it was critical that they survive.

While the she-wolf was nursing her pups in the familiar cage, a two-year-old male dispersed from the Crystal Creek pack and began hanging around her enclosure. In midsummer, he began courting her from outside the fence. In a storm, high winds knocked a tree down and opened a small gap in the enclosure, just large enough for her pups to escape. Biologists were worried that other animals might attack the vulnerable pups but her heroic suitor protected the pups from danger. Upon release in October, the she-wolf accepted the Crystal Creek male as her new mate.

Around the same time, a young female that took off on her own after her father was killed mated with a second young male—a temporary lone wolf—from the Crystal Creek pack and formed the first natural pack in Yellowstone Park: the Leopold pack, named for the famed hunter turned conservationist, Aldo Leopold. The author of the *Sand County Almanac*, Leopold broke free from the "wildlife management" ideology of his time. His honest observations of nature led him to see lands as interconnected systems where all living beings—especially keystone predators like wolves—played a critical role.

During the winter of 1996–97 the Yellowstone reintroduction program ended after releasing seventeen more wolves from four separate acclimation enclosures. The reintroduced wolves have continued to mate, produce new litters of puppies, and disperse to establish new packs in newly formed territories where wolves have not been seen in decades.

Creating a "landscape of fear," the presence of the Yellowstone Wolves changed the way their prey moved around the park. Elk moved more often and became less likely to overgraze in large, open river valleys. This gave willow, aspen, and other saplings time to breathe and to grow. An impact that cascaded down ecosystems, the introduction of wolves ultimately resulted in more habitat for beavers, fish, small mammals, amphibians, and insects. The presence of wolves was helping to maintain a balance of diversity, essential in the community of life. And with tourists streaming in for a chance to see wild wolves, the packs generated a massive infusion of revenue for Yellowstone and local businesses, estimated by the Greater Yellowstone Coalition in 2023 at more than $80 million a year. A 2014 film about the Yellowstone wolves on YouTube, *How Wolves Change Rivers*, has been viewed over 44 million times.

But outside the invisible boundary of Yellowstone, hunters wait.

TRACKING DEVICES

I have no phone signal here in rural Western Massachusetts. If I step beyond the wi-fi of my apartment, I can no longer be tracked or call for help. Growing up, it was like this. As a kid, I didn't think twice about leaving my house without a phone to walk to friends' houses or to play and wander in the woods. There was no checking in via text, just the stylish little Swatch on my wrist to keep track of time. It was like this when I moved to New York City in the late nineties, too. Although there were working pay phones on some city blocks, I wandered the streets with no tether. When I had my own apartment, I waited to get home to check my answering machine.

Landlines and answering machines seem archaic now, but there's a part of me that misses those days. Cell phones have made me more anxious. Here in Massachusetts, I'm trying to get at least one bar of service, just in case, and at the same time release the need to find and be found. While I enjoy the freedom of being untethered, without a partner in this rural environment I've been longing for, I feel lonely. I thought I would get a city guy to move out to the country, but that didn't work, and I worry that I'll be bored with someone here in Western Massachusetts, that a country guy will be too vanilla or something. I know it's ridiculous but I guess my New York City prejudice—the very place I had to escape—is still embedded in me.

Ever since my first love in high school, I've experienced a sense of longing if I didn't have a boyfriend or a partner. I enjoy solitude, even revel in it. Yet at the same time, I want companionship and deep intimacy. I know it's natural. All animals seek a mate, and I, like so many others, have been incredibly isolated during the pandemic.

Often viewed as rugged individualists, lone wolves are seen as animals who are uncompromising and independent, driven to forge their own path without the sentimental need for companionship or community. But in reality, few people would ever want to live this way and few wolves would, either. Wolves, males and females alike, may go through periods alone, but they're not interested in lives of solitude. A lone wolf is a wolf searching for love, for a mate, for other wolves. Everything in a wolf's nature tells them to belong to a pack. Like us, wolves need one another.

When I developed my partnership with the Wolf Conservation Center, I sat down with Maggie Howell, the WCC director, and asked her a million questions. During our conversation, she told me the heartbreaking story of a red wolf—the most endangered canid in the world—that they released to the wild. After being enclosed for a captive breeding program during the first two years of her life and spending more time in another enclosure in North Carolina for a soft release, she finally tasted freedom. No fence, no humans; she was blissfully wild. Something must have gnawed at her in those enclosures. She must have known something was missing, that something wasn't quite right.

The red wolves at the Wolf Conservation Center are not named in a conventional way, though they do have names like F134 (134th female). When they are released, it is with tracking collars. This is how the Wolf Conservation Center knows that almost all the wolves they have released have been shot by poachers. Just two days after the red wolf's joyous release, she was illegally shot. After all she had been through, a hope for her species, she was murdered. "It's intensely heartbreaking, and hard for us to bear," Maggie shared, "but I imagine it must have been absolute bliss to be truly free, even for a moment."

Following an on-again, off-again process that began in 2009, gray wolves have been absent from the Endangered Species Act list and fair game for hunters and trappers in Montana. For years, the state imposed strict quotas limiting the number of wolves hunters could kill in the two districts north of Yellowstone. But during the Trump administration, those restrictions were lifted. New legislation authorizes state commissions to allow wolf killing by cruel, archaic means—use of traps and snares—unlimited quotas, and extended hunting and trapping seasons. In Idaho, nighttime hunting, aerial gunning, and killing pups in dens is allowed. Idaho and the misleadingly named Foundation for Wildlife Management (a nonprofit in north Idaho whose sickening "Reimbursement" page shows hunters with dead wolves) also designated funds to "cover expenses incurred" by private individuals while killing wolves—essentially reinstating a bounty on the keystone species.

When the 2021 hunting season began, trucks appeared at Yellowstone's borders in anticipation. At dusk and dawn, hunters trained their scopes on the edge of the park, using electronic predator calls to lure innocent wolves over the border. Sadly, the wolves responded. The first killings were reported less than a week after the season opened: two eight-month-old pups and a yearling, members of the Junction Butte pack, offspring of the originally introduced packs whose very existence helped make 2021 Yellowstone's busiest year on record. As death tolls mounted, the area's most prominent anti-wolf families shared photos of the animals they killed on Instagram, occasionally tagging Yellowstone in their posts. Locals shared videos alerting fellow hunters to wolves spotted in the park's northern gateway community, and park guides were advised to avoid talking about wolves on their radios when they were in northern Yellowstone, lest their communications be intercepted by hunters.

When Montana's hunting season ended in March, the state's game agency reported 273 wolves killed. The National Park Service counted twenty-five Yellowstone wolves among the dead, with nineteen killed in Montana, all in the hunting districts where the quotas had been lifted, as well as four in Wyoming and two in Idaho.

Roughly a fifth of Yellowstone's wolf population was gone, with one pack eliminated entirely. By winter's end, the park's borderlands had been turned into a killing field.

In the trauma of the 2021 hunts, packs broke apart, lone wolves wandered through traffic, and Yellowstone's biologists noticed an unusually high number of female wolves—non-alphas who typically wouldn't breed—taking to dens. Coyotes have been known to ramp up breeding during periods of mass human-caused mortality. Park researchers were gathering data to determine whether Yellowstone's wolves were doing the same. It was one angle among many that Yellowstone's wide-ranging community of scientists were exploring in the wake of the hunt. Reproduction is a powerful force, but its potential doesn't erase the impact of the incredible trauma, or the cruelty.

Tom Rodgers, an enrolled member of the Blackfeet Nation in Montana and a nationally recognized commentator on Native American issues, politics, and ethics, spoke about the ongoing persecution of wolves, our wild kin, at a recent conference: "There are too many vestiges of colonialism still remaining in the U.S. Fish and Wildlife Department. I think there are still a number of career officials who anchor to a worldview and a culture of trophy hunting or harvesting, which is an Orwellian term for killing and massacring these beautiful, beautiful brothers and sisters."

Dr. Christina Eisenberg, a Native scientist and the author of *The Wolf's Tooth*, writes, "As an ecologist, I don't think we are capable of finding the solution [to our environmental problems] using western science without incorporating traditional ecological knowledge or Native science." I agree. For Ojibwe, Native Americans whose territory once stretched from present-day Ontario in eastern Canada all the way into Montana, the word for wolf is *Ma'iingan*: "the one put here by the All-Loving Spirit to show us the way."

Killing wolves to benefit other species is one of the many myths attached to wolf persecution. Among die-hard advocates of wolf hunts, the argument that the 1995 Yellowstone reintroduction destroyed the state's elk population is repeated even though, according to the park's researchers, there are roughly as many elk in Montana today as there were prior to reintroduction and even at any point in the past two centuries. Plus, Yellowstone wolves overwhelmingly hunt female elk beyond their breeding years, not the bulls hunters like to hang on their trophy walls.

Another argument for killing wolves is that they kill livestock, but a recent study by Washington State University found that lethal control of wolves actually, in the long run, leads to more dead sheep and cattle because hunters fracture packs. The isolated wolves are then forced to go after easier kills. Researchers looked at twenty-five years of data concerning lethal control of wolves from the U.S. Fish and Wildlife Service's Interagency Annual Wolf Reports in Montana, Wyoming, and Idaho. They found that killing one wolf increases the odds of predation by 4 percent for sheep and 5 to 6 percent for cattle the following year. If twenty wolves are killed, livestock deaths double. They simply need to eat, and we are stealing more and more of their land.

As our cultural landscape undergoes seismic shifts—injustice reckoned with, true history uncovered, and outdated myths composed—it is time to do away with the ridiculous myth of the Big Bad Wolf. Few animals are as misunderstood and misrepresented as the wolf, but wolves are very much like us: intelligent, family oriented, loyal. Although, unlike wolves, we have become a threat to the natural world from which we evolved. We might also need to examine our limiting, sometimes cruel inner dialogue, which encloses our own lives, and begin the work of rewriting stories. It's not just our experience that informs our mental and physical health but what we have come to believe.

In a recent dream I was trying to save a wolf—a beautiful, sweet lonely black wolf—but the doors in people's minds were closed. He was lingering around the house in my dream, showing everyone how kind he was by playing with other wild animals and even helping them find their way when they were lost. But present-day me and a younger version of myself were the only ones who could see him.

In the dream, a young me kept saying *Let's look up at the stars!* but no one would look up. Saying it over and over again, my excitement turned to sadness and then despair. The dream-people were living their lives in their heads, unable to see the living world outside. Literal doors inside their heads were closed. Rooms needed to be aired out but were shut. People were fainting from lack of air, for lack of being able to see. There was no resolution.

When I woke, my dream lingered—the lonely wolf was still wandering around the perimeter of the house under a beautiful starry sky.

Rusty-Patched
Bumblebees

Rusty-patched bumblebees are fuzzy, adorable bumblebees with a small rust-colored patch in the middle of their bodies. Native to eastern North America, rusty-patched queens are one of the last bees to go into hibernation in autumn and one of the first to emerge in spring. When a queen wakes from her solitary winter slumber in abandoned rodent cavities, in rotten wood, in clumps of grasses, or beneath the soil and a blanket of autumn leaves, she is groggy, starved, and in need of nectar.

Hovering over manicured lawn after manicured lawn, she struggles, searching for wildflowers. She needs consistent bloom in order to survive.

If the bee disappeared off the surface of the globe, then man would have only four years of life left. No more bees, no more pollination, no more plants, no more animals, no more man.

—ALBERT EINSTEIN

13

Searching for Nectar

After a long, cold winter, the ground is softening. Deciduous trees are waking, their sap rising, and I feel myself thawing out, too; my blood quickening under the warming sun. As I walk through the woods, I sink into tender earth and see deer tracks, dark depressions now, disturbing the soil, making space for new life to grow. Geese are returning north. Their loud calls come and go above me as I step inside and out of my muddy boots.

It is time to rearrange my apothecary, decant herbal medicines, and have new tinctures and teas ready as my body adjusts to spring. I reach for dried nettles—a so-called weed—to forestall spring allergies and find a turquoise jar filled with delicate petals, serrated leaves, tiny branches, and protective thorns of wild rose harvested last summer. Each part of the plant is a precious piece of nature containing all seasons of growth: the seeds of autumn, the restorative darkness of winter, the potential of spring, the bloom of summer. I unscrew the cap and pour a beautiful amber liquid into a tinted green glass and place a few drops under my tongue. It is heart medicine, boundary medicine, wild and sweet.

To many humans, wild rose—*Rosa multiflora*—is a nuisance; an invasive, non-native species of plant. But the abundant, showy pollen of the flowers of the medicinal plant attracts various long-tongued bees, including honeybees and bumblebees. *Rosa multiflora* is a member of the rosacea family, of course, a large bee-loving family that includes trees like apple, plum, and pear, and vines like raspberry and blackberry. The rose family also includes common wildflowers like agrimony and cinquefoil, whose five-petaled flowers offer considerable amounts of nectar and pollen. Since bees see UV light, which does not include the color red, the cultivated red roses humans exchange on Valentine's Day are invisible to their pollinators. Not to mention the fact that, like many cultivated flowers, the red roses ubiquitous at the florist's are sprayed profusely as they grow and are highly toxic to bees (and others). Plants like clover, goldenrod, motherwort, dandelion, and thistle that humans consider to be weeds (or less attractive than ornamental flowers) are beloved healing allies for herbalists and are important bee plants. Bees tend to prioritize flowers with a sweeter or minty scent to pollinate, so a fragrant flower has the ability to attract a bee over long distances.

Many bees have evolved in partnership with particular flowers. Those with shorter tongues, like the buff-tailed bumblebee, prefer short, open flowers like white clover and yarrow, which have nectar within easy reach. Those with long tongues, like the garden bumblebee, rely on deeper flowers like honeysuckle. The large red-tailed bumblebee likes flowers with platforms, like echinacea and foxglove, so they can land and relax their big bodies while doing their work. Rusty-patched bumblebees are generalist foragers with short tongues that they sometimes use to poke a hole in the back of the flower to access nectar. Rusties enjoy a wide variety of flowers for pollen and nectar but have certain flowers, like lupine, aster, and bee balm, that they like best. Once a prolific pollinator of cranberries, plum, apple, alfalfa, and countless wildflowers, the rusty-patched bumblebee is now endangered. They were the first bumblebees to be listed as endangered under the Endangered Species Act.

When in love—like a bumblebee and her favorite wildflower—it can feel as though we are made for someone, that we won't survive without them. I think that's why it worked with Rafael for so long. We loved each other, but we didn't become one. We weren't so absorbed in our relationship that we got lost or forgot ourselves. Maybe our slight distance from each other made our relationship safe, but in the end, the distance had a lot to do with what did us in. We became too different and it was difficult to reconcile a life together. He didn't limit my growth, but I felt rootbound by the city. I needed more soil, more space.

I suppressed my animal desires for too long in our relationship and I am, honestly, a little afraid of them now. Not of myself, really, but of the addiction that can come with that kind of longing. I worry about losing myself in a man or not trusting him. Either way, being preoccupied. My body is nervous. She doesn't want to be under someone else's scrutiny or even gaze.

What I liked about the dating app Bumble is that women choose. There was no chance of opening my inbox to creepy messages from guys I didn't want to interact with. If a conversation I initiated got weird, I could easily block the offending dude and make him disappear from my hive. And I had a tactic: I didn't show my face. I wanted to look but not be looked at. I wanted a guy to be interested in who I was, not just what I looked like. To be intrigued by the essence of what he saw and what he read. Plus, I was ambivalent about Bumble and didn't know if I was ready for online dating. Really, I just wanted a friend I could hike and explore with. I also wanted to know if Western Massachusetts is an area where I could find a companion and truly settle. The problem was, the app's word count was low for all I had to say—300 characters maximum—so I had to choose carefully. I figured I'd share photos once I felt a connection.

In my journal, I explore what I'm looking for:

I'd like to develop a friendship with a warm, compassionate, open-minded man who laughs easily, and loves and cares for the Earth. Ultimately, I want a life partner who is a dear and devoted friend who has my back (and vice versa, of course) and who can enjoy simple things in life as much as adventure. Someone who is honest, sensitive, reliable, intent on personal growth, and comfortable in his own skin.

Together, I want to preserve and learn from the land, live simply in nature, enjoy quiet, have bonfires, read in bed together—sometimes to ourselves, sometimes to each other— have picnics outside, cook delicious meals, and laugh a lot. I want to learn more about growing edible and medicinal mushrooms like reishi, chaga, and oysters, especially in a way that mimics their growth in the wild. Moving forward, I want to be engaged in permanently protecting land to give sovereignty and dignity back to all wild spaces. Though I don't believe land can ever really be owned, I want to buy as much land as possible and/or find other ways to set aside protected land for restoration (if needed) and for wildlife while I'm living and long after I'm gone.

Life is full. And while I have incredible friends and family, it just isn't the same without a partner.

In the small space allotted, I wrote, edited, and rewrote my Bumble profile. I chose prompts like: *Things I cannot stop talking about.* That one was easy: *Banning leaf blowers.* Apart from the legal, inhumane hunting of animals like coyotes and bears, leaf blowers have been my nemesis here in the country. I cannot stand those harmful, ridiculously loud noise-polluting machines that look like military weapons.

I hate leaf blowers for many reasons: gas-powered leaf blowers pollute the air with intense noise and CO_2 emissions (far worse than cars) while being harmful to wildlife. The average, unnecessary leaf blower emits noise at levels of about ninety decibels, according to the Centers for Disease Control and Prevention. About two hours of exposure to that level of noise can damage hearing, and prolonged decibel levels at or above sixty-five can trigger adverse health effects, including an increase in blood pressure and heart rate. Leaf blowers are also incredibly irritating for the increasing number of people trying to work at home. Most importantly, leaving leaves is essential for the health of ecosystems.

As a layer of organic materials aboveground, autumn leaves provide food, shelter, nesting or bedding, and overwintering materials to a variety of wildlife, including queen bumblebees. The majority of butterflies and moths overwinter in the landscape as an egg, a caterpillar, a chrysalis, too, and use leaves for winter cover. One of the most valuable things we can do to support pollinators and other invertebrates is to provide them with the winter cover they need in the form of autumn leaves. The soil itself is also a beneficiary of fallen leaves, as the leaves are essentially composted over time into nutrients that feed a vast number of microbes in the soil.

Recently, when my mom, my sister, and I were social distancing on the deck of my brother's new home, his neighbor started using a deafeningly loud, gas-powered leaf blower. Amid the deafening noise we spoke about how insane it is that we're not taught how to care for land and other creatures in our schools. In most places, it is left to our families and our neighbors who may have forgotten how to live in harmony with the Earth to teach us, or worse yet to our capitalist society, whose objective is to sell us things. Each of us, with "our own" little patch of land, is doing something different. One neighbor strives for a lifeless, carpet-like lawn, another wants to grow food, and another wants to create habitat for the wild. But the wild knows no boundaries, and these strange fractured ecosystems are disruptive. Pesticides don't know boundaries, either, and float in the air, killing the wildlife elsewhere. We need more neighborhood networks and education programs like Food Not Lawns that encourage people to turn their lawns into permaculture gardens and uninterrupted landscapes, leaving so-called weeds and native plants that support wildlife and essential pollinators.

Losing our voices, my family and I could no longer hear one another and, after a while, decided to head back to our respective homes.

I choose to sum up the "three things I cannot stop talking about" like this: *Banning leaf blowers, the sentience of nature, the healing power of so-called weeds.* I figure that will eliminate the wrong men while attracting those who are curious, open, or on the same page.

BUMBLES

In the wild, bumblebees can be found in burrows or holes in the ground and make messy little nests with enough honey just for them. Essentially, we can't extract honey from wild bumblebees, and I love this. As bumblebees feed only on flowers, they need far more plants than equivalent species who are also able to eat leaves or roots. It has been estimated that a stomach full of honey will give a bumblebee about forty minutes of flying time, so they need to forage regularly to survive. Without the energy in nectar, a bumblebee cannot fly, and if she cannot fly to reach flowers to get nectar, she will die. Thus their population is dwindling due to habitat fragmentation and a scarcity of wildflowers, among other things. They are suffering from a lack of natural, uninterrupted beauty.

In the city, bumblebees liked to land on me. It must have been all the herbs and wildflowers seeping through my pores. "They are attracted to sweetness," a friend told me when bumblebees in Tompkins Square Park crawled along my arm. I took it as a compliment but I worried about their confusion. I often walked with bumbles on my body until I found a pollen-rich flower to bring them to. It may sound like I was rescuing these pollinators, but in the city, they rescued me.

Despite their reputation for being busy, bees forage only when nectar and pollen are at their highest levels. When weather or timing isn't ideal, they remain cozy in the hive, conserving energy that would otherwise be exhausted on nonproductive foraging flights. They stay in their hive when temperatures drop into the fifties, if it might rain, or if there are winds above about fifteen miles per hour. If a bumblebee feels tired after a long day of pollination, she might rest inside or around flowers to take a well-deserved nap.

The bulk of the bumblebees' work is performed by the females, who go out to pollinate, gather floral food, and produce wax and honey from their bodies to feed the drones, larvae, and queen. It is the female bumbles that sting and solely the queen that can reproduce. Although worker bees live for only approximately six weeks, they spend their lives performing tasks that benefit the survival of their colony. Every single bee that works within the colony is born from the queen. She is the mother of the hive. Devoted male drones serve her by cleaning and guarding the nest. After a bountiful spring, summer, and early autumn, an entire bumblebee colony will die except for the queen. She hibernates underground and rests, often blanketed by autumn leaves. After winter, she emerges to set up her new colony in spring.

When a bumblebee queen rises in spring, she seeks early forage sources for fuel and to provide food for her first brood of offspring. If just one queen dies, an entire potential colony will be lost. We can help her by leaving our yards, parks, and outdoor spaces a little more wild for nesting sites and ensuring that early blossoms like dandelions and late blossoms like goldenrod will be available to prolong the nectar season for bumblebees.

I loved to sit and watch bumblebees pollinate flowers in my Brooklyn community garden. A daily ritual in spring and summer as I gathered herbs from my garden plot, I watched as fuzzy bumbles weighed down with yellow pollen occasionally paused on flower petals to rest and run their little claws over their fuzzy heads to clean themselves. It's the kind of simple sweetness that fills me up, reminding me that I am inextricably connected to the smallest of creatures. I know the statistics—one out of every three bites of food we eat is made possible by pollinators such as birds, bats, butterflies, moths, beetles, small mammals, and especially bees. But the commercial bee industry is not the same. Commercial bees have spread pathogens to bumblebees, and according to the U.S. Forest Service and the Xerces Society, the commercial bee industry is "cited as the most probable rapid decline of the rusty-patched bumblebee."

There are many other threats to wild bumblebee populations, including agricultural and urban development, grazing (since cattle eat off the tops of flowers), insecticide and herbicide, and fewer natural nest sites for overwintering queens. The use of deadly neonicotinoids and the horrendous but widely used herbicide glyphosate have intensified within the rusty-patched bumblebee's range during the same time period their populations have declined. It's critical we learn what bumblebees like and move beyond the propaganda of plants we're conditioned to hate. While many bumbles are generalist foragers, there are many species of wildflowers that depend on them. The transferring of pollen from flower to flower is how most plants have been capable of reproducing for millions of years.

A bumblebee's life may be fleeting, but we all measure time differently. These small creatures are always seeking the sweetest nectar,
reminding us that the land is alive, built on attraction.

ATTRACTION

I had dates with three men before I met you. I went hiking with all of
them. I guess my profile made it clear that hiking was a turn-on. The
first two dates were with a therapist, a sweet guy whose boots were
worn down at the edges of their soles like mine used to be. For years,
I leaned to the outer edges as though trying to climb out of my body;
I've had to consciously work on centering myself. I wonder what
quirks he noticed and assessed in me.

I had another hiking date with a professor and two with a foraging
musician. They were interesting guys I could definitely be friends
with, but ultimately they weren't the right ones. You were astonished
that I didn't even hold their hands.

It was late summer, a week or so before the fall equinox—my
favorite time of year, when bumblebees linger around fields of
goldenrod—when we first spoke. We had been messaging each other
on Bumble off and on and I disappeared for a little while, overwhelmed by it all. Thank goodness you were still there when I
emerged from my mini-hibernation. It was then that we finally decided to speak and agreed that if the phone conversation went well,
we would meet at a neutral place, a farm and Airbnb run by your
friend, a well-known sustainable food chef. The farm was an hour
and half drive, so the option to stay for the weekend at a legit Airbnb
was appealing. I was getting a little more comfortable driving but not
so comfortable that I would want to go back and forth in one day.

On the phone, we talked about the ideal vision for our lives, our past relationships, our current situations, and what we were looking for. You told me you wanted to live in the forest even though you've lived only in cities so far. You imagined one day buying land in Puerto Rico, living in the mountains where your family has existed in relationship with the land for generations.

Our conversation was going well enough, so midway through, we agreed to meet, and soon, we began talking about things we could do together at the farm. I would take you on a plant walk, I would bring my bow and arrow and you would bring yours. We would talk more, of course, go for hikes and get to know each other among like-minded people you thought I'd appreciate. "If you're not attracted to me," you said, "you'll probably be into my friend. Most women are, but he's also kind of a man-boy." I wasn't quite sure what you meant by that but agreed to go that weekend.

In my dream that night, after our phone call, we were in Puerto Rico lying in bed together and you were spooning me, caressing me sweetly. We said little but I knew we were close. It felt safe and familiar to be in your arms. Your face was shaved, not the way I had seen you in pictures. When we dressed and went outside, we got into a black Jeep and drove through curvaceous mountain roads, lush green as far as our eyes could see. You were driving, and a storm was coming, but we were ahead of it. You weren't worried about the increasing clouds and ominous graying skies. I was worried you might be oblivious to the looming threat, but I trusted you and chose to align with your optimism. The last thing I remember from the dream is that we continued ahead of the storm. The sun was lighting our path and the gray clouds were left behind.

We would weave through those dreamy mountains just five weeks later in waking life, twenty minutes from Aibonito, your ancestral land, whose name means "oh so beautiful."

———————

When a bumblebee finds an abundant flower at a particular time, she will remember her interaction and the time pollination was completed, and visit the flower at the same place and time the following day. A bumblebee will synchronize her behavior with daily floral rhythms, essentially measuring her time with flowers. Imagine if we measured intelligence by how well we knew the location of and behavior of local flowers, navigating the world through landmarks of wild beauty. What an intoxicating world that would be.

Wood Thrush

Some birds are born knowing the songs they will sing, whereas true songbirds, like the wood thrush, have to learn their songs. They begin learning as nestlings, listening closely to adult birds in their neighborhood and committing their songs to memory. But it is only after they've left their nest that young birds begin to sing aloud. Early songs are messy and unstructured, a lot like the squeaky howls of a wolf pup. But after months of practice, a young wood thrush will refine their songs and settle on a repertoire.

Just as humans have regional accents, some bird species develop distinct, area-specific dialects. Variations in birdsong can arise when populations of the same species are isolated by mountains, bodies of water, or miles of fractured habitat. Local dialects are then passed on to the next generation of young birds, who hear songs performed by their father and other local males. After many generations, the birds of the same species from one area can sound different from those across the pond.

A male wood thrush can sing over fifty distinct songs. While most male birds square off by answering a rival's song with the same one—perhaps seeing who can sing better—the male wood thrush likes to be original and will almost always answer a rival's song with a song of their own.

Between the lips and the voice something goes dying.
Something with the wings of a bird, something of anguish and
oblivion
The way nets cannot hold water.

—PABLO NERUDA, "I HAVE GONE MARKING"

14

Semantics

I couldn't roll my *r*'s so I could barely say your name, or at least I couldn't say it right, and you kept forgetting mine. *You don't look like a Vanessa, I have never known a Vanessa.* And yet, somehow, we were already committed.

It all started by the fire: our first touch, our first kiss on the Saturday before the fall equinox. Hours earlier, you sauntered across Earth with effortless, natural swag to meet me at my car. I liked the way you raised your right eyebrow, your easy smile. You would later tell me that as you walked toward me and I leaned over to get something out of my car and flipped my long hair when I stood, *Cindy Crawford Pepsi commercial–style*, you knew you were in trouble. The animal attraction was instant for both of us. I was flushed as you introduced me to your friends, who were busy harvesting plants from the small farm and setting up picnic tables to prepare for an outdoor gathering.

Soon it started to rain, so the two of us ran to a camper van on the far side of the farm where we could be away from the commotion and get to know each other. We knew from our brief phone conversation that we both wanted something real. We were too old to waste any time, so we dove right in, asking probing questions, feeling each other out, and searching for reasons, any reason to walk away.

You spoke about the limits of communication, the loneliness of being in a body. And it's true that often what my body feels and wants to communicate cannot be translated into words. "Between the lips and the voice something goes dying," Neruda writes, and it is oh so true. Words are insufficient for the depth and breadth of what my body wants to say. Sometimes my mind feels like a sieve; information just seeps through. I don't know how people remember everything they read. I have to feel, touch, taste in order to remember. Sometimes I just need to be held and seen or be the one holding and seeing. Sitting in the camper, we quizzed each other through words and watched each other's body language, trying to determine if it was safe enough to let go. And if we did let go, how far we might fall.

You chose words to paint a picture of your background, your family, and your belief systems. You explained why—in spite of, or perhaps because of—having grown up in a devout Catholic family you are intensely allergic to organized religion. You went to Catholic school and, while there, in high school, questioned the existence of God and eventually came to the conclusion that he didn't exist. You became an atheist, a difficult thing to become within a religious community. To find your footing, you sought scientific and naturalistic foundations for your belief systems. Proving the "real real" became increasingly important to you. Any mention of "the divine" makes you cringe. *People think atheists don't believe in anything, that we don't experience wonder, but I believe so many things, too many things, and experience wonder all the time.*

I listened, and though we were mostly on the same page, I worried that you believed everything could be explained through human technology. But we agreed there is infinite mystery. We debated semantics—the word *spirituality* versus *genetic memory*—and you questioned if it made sense to use the word *sentient* for nature. I pointed to the work of the scientist Suzanne Simard, and while you didn't doubt that trees and fungi share resources, you wondered if it was squishy science. You were shaking your leg the way I now know you do when you're keeping pace with your busy mind, but I thought you were nervous. Still, I glimpsed your depth and could tell that you were a poet, a deep thinker, a philosopher. *I may seem austere in my way of thinking but those boundaries go deep*, you tell me. *If you threw a coin into my well, bounded by the constraints of my beliefs, you'd never hear it touch the bottom.*

Finally, you elaborated on the many reasons you want to live in the forest even though you've lived only in cities so far. We shared the same sentiments about the ecosystem and I liked that you consider yourself another animal on this planet, not something divine. As we spoke, we found synergy and, tentatively, moved closer.

In the days and weeks that followed, we bought books, underlined and read others' words, and talked about them. You read Bertrand Russell and Richard Dawkins to me and I read poetry and books about ecology and plants to you. We watched *Fantastic Fungi*, shared articles and quotes. We wouldn't admit it but we were trying to convince each other of something. Or maybe we just wanted to be understood; to find words to describe the depth of our feelings and distill the multitude of experiences and ideas inside; to share those incommunicable thoughts resigned to our lonely depths for lack of finding the right words. We touched, cooked, shared, tasted, and traveled to meet each other's friends and families. All ways to assess each other, the person we might, eventually, call home.

The courting of the wood thrush begins in spring. The male arrives first on breeding grounds in the understory of mature deciduous and mixed forests in eastern North America. Once there, he establishes territory averaging a few acres in size, and defends it by singing. His flutelike songs add beautiful music to the forest. His is one of the first songs to be heard in the morning and among the last to be heard in the evening.

Within days of his arrival, a female will initiate pairing by enticing the talented singer to chase her in silent circular flight among the trees. Flying and diving three to six feet aboveground, the prospective couple weaves in and out of maple, oak, and pine branches. Between flights, they rest and share a perch. If all goes well and the female chooses her singer, they will move quickly and find a place to nest. A male may call attention to a tree nook, a potential nesting place, with a song or by placing building materials nearby. But the final decision is the female's. If she approves of his choice, she will build a beautiful open cup of grass, leaves, moss, weeds, and bark strips, mixed with mud and a lining of soft materials like rootlets, to support their eggs. Once settled, the female, in her quiet way and with bold body language, will help her chosen partner, her singer, defend their territory from intruders.

After our first weekend together, you came to my apartment for an equinox celebration to meet my friends. You brought green coffee beans from your mother's backyard in Puerto Rico. Harvested by hand, the old way, some were fermented in their red cherries. When we broke open the fruit, we found two green seeds. You wanted to roast them for everyone before they arrived, so you sat at my kitchen table and slowly, patiently sorted the small beans. Looking closely and setting broken pieces aside.

You also sensed my broken parts. But instead of setting them aside, you turned to them. You read me closely, alert to changes in the rhythm of my breath, expressions on my face, and trembles beneath my skin. A sculptor, you make stone come alive, so it is no surprise you do the same for me, touching places that were raw and others I didn't even know were numb. You are patient in a way I'd been longing for, you make me vibrate with a buzz that moves through stagnant places inside. While we merge seamlessly when we make love, it is temporary. Between those moments we search for the right sentences to hold us together.

If your body is a house, I am going into every room, every corner to air it out, opening every door, you tell me. You are not only moving beyond physical boundaries but also entering my psychic space. You're not asking me to erase my past, but sometimes it seems my past makes you uncomfortable. You want to pull up tangled, invasive root systems and rewild the landscape of my skin. You are determined to learn and outdo all the other songs.

You have a past, too. You recently left your nest of almost thirty years. A family, two daughters and a former partner, their mother. It is a different sort of past. One that, you insist, must eventually be integrated into our present. I agree, they will always be a part of your life, our life. But right now the pain of your separation is still palpable, so we are treading lightly there. Sometimes you refer to them as your family and it confuses me. Not your daughters and your ex but *your family.* You say *we* got pregnant and that you told your old boss, *I'm pregnant.* It all happened to *you,* too. Of course it did, but I rarely hear it said that way, and I think it's beautiful. You and I will never *be pregnant,* not with a child, at least, and sometimes—even though I am at peace with the decision not to have kids—sometimes it makes me feel sad.

A few months into our courtship, we sat in bed to watch *Dancing with the Birds,* a documentary that shows the elaborate dancing, building, sculpture-making, and performances male birds use to attract a mate. Many of them spend days upon days practicing their routines or creating art, trying their absolute hardest to court a female. My favorite were the bowerbirds, architects who construct elaborate stick sculptures—decorated with everything from dead insects to leaves, shells, and colorful berries—to impress females. When the artwork is complete, the male sings to beckon a female. If she likes what she sees, they dance and mate.

Apart from watching the occasional movie with me, you are comfortable with silence. You don't even reach for the radio. You listen closely when we talk and turn things over and over and over in your mind. *I have a rich inner life*, you often tell me, and yet you are able to be intensely present. I love the way your words get soft and trail off at the end of a long thought or sentence. Sometimes you talk, working your mind into a froth of ideas and dreams, when I'm tired or crave silence. But still I want to hear every single word. Here you are in front of me for who knows how long. I hope it's forever, whatever that means. I am listening. You talk about deep monogamy and it is music to my ears.

After much back-and-forth and song and dance, we choose each other. It is a wonderful thing to feel chosen as a partner. Like a wood thrush pair, we assessed each other, trusting our animal instincts. We knew. To those on the outside, it may seem that our knowing was relatively quick, but we courted—splaying open to share our deepest thoughts, desires, and dreams—enough to know. Why waste time when we were brave enough to admit we wanted each other? Claiming each other and being claimed allows me to feel free. The possibility of our future allows me to let go. Without that potential, I would be more guarded, my borders would be harder to cross.

Birds from across the pond, we have learned a whole repertoire of songs from other places. Part of our new reality is accepting each other's songs and integrating the language of our experiences, of other loves, into our future.

QUIET

I've ruined my view at the farm and placed prisms and other trinkets in the center of my windows so birds don't crash into them. This Earth, pulsing with life, is always giving so I give back, and care for her and her creatures in small ways like this, too. I tend to soil that has been depleted, allow fallen leaves to compost into fertile ground, and offer native plants to naked earth. I fill the stone birdbath on hot summer days and watch songbirds get sips of water and take their last baths of the day before the sun goes down.

As I write today, it is autumn. The wood thrush has already migrated to spend late fall and winter in warmer places. Fall migration begins here in mid-August and continues through mid-September. While we humans plan our last-minute summer getaways, the wood thrushes are busy planning their trips, too. They fly hundreds of miles at night, using the moon and stars to help them navigate, stopping along the way for days or weeks to refuel. Free of daytime thermals, the nighttime atmosphere is more stable for small birds, and daytime predators like hawks are sleeping.

When we notice that the forest has gone quiet, or by tracking the migration through citizen scientists, we can help the wood thrush and other nighttime travelers by turning down our lights as an evening ritual of solidarity. A ritual in memory of their song, in hopes of their safe return. Sadly, like many songbirds—especially those of the forest—wood thrush populations have declined seriously in recent years due to human development and fragmented landscapes. They are included on the Yellow Watch List for birds most at risk of extinction unless significant conservation actions are put into place.

If the wood thrush survives the harrowing migration, finding safe places to refuel, they may spend winter in Central America, sometimes nesting on shade-grown coffee farms in Costa Rica amid a multilayered tree canopy. They'll return to forests of the north in the spring, journeying almost 2,000 miles from Central America, across the Gulf of Mexico, to their summer breeding grounds.

I miss them while they're gone. The forest feels lonelier, too empty and too silent. I look forward to spring when they start their cycle of courtship again. When it is time, in late April and early May, I will turn off the lights in the evening so the small travelers can see where they're going. A small gesture with hope they'll return safely. To fill my heart, and the heart of the forest, with their songs.

Seahorses

Seahorses are incredibly romantic. In their elaborate courtship rituals, the unusual fish hold tails, swim snout-to-snout, and change colors to show they are ready to mate. Seahorse flirting can last for days. The romance usually begins with the male and female anchored to the same plant so they don't float away while facing each other in bright beautiful color.

After days of romance the seahorses swirl around seagrass to engage in their true courtship dance. As they move, the male pumps water through the egg pouch on his trunk, which opens to display its emptiness. In this show of vulnerability, the pair let go, release their anchor, and drift upward snout-to-snout, out of the safety of seagrass, spiraling as they rise. It is then that the female fills the male's empty pouch with her precious eggs. He will carry them while his partner keeps him company, holding his tail, changing colors, and supporting him until their baby seahorses are born.

Love is born of memory, lives from intelligence and dies from forgetfulness.

—PABLO NERUDA

15

Remember Me

The first time you told me you loved me, it was November. We were outside by the fire, sitting on tree stumps at your friend's New England farm. The same place you asked to hold my hand, and where we had our first kiss. It was a chilly night, and as you stoked the waning flames, you turned to me and said, *I've admitted to myself that I love you, and now I'm admitting it to you.* Then, you paused, looked me in the eyes, and said, *I love you, Vanessa.* The words hung in the air and I held my breath. As though by holding my breath I could suspend time. I had been waiting to hear you say it, so hungry for the words. I felt compelled to say it back immediately but I wanted to stay silent, savor the moment, and take the weight of the words inside me. I breathed deeply so they could sink in . . . *Is that okay?* you asked in my silence. *Yes*, I said, finally. *You know I love you, too.*

I had said it first. A week earlier, the words, with a life and will of their own, burst from my mouth before I could stop them. *I love you* had been trying to escape from my body—burning in my gut, rising up and into my exploding chest for days—but my mind halted the momentum: *Too soon, too soon!* So I swallowed the words but the momentum kept going. The heat rose, blood rushed to my head, and the suppression of all that energy gave me a headache. When I finally said the words aloud, my body felt relief, but my mind wished I had waited longer, wished I'd let the tension and feelings build even more. And I worried that something dissipated the moment I said *I love you.* You didn't seem surprised, didn't run away, but you didn't say it back, either. After the words were said I felt an emptiness. Empty of all that heat, pressure, and energy.

———————

My therapist said that falling in love from a psychological point of view is akin to madness, and the psychologist Erich Fromm defined love as a practice. He also said that we expend too much energy on "falling in love" and need to learn more how to "stand in love." I agree. Though sometimes I am so overwhelmed with feeling that I want to burst out of my skin. Other times I feel like I'm descending or floating, out of control like a seahorse unwinding from the safety of their seagrass, spiraling to the surface of the sea.

We once lived in a cave underwater. It was autumn. Days grew darker earlier and earlier, and day blurred into night as light barely glimmered into the bedroom where we tumbled deep into the abyss of love. It was just weeks after we met but time was irrelevant. You felt familiar, like I'd always known you, or maybe, had been waiting for you. Whatever it was, I knew I could surrender. I have never met a man so brave, so willing to let go so soon.

During those dreamy days, we came up for air to hike among fiery colors of dying leaves. We hunted for mushrooms—maitake, chicken of the woods, turkey tail—sea creatures of the forest floor. You, determined, scanned the edges of trails and found them. I infused our morning coffees, soups, and stews with our bounty, and as we sipped and ate, we searched for words to share our deepest thoughts, ideas, dreams, and desires. We wanted to expose ourselves, to be seen, to offer each other a nakedness beyond our skin.

Scientists have peered into the brains of people in the early stages of love and found that when they are shown pictures of their beloved, dopamine—the "feel-good" hormone, part of our reward system— floods their brains. That's no surprise, really, but the interesting thing is that our brains need to release dopamine to store long-term memories. Being madly in love creates more dopamine, and more dopamine leads to better memory. Of course, the lens through which we see our partners skews the memories we store for better or worse. Those who trust their partners look back in time and remember moments together more fondly, while those with low trust tend to hold on to negative moments. Trust or lack thereof changes how our brains on love process memories. And the hippocampus, a seahorse-shaped structure in the brain, is where we store many of those memories.

Nine months later, it is summer. Bright rays of sun pierce our sleep and pour into our bed through the skylight. We wake in this new habitat, squinting, and smile at each other. You caress me gently and kiss me wherever you find my star-kissed skin—my back, my forehead, my shoulder. You remind me that these photons, these beams of light that touch me, are incredibly precious, *they have been waiting, bouncing around for roughly 100,000 years inside the core of the sun, waiting, struggling, fighting to reach you.* I know that all life on Earth is nourished by our committed star. I also know that suns and stars engulf their planets, eventually. Sometimes I think I, too, will burn up, be consumed in your light.

Ten months later it is night, the eve of your birthday, your fifty-fifth trip around the sun. Our bodies entwine, legs tangled together like prehensile tails as you dream. Every once in a while, I hear you murmur in your sleep. I kiss you and you tug me closer. I compose your birthday card in my mind, trying to find the right words to express how I adore you. *I'm grateful you were born on this day, I'm grateful for your ancestors, for the land and food that nourished them, and that nourished you. I am grateful to everyone who loved you . . . I love the way your voice trails off and softens at the end of a long train of thought, the way you wrap up phone conversations with adorable little quips like "It'll be fun!" . . . or "Well, that's that!"* and other sappy, imperfect words to express how much I love you. But I couldn't slip away to write them. I wanted to be with you. *What if I go to the store and something happens? Why take time away to write it when I can be near you?* I chose to savor our time together, show you how I adore you. I'm sorry you didn't get a card.

Eleven months later, you make me a breakfast of miso soup filled with all of our leftovers—kale stalks, shiitake mushrooms, carrots, onion, foraged greens—the entire vegetable drawer. You brush my hair as I write and insist on buying detangler for my knotted mane, so we shop at the local co-op and you roam the aisles with such earnest patience, reading labels, clipping coupons. At night you ask probing questions, turning things over and over and over in your mind. You say you are proud of me, excited about my writing and work, when I doubt myself. But still, I get lost in you. We are melding into each other, trying to find our way.

Like a pair of devoted seahorses, the hippocampal neurons string together past and future, consolidate new memories and weigh possible outcomes. Humans and other mammals have two symmetrically curved hippocampi hidden within the cerebral hemispheres. It is our hippocampal neural system that binds common features of different moments separated in time—our first date, first kiss by the fire, watching the full moon rise on the equinox, when you said, *I love you more than seems possible after six months*, and *You know, I love you more every day.* The hippocampus also plays a role as a differentiator of social memories when enabled by the neurochemical oxytocin, the "love" hormone known for its role in bonding, empathy, and sexual pleasure.

In 2014, the neuroscientist May-Britt Moser won the Nobel Prize for discovering grid cells, neurons that inform an animal's hippocampus where its body is located in space. These grid cells create maps of the outside world so the hippocampus can store and retrieve movement in space, and we can find our way. Moser suggests that remembering where we are in our environment—where we are and where we come from—may be the basis of all memory. Place holds the imprint of memory—*Do the tree and the mycelial roots under our feet where we kissed remember us, too?*

While we need and want to be present with each other, our memories give context, depth, and richness to our love. We have history, we reminisce, we have inside jokes. You know that I like to sit at the corner table of a restaurant with my back to a wall (my "Al Capone seat"), that I will cry if I see a dead fox on the road, that I will feel a wild rush of excitement when I hear coyotes howling at night, and that I hike slowly to see everything, touching and tasting the land. You enjoy the slowness now, too. We pay attention to the land and to each other, anticipating each other's needs and picking up each other's slack. Our memories weave together and unify our sense of being. But there is a conundrum between presence and memory. The same memories that brought us so much joy can bring us equal pain.

Now it is nearly a year and we are apart. I'm away at a writer's residency so I can focus and dive into this book. Without you, this big bed feels like an ocean. I wind my weighted blanket around my body so I don't float away. I don't want to relieve myself from the sadness of missing you because then you would truly be gone.

At least you're here, a palpable ache inside this melancholy. Not so far away.

SEA MONSTERS

My great-grandmother, Ada Graham, an amateur naturalist, was very crafty, and for some bizarre reason she liked to make dried "smoking" seahorses. I still have one. She would roll up a little piece of paper and put it in the dead seahorse's open mouth. As a kid, I didn't consider how weird they were or how she got these creatures, I just adored them. I was fascinated by their odd shapes and rigid, ring-shaped bony plates with thin skin stretched over them. And, of course, their tiny cigarettes.

Sadly, these gentle beings, clinging to their seagrass, are shy, vulnerable, and easy to catch. Millions of seahorses are stolen from the ocean yearly, for fish tanks or to be dried and sold as souvenirs or ground up as pills, powder, or tea in Traditional Chinese Medicine. And as medicine, they are used to help with kidney health, invigorate the blood, and treat asthma, arthritis, and male sexual dysfunction. While they have been found to be useful in treating arthritis, there is little scientific evidence to support the other claims, and there are many other ways to treat arthritis. Like many creatures of the ocean, seahorses are threatened. The IUCN Red List of Threatened Species has listed several species of seahorse as endangered or vulnerable.

For a fish, seahorses are terrible swimmers. Rapidly fluttering a dorsal fin and using pectoral fins to steer, these vulnerable creatures are usually found with their prehensile tails wound around seagrass, coral, or underwater debris so they don't float away. But when they find the right partner, they release their grip, unravel . . . and let go. It's a terrifying prospect, to love.

We can love so hard and so deep and make someone our life and then all of a sudden, one day, they could be gone.

Transitions are hard, like seeing your smiling face drive away after the perfect weekend and having little control over what happens next. We have plans to see each other next weekend, and the next, and the next, and to build a life together, but I harbor the fear that something might interrupt that. *What if this is the last time I see you?* Yet we must plan for our future and go on as if it will all be okay. We will plan as though we will grow old together, not that I fear I could lose you tomorrow. Now you are here, with me, in love, alive, and I don't want to waste time grieving your loss while you're next to me.

We both have our fears that we will leave each other, in different ways: I am hyperaware of impermanence, of the fragility of life, and am afraid that something unexpected might happen to you. *Drive safely, my love*, I text you all too often. Even though I doubt it will change anything, I feel better when I say or type the words. You have a different sort of fear, afraid that one day, I will wake up out of the trance of love and leave you. That I'll release my grip for some unknown reason or for an accumulation of small reasons and just . . . go.

As romantic as seahorses are, the fate of their offspring is left to chance. When the male gives birth—after his belly swells and he has muscular contractions—tiny, fully developed seahorses are born. These vulnerable babies float away on the current. Some species give birth to as many as 200 at one time.

Seahorses may not worry about the fate of their babies or contemplate, anticipate, or worry about the inevitable death of their partners, but it is said that they die of love. For when a mate dies, their partner dies afterward.

There is constant ache and constant tension to be so in love, and so aware of our mortality. I feel as though I have been waiting my whole life for you. At middle age, we are already halfway there, halfway finished, and I wish we had more life left. What I do know, though, is I will savor this time together with every second we have.

In love, we let go, we lose ourselves, forget ourselves, and when we eventually land on solid ground—with our beloved or without—the *us* we remember is not quite the same.

Sea Lions

From youth through adulthood, sea lions chase each other, push and shove each other off rocks, and dive into the ocean to harass other creatures of the water. They play tag and fetch with "toys" such as starfish and, in the Galápagos, have been known to antagonize marine iguanas. Like cats, they also "play" with their prey.

Sea lions can walk on all fours and have external ear flaps, short, thick hair, and transparent coverings over their eyes that reflect light, which gives them excellent underwater vision. Their natural habitat is sandy beaches or rocky shorelines, where they often lie in the sun and relax together. In some parts of the world, sea lions are tolerant of humans and can be seen lounging on moored boats, beach chairs, and park benches.

Too much joy, I swear, is lost in our desperation to keep it.

—OCEAN VUONG, *On Earth We're Briefly Gorgeous*

16

Play and Pleasure

Play is an instinctual act, essential for brain development and life skills in all animals, that involves imagination and imitation. In a soft release situation, the ability to play acts as an indicator that the animal is ready. When we can play, it usually means our guard is down. If an animal in captivity hasn't reached the stage of play, they probably aren't ready for release. Play is an indicator of security. We are released into our own wildness through play. When sex gets playful, it's usually because we feel safe.

I thought I could take a break, be absent from work for a while, but years of effort seemed to dissipate quickly amid an endless pandemic and our months of play. In our bubble—falling in love so hard and so fast—we ignored outside pressures. Now, in order for us to pay our bills, we have to work and limit some of our play. Though I don't really know where to begin again.

With no travel to retreats, no workshops at the Wolf Conservation Center, and no in-person classes, I'm at a bit of a loss. I still have my online groups, which are wonderful, but they aren't quite cutting it financially and it seems I have to wrestle through much more noise, through more glamorous, shiny people who are far better than I am at marketing themselves to be heard. It was easy in Brooklyn, so many people to meet and so many people who needed what I had to offer: a connection to nature in the city. But now I live in a place that is surrounded by forests, meadows, and endless green. I don't even know if it feels right to travel these days or if I want to in the same way. It seems like a contradiction—traveling to feel content at home. Is ecotourism even possible? Isn't it an oxymoron, burning greenhouse gases to nurture Earth? I don't know, everything outside our bubble feels heavy and I just want to play.

As a child, play meant drawing for hours, getting lost in the woods, creating multicolored animals out of playdough, stretching silly putty, making elaborate gingerbread houses, beading jewelry, and other pointless arts and crafts. Now I know how precious time is and I imbue everything with meaning. I meditate to be more present, walk in the woods to learn from nature. But pointlessness? I know it would be therapeutic for me to draw again for no reason at all. Not to heal, not to post on social media, not to show in a gallery. Just to draw, to express whatever my body wants and needs to express, whether it's good or productive or not. Conditioned to be "productive," I have to remind myself over and over and over again that a drawing for pure play has value in and of itself. I also know that when I create for no reason, I make good art, so there's that. When I take time to unravel through art during a workday, I wind up going back to work with more focus. Wasting less time. It's amazing how quickly play can be drained of pleasure when it becomes work, it's met with expectation, and we get paid for it.

It seems that sea lions not only play but have a sense of humor. I remember going to SeaWorld as a kid, before I knew SeaWorld was evil, and laughing at the antics of the sea lions who learned stupid tricks like balancing balls on their noses, jumping through hoops, and sometimes kissing an audience member to entertain us. What weird creatures we are—getting voyeuristic pleasure from their manipulated play. Often referred to as "dogs of the sea," sea lions are among the most intelligent (via humans' measure of intelligence, anyway) and talkative of all marine mammals. And like dogs, they tend to be kind, curious, and easy to take advantage of and domesticate. In one SeaWorld-like ocean park, you can pay to pose with sea lions "for the cutest pictures ever!" SeaWorld trainers, circus trainers, and all those who work with animals forced to entertain are playing with broken creatures.

Sea lions are pinnipeds, a group of fin- or flipper-footed marine mammals who live in the ocean but are able to come on land for long periods of time. The evolutionary origin of sea lions can be traced back to ancient bears and the mustelids (otters, weasels, ferrets) who stayed on land, while sea lions chose to return to the sea and developed fins. The oldest definitive pinniped fossils date from approximately 23 million years ago in the North Pacific.

A sea lion's behavior in the wild is inspired by the dynamic ocean environment—changes of weather and sea conditions, fast diving, and long-distance swimming in sync with the movement of prey, and strong social and emotional bonds. In impoverished aquariums and small pools where they are held captive, some facilities try "enrichments" to alleviate stress, depression, and boredom like plastic balls, squeaky toys, or large ice cubes that contain fish pieces inside. These diversions are a tragic and sad substitute for the wondrous environment of the ocean. Captive California sea lions may live longer than their relatives in the wild, but does a long, dull life justify unnecessary captivity for entertainment or educational purposes?

The captive sea lions remind me of stories of the selkies, the seal people from rural coastal communities of Scotland, Ireland, and Iceland, which are often told as tales of longing. They are stories of separation from home, from nature, from community. They speak to a gnawing ache for our animal nature, for who we really are. In order for a selkie to come ashore, they must shed their sealskin and transform for a time into a human. And if one managed to find a selkie's skin and hide it away, the seal person could not return to sea.

In the story of the selkie wife, a wild seal woman is held captive for a man's pleasure. Though she is treated kindly and fed well and even has children in captivity, the selkie always craves the ocean—her true home—and freedom. Some tales say that on an autumn night, under a full moon, a lonely fisherman wandered along the edge of the ocean and came upon beautiful women playing and dancing in the moonlight. Stunned by their beauty, he hid behind a large rock to watch them, and as he did, his lonely heart awakened and he fell in love. While one of the selkie women was dancing, he stole her skin, knowing that without it, she could not return to sea.

One by one the seal women jumped into the water, but without her sealskin, the lone selkie could not follow. She was frantic, searching everywhere for her skin. She was desperate, naked, and in tears when the fisherman finally revealed himself. With no one else to turn to, she begged him for help. But instead of giving her the sealskin and a choice, he hid her freedom, professed his love, and promised to take care of her if she married him.

The seal woman began a domesticated life and, in time, accepted her circumstances, learned to be somewhat happy, and even enjoyed a loving relationship with her captor, the fisherman, with whom she bore children. Some stories say she had a close relationship with her daughter; others, her son. But despite any joy or momentary pleasure, she was always longing, gazing out to sea while the fisherman, preoccupied with hiding her skin, checked and double-checked his hiding places and locks to be sure his selkie wife could not flee.

In most versions of the story, with the help of her children, who love her and whom she loves unconditionally, she finds her sealskin and leaves. A bittersweet ending, since she had grown attached to her captor, and especially the children she had raised in captivity. But the pull of the wild, the desire for freedom, for who she really was, was stronger than any domestic attachment.

Huge numbers of malnourished California sea lion pups have washed up on Southern California beaches in recent years, an emergency situation that led the National Oceanic Atmospheric Administration to declare the circumstances "an unusual mortality event." In response, the National Marine Mammal Foundation's animal care experts provided support to California marine mammal rescue facilities as they faced an elevated number of patients. Biologists and veterinarians worked to determine the cause of the starving, stranded babies, and scientists now believe changes in prey availability—especially sardines, a vital nutritional source for nursing sea lion mothers—are the culprit. In this case, I'm grateful to the people who have rescued starving babies and to everyone caring for traumatized sea lions in captivity. While researching the stranded, rescued, and released sea lions, I learned that SeaWorld now has a rescue and release center. Things are changing. Hopefully, like many aquariums and zoos who exist at the edge of harm and help, they are leaning more toward rescue and release these days.

By disentangling marine mammals trapped in fishing nets and trash, providing a hospital where rescued marine mammals receive necessary care and teaching the public how to become stewards of ocean ecosystems, the sole purpose of the Pacific Marine Mammal Center (PMMC) is to help. Their mission is to "inspire ocean stewardship through animal rescue and rehabilitation, marine mammal research, STEM education programs, and advocacy for a healthy ocean." Children can learn how to be ocean stewards by attending Camp Pinniped in person or Camp Pinniped at Home, where they attend live chats, watch educational videos, and learn how the

PMMC rescue and rehabilitate seal and sea lion patients. Much more enriching and fulfilling for children and for marine mammals than watching captive sea lions play with plastic toys.

SENSORY AWARENESS

I've been catching up with work and have been teaching a lot lately. A lot of "space holding." Maybe what my animal body needs today is not to speak or to write but to listen. I have spent less time listening lately. The sight and sound of water on the skylight above makes me want to curl into you, your warmth, your soft, silky skin. The rain is such a relief; it has been so hot and dry this summer, the land so thirsty. I have things to do, but instead, I snuggle into your chest. This is why I have worked so hard the past few weeks, to melt into moments like these.

The more I drop into my body, the more I am here with you. When we were hiking the other day, I was so absorbed in our conversation, I looked around after a while and I didn't know where we were. No phone connection, no time ticking away, I forgot myself and my surroundings. All that existed were the nearby plants, trees, birdsong, and you. Moments of deep connection and acts of creation—making love, making art, bonding with loved ones and with nature, reading poetry, or listening to music—are where I forget myself most. Immersing in bodily sensations of taste, touch, sight, and scent allow me to dissolve and become more myself at once.

You have been helping me remember the sensual part of me, the natural part of me that enjoys sex. Not only what the creative act opens up in me, but how it makes me feel more alive. My desire wasn't gone or waning, just waiting. I can grab you and you welcome me. I don't have to hold back anymore. I am recalibrating, discovering my body again. A body I thought I knew so well. I am flushed; more blood is rushing to my face and my friends say I look different, more juicy. I am less of a raw nerve. We are 98 percent monkey; you remind me to "let the monkey do the talking." Though you often make me feel more like a creature of the sea. Boneless, like a jellyfish, or heavy like a waterfall; liquid that desperately needs to pour down and keep going and going and going. I want to float free in a body of water, melt into earth.

We have been together for over a year now and we are apart again for some weeks so I can focus and write. I just arrived at an artist's residency and it is pouring outside. I am tired. A bone-deep tired that comes from too much talking, lots of work, and not enough playtime in nature. I don't need to use this time to be productive even if I have a book to write, even if I came out here for inspiration. I don't want to open my computer for a while, I don't want to produce. I just want to slow down, to savor each moment. To lie in the hammock, eat delicious food and linger in each taste and texture, to sit in the waning sun at the end of a long, easy day and drink organic red wine from a delicate glass. To bathe in feeling.

Pleasure requires presence, sensory awareness, and slowing down. In my experience, writing requires the same. The practice of writing helps me attune my senses to greater awareness and pleasure. Writing also comes alive through the senses. We are sensual animals, after all.

It can take time to drop into a mental, physical, and emotional space where we savor moments with all of our senses. Before I can drop into a deep space of sensory awareness, I might have to do nothing. Jenny Odell, author of *How to Do Nothing*, writes, "To do nothing is to hold yourself still so that you can perceive what is actually there." When I've been busy, this nothingness can be uncomfortable. Thoughts and emotions I haven't made space for begin to emerge. But as uncomfortable as it can be, I've learned to be with what is and to feel what I feel instead of distracting myself. Often the thoughts and feelings that arise are the same ones that enrich my experience of life. I can experience grief and pleasure at the same time. I can be more receptive to the touch of a late summer breeze, the welcome touch of my beloved, or the scent of a wildflower.

We all engage in activities solely for pleasure—decadent desserts, lovemaking, sensuous baths, unplugging from work, and wandering in the woods—but we often judge the calories consumed or the hours spent in bliss as something to feel guilty about afterward. Puritanical ideas or our productivity-obsessed culture may be to blame. Religions have woven guilt and sin into our sensuous flesh. Abstinence and sacrifice of our longings are often lauded and those who deny themselves might believe they've been good.

Of course there are edges: sometimes we equate expensive, intangible things with pleasure. Those of us who live under capitalism are led to believe that material possessions can heal our deepest wounds. As with the plastic toys in aquariums, we're left grasping for luxurious bags, clothes, or cars—poor substitutes for the miraculous complexity of our bodies. Bags cannot offer us warmth, touch, or kind words, or love us back. Pleasures may also be used to bury pain or trauma, becoming escapes that lead to harmful addictions. But eventually, those pleasures are fleeting and their pursuit becomes a nightmare. And, of course, sometimes we define entertainment as a pleasure and attend circuses like SeaWorld that exploit our underwater relatives.

My pleasures are heightened the more I realize I am nature. Feelings of deep remembering may wash over me suddenly, triggered by the sound of a stream that echoes the flow of water in my body, the glow of goldenrod that touches the sun inside me, the intoxicating scent of lilac carried in a warm spring breeze, the poignant change of autumn leaves, the haunting song of mourning doves.

I love watching other animals experience nature's pleasures, too. Bears bathing in rivers, sea otters cuddling as they float in the ocean, chipmunks basking on a rock in the sun, and plump sea lions sunning themselves on the shore, dancing through the ocean and playing without obstruction. Wild and free to play and experience pleasure, the way they are meant to be.

Red-Tailed Hawks

Red-tailed hawks ride the wind with keen eyes on the ground, zoning in on prey. With excellent eyesight and sharp beaks and claws, hawks are efficient hunters who dive with precision—sometimes at speeds of up to 120 miles per hour—to secure fast-moving squirrels and small mice. Hawks can see up to eight times farther than humans and have a total field of vision that extends to 280 degrees, giving them access to panoramic views to spot faraway prey. With binocular overlap, hawks can focus on one object or prey using both eyes simultaneously, creating a single clear image for optimal precision when attacking. The most common species of hawk in North America, red-tailed hawks are highly resilient and, like the coyote, can live in a wide variety of habitats—from desert to grassland, fields to parks, and even tropical rainforest. Some red-tailed hawks are migratory and others are not. Many living in the northern portion of their range in southern Canada and the northern United States migrate to warmer locations for the winter. But a few remain in their breeding territories even in severe winters. Many red-tailed hawks in Western Massachusetts seem to be here year-round.

I will not be like a bird bred in a cage, I thought, too dull to fly even when the door stands open.

—MADELINE MILLER, *Circe*

17

Local Cosmology

R ed-tailed hawks appear in moments of frozen indecision, or maybe it's that I gaze out the window and notice them when my emotions entangle me and it's hard to put one foot, or one word, in front of the other. I look out the window, breathe, and see them soaring. *Remember the big picture,* they nudge. *Will this choice take you where you want to go?* Sometimes they ride the wind above me, perch nearby, or come down to my level to feed. I've seen them in the strangest places lately, and now a gorgeous pair has nested close by. The huge female is perched on a tree limb as I write.

It was November 2020 at Sawmill Herb Farm when I first encountered her. I arrived a little early, before my students, to set up our gathering space under a gazebo. It was my first in-person class with students since COVID, and a tiny one, just three of us. We were in the midst of the blue moon and the time when the veil between worlds is said to be thin—Allhallows and Samhain.

I greeted the land and plants and opened the greenhouse to find our benches. It felt like a massive homecoming. It had been over a year since I'd been there. It was so good to see the medicinal plants and land I'd come to know so well. I placed a warm hawthorn infusion on the ground, arranged the benches and other ritual items under the gazebo, and came back to get more from the greenhouse. And that's when I saw her. A gorgeous red-tailed hawk perched on the top of the entryway less than four feet above my head. She stared at me with her intense amber eyes and I stared back. Locked in a staring contest for what seemed like minutes, she turned her head first, feeling like she'd sufficiently taken me in, and moved her neck from side to side to survey the landscape. Besides the huge community of plants, it was just us on the farm and, I imagine, plenty of tiny prey.

After a while, my students arrived and as we continued to set up, she flew to another post and watched over us. And then the most amazing thing happened: she flew to our tiny gazebo and perched right above us, anointing our space. She stayed nearby for the entire three hours, moving from perch to perch, weaving a circle around us.

When I told the story to some, they replied with sayings like *The hawk was there for a reason, There are no coincidences, It was meant to be, She was a sign.* Sometimes experiences do feel that way. But if I really believed everything happened for a reason, I might believe that some of us were being rewarded and others were not, or that my heartbreaks, losses, and illnesses were designed to teach me some fateful lesson I had been preordained to learn. If I believed there were "no coincidences," it would mean the wonders I stumbled upon or the terrible accidents I experienced were choreographed just for me. And if I believed everything was "meant to be," it would mean that people deserved what life handed to them, absolving me and others from righting heinous wrongs and alleviating suffering.

In *Between Two Kingdoms*, the author Suleika Jaouad writes about well-meaning but harmful platitudes people offered to her and other cancer patients in the midst of unbearable illness. She was told "to find the silver lining, that everything happens for a reason," and the one she hated the most: "God doesn't give you more than you can handle." "In my case," she writes, "it certainly felt like I had been given more than I could handle."

———————

I don't believe the red-tailed hawk at Sawmill Herb Farm or any other hawk is showing up for me but that I have been lucky enough to see them frequently and sometimes to notice them notice me, too. I don't believe the hawks soaring above or perched in odd places are signs but that I am making meaning from their presence. Maybe that's what signs are—signs that we are paying attention, that we are awake to our environment and stepping out of ourselves with an open mind. Looking, seeking, noticing other species and ways they navigate the world. In wildlife tracking, *sign tracking* is a term used for scat, footprints, trails, scent markings, and other physical evidence that animals were there.

God never made sense to me. But for a while, I kept my doubts to myself even though there was no cohesive religious belief system in my family. My grandfather was raised Jewish, but all in all, he was an atheist. My grandmother read her Bible when he wasn't home and my mom, well, I know she feels one with nature like me, but growing up she seemed open to it all. We didn't really discuss religion and she didn't contradict my stepfather when he told me God was watching me and not to use God's name in vain. Occasionally, we went to his father's Baptist church, which worshipped a judgmental Christian God who was quick to punish. This male God seemed incredibly insecure and invasive, nosing into everyone's private thoughts—and he didn't seem to like women very much.

As much as I felt like I was being watched by this supposed all-powerful being, deep down I was skeptical and resentful of him. The stories didn't hold. Nature is what made sense to me and I certainly didn't believe humans have dominion over Mother Earth. In forests, wild meadows, and waterways, I felt kinship and what some might call a spiritual connection. I also felt fiercely protective.

_____

Circe is a sorceress in Greek mythology whose name means "hawk." She is now a favorite mythical being thanks to Madeline Miller's book *Circe*, which gives her a voice. The sorceress is the daughter of Helios, the sun god, and Perse, the ocean nymph renowned for her knowledge of herbs. Circe inherited her piercing hawk eyes and intensity from her father and her intuition and plant wisdom from her mother. With the help of plants and her magical wand or staff, Circe could transform anyone who offended her into an animal. She has been depicted as a predatory, sexually promiscuous female whose violent jealousy made her a source of fear as well as desire. She is famous for changing Odysseus's crew into hogs. In Circe's voice, Miller writes, "I thought once that gods are the opposite of death, but I see now they are more dead than anything, for they are unchanging, and can hold nothing in their hands."

The hawk is sacred to the Greek gods Hermes and Apollo and the moon goddess Artemis—a hunter and protector of children, women, nature, and wild animals. In ancient Greece, certain hills and valleys were known to belong to Artemis, along with forests, streams, meadows, and marshes. The presence of the goddess in the Greek pantheon inhibited human invasion of sacred waters and forests and helped to preserve acres and acres of wilderness along with the wildlife that lived there. Since her groves were numerous and often large, they protected diverse species of flora and fauna for hundreds of years. Where lore of the land and stories of respecting wildlife are strong, land and wildlife are often protected. But in most places today, instead of goddesses or taboos that protect and honor land, we have laws. Luckily, it is illegal to kill a hawk, but other animals and areas of land are not so fortunate. Like the wolf, many are trapped in harmful mythology.

While I love nature lore and stories of animism, I'm most interested in learning from and protecting the animals themselves, in the flesh, here and now. Sometimes I grow tired of trying to convince people not to poison land and destroy the wildflowers, tired of trying to show people how beautiful it all could be if we stopped the endless wanting, if we slowed down and remembered we were animals, too. Not something divine that will someday transcend this world but that the trees are our relatives who were here before us and that it is because of them that we can breathe. As an herbalist, I'm less and less interested in what plants can do for me and more and more interested in what I can do for the plants.

WINDOWS TO THE SOUL

I dreamed of drawing eyes. *I drew eyes when I was little too*, I told myself in my dream. I am writing and reflecting on this nonsense and you are making breakfast. I know soon you'll come over and brush my tangled hair. I like my messy bed head, I think it's sexy, but I love your tenderness, so I let you untangle me. You tell me that you are *just trying to be a good monkey*, and you are. You tell me how you brushed your daughters' hair, too. Grown women now, they are so lucky to have a father like you.

It is the small tender things like these that matter. The way you reach for my hand when we're walking outside, the way you pull me in to lie on your chest while you're reading, the way you express gratitude every morning when I bring you hawthorn tea and fruit, the way you gaze at me as though seeing me for the first time when we wake in the morning. "My local cosmology has shrunken down to my kitchen and the people I love," you tell me. It makes sense, and I think it's beautiful. I gaze back into your eyes, in awe of you. In your eyes, I see the depth and mystery of your past and the light of our possible future. As endless as you seem, the fleeting nature of your flesh reminds me I must be present in case this moment is all we have.

Eyes—windows to the soul—were what I always drew and doo-dled growing up. They fascinated me. As I grew older, it seemed eyes were where I could see a person's depth (or lack thereof), their intent, what they held inside, and whether or not they saw me. One piece of artwork I created in my late twenties during a period of disciplined Buddhist meditation is a large eye composed entirely of tiny, uned-ited words. A seeker, I wanted to uncover truth and see beyond life's illusions. I wanted to empty myself of all the chatter in my head: *How could I see with so much noise clouding my perception?*

While I may no longer be curious about the traditional idea of past-life karma, our actions and choices do have repercussions within and beyond this lifetime. Everything we do—from the food we buy, to the stories we internalize, to the land we harm and the plants and animals we misunderstand—has an impact. This in-cludes small things, too. When you slow to let drivers merge ahead of you on the road, you tell me, *I may have prevented an accident or alleviated tension in someone's day. Being kind makes the world a little kinder.*

Now it is early spring. We walk around Puffers Pond and the Mill River Conservation Area, whose woodland paths are just beyond a house where I lived until I was twelve years old. We are silent as we watch a pair of hawks circling above us in their dynamic courtship flight. Scientists have concluded that hawks and other birds are de-scendants of predatory, two-legged theropod dinosaurs like Tyran-nosaurus rex and velociraptors of the Cretaceous period, about 100 million years ago, long before humans walked upon Earth. Hawks are unusual among birds in that the female is larger than her mate. In some species of hawk, the female is twice the size.

Monogamous birds, red-tailed hawks pair for life. When the breeding season begins, so does their mating ritual: clasping talons, male and female hawks fall in spirals before breaking apart in dramatic twists and turns. Sometimes they plummet to the Earth in a passionate tangle before pulling apart from each other at the last moment. If the hawks bond and choose each other, the pair will nest on a high perch, preferably an open area with patches of trees. They will use and remodel the nest, made from bark and twigs, for many years.

I feel a profound connection to the hawks, the water, the land around us, and so do you. We speak about the feeling of wonder—a familial connection, a sense of recognition—and about the imperfect words used to convey its depth. You describe the feeling as ancient, not spiritual; not tapping into something otherworldly but *a genetic recognition of our deep time connection to this world*. I feel it in my bones, too. We talk about freedom to believe what we believe, believing in stories that don't harm others, and the freedom to find our truth.

Standing together surrounded by distant relatives, we feel into our ancient and deep interdependence. Looking up, we watch small dinosaurs in their mating dance, diving and spiraling above.

PART FOUR

Homing

Homing refers to an animal's ability to return to a den, a nesting place, a cabin, an ancestral land, a river, or a stream after traveling a distance away. Sometimes it means migration—both forced and chosen—or swimming upstream to spawning grounds and retracing steps to the source of life. For some creatures, being carried by the currents or blowing in the wind leaves few regrets as long as the unknown destination provides food, a mate, and shelter.

But homing is not so easy these days. For us, and unfortunately for all life, there are pressures of humanity to avoid. Areas animals called home are changing—climate change, human housing developments, fragmented landscapes, and loss of migration corridors make it hard for animals to return home or to find new, safe places to live.

Nature is not a place to visit. It is home.

—GARY SNYDER

Pigeons

Pigeons don't migrate; they're homebodies. Feral descendants of the rock dove, the ubiquitous pigeon was once revered and bred as a messenger because of their profound homing ability. Using the position and angle of the sun and Earth's magnetic field to navigate the sky, these amazing birds can return home from as far as 7,000 miles beyond familiar territory. Pigeons may also rely upon low-frequency infrasounds—movements of the Earth's crust and changes in the tides—to find their way.

Watching the birds, I felt I shared in their freedom. But nests and eggs tied birds down. They made them vulnerable.

—HELEN MACDONALD

18

Finding Home

HOMEBODIES

I've lived a transient, almost nomadic lifestyle for the past decade, yet I get very attached to place. To land, really. To wild places especially. My way of homing is going where I feel pulled. But home? I don't really know where that is.

I nested at the farm in Western Massachusetts, spent money to fluff up my den with ethically sourced linen curtains, sheets, mustard-colored bedding, and embroidered pillows. I took dried, wildcrafted herbs and fungi out of bags and filled and labeled glass mason jars that lined my kitchen counters. It felt good; it had been years since I'd had a space that felt like my own. But still, something in me sensed this was a pit stop. I never really settled.

Now it is March 2022 and I'm leaving my apartment in Western Massachusetts with the promise of living with you, my chosen partner. The nearly two-hour commute has been wearing on us and I worry about you driving back and forth on icy winter roads. I want to be in the same place, wherever that is. Unfortunately, "wherever that is" keeps changing. We've talked about traveling and studying tropical permaculture to pursue your dream of stewarding forest in your ancestral lands of Puerto Rico. You would transition from your life in the Northeast and sell your business so we could live off the land.

We went to Puerto Rico to explore recently and drove along the Ruta Panorámica, a stretch of steep, skinny, winding mountainous road that makes up the spine of the island, where Christian crosses and vases full of flowers marked places where people flew from ledges, presumably to their death. The drive was beautiful and terrifying. But it didn't take long for the beauty and possibility to grow stronger than the fear. We parked at Torro Negro State Forest where the sign in front read IN THE FOREST AND MOUNTAINS, ANIMALS DO NOT LEAVE TRASH, HUMANS DO. PLEASE BEHAVE LIKE ANIMALS. We hiked like animals amid tropical rainforest and imagined that this could be our life. Back at your mom's house in Aibonito, we walked through her backyard to pick coffee beans and dig taro roots, and we found delicious passion fruit rolling down the gutter. Living off the land felt possible there. But then there was life up north to consider: your kids—one graduating from college and one graduating from high school—the work you are still transitioning from, the change of seasons we both love, my family.

On our way back from Puerto Rico, I ask you if you have a strong sense of where you're from and you tell me, *Not really, but I do have a strong sense of who I'm from.*

Back in Massachusetts, I sort through my stuff—books I've carried from place to place but have never read, albums I've lugged around for years after my turntable broke, fancy clothes I will wear someday, jars and jars of plant medicine I've yet to decant. I sort through the ideas, dreams, and memories tied to belongings. *What do I cling to? What do I give away?* I am trying to stay grounded even though the ground feels like it is shaking beneath me. Or maybe the ground is just waiting for me to stop. I'm not staying still enough to grow roots, let alone incubate and settle into soil.

With no children, fewer responsibilities, and remote work since the pandemic, I have been going with the flow and open to possibility when maybe, instead, I should have been anchoring us. Maybe I should have held on to my apartment for both of us. Caught up in love's momentum, I haven't really taken a moment to step back and breathe, to see how it is all going to settle and ask, *Where are we going?* We are in midair and it is uncomfortable. If I were a bird, I would orient myself mid-flight, using Earth's magnetic field to navigate and know exactly where to go.

One of the things that kept me in New York City for so long is that it attracted people from all over the world—some pursuing dreams, others escaping violence—all looking for a better life, a new definition of home. It isn't always possible to stay in one place. Colonization, climate change, gentrification, and loss of common land and migration corridors (paths followed by animals, birds, or fish when traveling between winter and summer habitats) are among the many reasons it is becoming harder for animals of all kinds to return home or to find safe places to exist. Today, as land and waterways struggle to adapt to unprecedented changes, humans and more-than-human animals embark on natural and forced migrations, with many obstacles: resource and food scarcity, and air, water, light, and noise pollution. Paths that once connected wildlife are disconnected by paved roads and shopping malls, and interrupted by fenced-in land.

Animals move burrows, nests, and dens for love and for safety, prompted by hunger and survival. But for a pigeon, no matter where they are, home is where they were born. It is a clarity some might envy, but pigeons are attached to their birthplace even if it is, or eventually becomes, inhospitable.

In New York City, pigeons were so common they became almost invisible to me. But the longer I lived in the city and the hungrier I grew for nature, the more I noticed its wildlife, which I had been blind to. I marveled at the incredible beauty and resilience of plants that grew through the cracks in the sidewalks, learned about urban bats, coyotes, foxes, and countless migrating birds, and, of course, noticed the beauty of pigeons, each with their unique luminescent markings of lavender, silver, and turquoise. The more I learned about their history, the more the hatred of pigeons made me sad. With ancestral lineages of heroes and heroines, I wondered if they, too, lament all that has been forgotten.

The pigeon's full backstory is often confused by the species names *pigeon* and *dove*, which are used interchangeably. The exalted white dove of peace and the reviled urban pigeon are descended from the blue rock dove—a species often interbred with the feral birds we're accustomed to seeing in cities around the world. In the wild, rock doves make their home in steep craggy ledges, and coastal and inland cliffs whose natural structures resemble the windowsills of New York City high-rises. Which, sadly, are often adorned with spikes to keep pigeons from roosting.

While crossing a busy pigeon-filled street in Glasgow on a recent trip to Scotland, I overheard a woman saying, *I feel bad for pigeons, they just want to be around people and we shun them. It's our fault there are so many. We bred them to be with us, to help us, and now we hate them.* It's true. Just as technology has made many of our jobs obsolete, the same can be said for pigeons. Domesticated about 10,000 years ago, humans have had a long relationship with pigeons. The feral pigeons in New York City and throughout the world are likely ancestors of domesticated pigeons from large, abandoned pigeon houses called dovecotes. Dovecotes were once status symbols in medieval Europe, so only the wealthy were allowed to build them. The earliest known dovecotes were built in Mesopotamia around 4000 BCE. The largest dovecote in the world is located in England and has over 16,000 pigeonholes.

Companions to the love goddess, Aphrodite, pigeons carried poems and notes between lovers, and were life-saving messengers during war. Pigeons would typically be transported to a destination in cages, with outgoing messages secured to them. Once the messages were received, the recipients would write down their replies and release the pigeon to fly back home, return message in tow. War pigeons like the famed Cher Ami (French for "dear friend") received awards for saving lives after being wounded in battle during World War I. In November 2019, Cheri Ami became one of the first recipients of the Animals in War & Peace Medal of Bravery, bestowed on him posthumously at a ceremony on Capitol Hill in Washington, D.C. Now these intelligent birds with a long history with humans carry on with little recognition or respect. These heroes and heroines eat old pizza off city sidewalks—a testament to their resilience—and are referred to as rats with wings.

One of the most widespread misconceptions about urban pigeons is that they are carriers of disease. Pest-control companies accuse them of transmitting a number of diseases, but the truth is that pigeons pose little to no health risk to humans. To contract a disease from a pigeon, a person would need to inhale or ingest their poop. And even if they did, disease-causing organisms are unlikely to survive for a long period of time since droppings are typically dry and exposed to sunlight. Pigeons' only real crime against humanity seems to be their success as a species. Do we revile them because they can cope with our mess?

I think about the fact that for over 95 percent of human existence we have been nomads, carrying and taking only what was essential. Our supplies depended on the availability of forageable fruit, nuts, roots, and greens, the movement of animals, and changes in weather. Sometimes I wonder if we humans are even meant to stay in one place. Certainly, we're not meant to accumulate so much unnecessary stuff—from plastic toys and trinkets to tacky souvenirs, decorative furniture, and vanity cars (and the containers and buildings in which to store them)—that exhausts the Earth while keeping us bogged down and tethered.

I know my Middle Eastern ancestors were nomadic; they were forced to be. My mother said they were from Palestine, and my brother and sister, who did some digging, said they were from Syria and went to Siberia and Eastern Europe from there. My Scottish ancestors were planted in place the longest, from the little I know. Maybe that's why my body registers the land as a familiar taproot. But many of them were forced to surrender their land.

Massachusetts is where my family lives now, and where I was raised. But I've had one foot off the ground from Western Massachusetts, questioning whether or not I belonged, as soon as I learned it was stolen, unceded land. *Do we grow where we're planted even though the land was stolen? Can I call this place home?* I lived my entire adult life in Brooklyn, a city of displaced people, and at times I felt called to go back to Scotland, and while it feels right on some levels, I've also been curious about the places inside me, the blood that runs through my veins and remains a mystery.

If I were a homing pigeon, where would I go?

SETTLING

I thought about the strangeness of vacation while in Puerto Rico. The harm we can cause when "getting away" from the stress of our daily lives and the places that have come—often reluctantly—to depend on tourists descending on their lands and spending lots of money to be pampered, catered to, and entertained. Travel also can be enriching and beneficial, of course—opening hearts and minds to other cultures, landscapes, and ways of existing in the world; even helping sustain ecological projects—but when it comes with a sense of entitlement, travel can be incredibly harmful.

For me, travel is connection. I don't want to escape my daily life, I want to enrich it—though sometimes it is nice to get away and come back with new eyes. When I travel, I go to the same places over and over again. I want to learn from the plants, the people, the culture, the wildlife. I have only so much time on Earth and I'm much more interested in deepening existing relationships than skimming the surface of new ones. An introvert at heart, I want to soak in the beauty of rustic, quiet places close to nature where I feel emotionally pulled and connected. With increasingly strong relationships to land, plants, people, and other animals in places I've returned to, I've fortified friendships. I am now welcomed with the warmth of loving hugs, open doors, and open arms, and these places have all come to feel like home.

I also know the world is burning and that a single flight releases into our atmosphere hundreds of pounds of CO_2—a huge contributor to global warming. When I think about this, I feel as though I should just stay put, live simply, and make a home where I am. But with friends and family scattered around the world and deep emotional connections to other places, here doesn't feel like enough. My friend Àdhamh, a Gaelic cultural activist in Scotland who speaks the Gaelic dialect of my ancestors, put it succinctly: "We want to find our connection to place but we don't want to be in that extractive position that so many are, so we're perpetually displaced." As much as I've come to feel a sense of belonging in Scotland and the places I return to, my accent always "others" me and gives me away. When I see and hear loud, entitled tourists from the United States around me, I want to shrink.

I travel to Costa Rica because I am in love with the land and with the countless animals, and I marvel at the biodiversity. I'm lucky to have close friends there like Encar, the primatologist and founder of the Jaguar Rescue Center who does incredible work on behalf of Costa Rica's wild animals and rainforest. I collaborate, hoping to do my part to keep the wild wild, too.

I travel to Scotland because it is ancestral land. Something happens to me when I'm there; I feel like I belong. It is land that my bones know, where my ancestors touched the soil and spoke to the sky for thousands of years. Since I am of mixed ethnicity, there are other ancestral lands of mine that I will probably never see or know, but at least I have Scotland.

I travel to Puerto Rico with you, my beloved, where your family resides. It is land that your bones know. You flinch when non–Puerto Ricans tell you how much they love to vacation there. You want them to leave Puerto Rico for Puerto Ricans. *What about me?* I ask you. *It's different, you're with me and you were invited*, you tell me. But the old white ladies with overly tanned, sagging skin in San Juan unsettle me. I don't want to be like them; they aren't supposed to be here in this latitude. I agree with the graffiti and posters that read "Colonizers, Go Home!"

When I first traveled to Puerto Viejo de Talamanca, Costa Rica, in 2008, it was a quiet place, with gravel roads and contiguous forest. I am a skittish bike rider but I felt safe riding my bike everywhere there. The area was rustic, with no phone signal or easy wi-fi. Yes, there were parties on the beach and lots of activity, but it felt like a special nook, unmolested by human development. I didn't know it then, but 2008 was also the year that my friend Encar founded the Jaguar Rescue Center with her late partner, Sandro.

Now the main road is paved, and despite SLOTH CROSSING signs, people drive too fast. There are more cars, and as the area has become more popular, there is more development and more deforestation. Airbnbs, new vacation homes, and beautiful escape dwellings in the jungle are displacing sloths, howler monkeys, and countless other creatures who already live there. Encar has rescued too many sloths still clinging to their trees, now logs on the ground. Increasing pressure from a growing human population has been most significant in recent years following the pandemic as people seek bucolic landscapes away from the stress of city life. Encar's work is getting harder. She rescues animals almost every day now. And yet she and her team (at least for now) rely mostly on tourists that come to daily public tours of the sanctuary to keep their work going.

Encar and I have been talking at length about ways she can raise money to buy more land. The preventative medicine is to preserve forest, to save animals' homes.

The pandemic increased the appeal of rural areas to other city dwellers, too. With so many people able to work from home now, home can be almost anywhere. Rents have soared during a time when income was unstable for many. Property owners have cashed in with Airbnb, making it difficult for us to find a long-term rental once I left my apartment—my treehouse—on the farm. Short-term rentals are exorbitant and there are very few long-term rentals in Western Massachusetts. Like other displaced animals, we have been moving from place to place, and with modern humans' idea of being settled by middle age—owning a home, welcoming friends and family into a cultivated space—it's embarrassing to be so unsettled. Then again, we're not quite sure where we want to be.

Shuttling through a succession of short-term rentals, we've been wasting so much time finding a place to land that it's hard to get into a groove and get anything done. It's difficult to write and rebuild a routine without a consistent base, when we're packing and moving and spending energy trying to figure out where to be. I feel palpable panic when it's time to pack boxes again. When the ground falls out from beneath me it doesn't feel like I'm flying but spiraling.

When I felt stuck, frozen, as though I were spinning in place, I remembered to move my body, to go for a hike, and the movement grounded me. The scent of moist soil after rain calmed my nerves. I took a deep breath, sank into the land, and remembered. Remembered that I am related to the land, Earth, and just one part of a vast, complex ecosystem. Breathing in the forest, I felt a profound sense of belonging.

As I walked in the woods, I reflected on the sentimental yearning for home. A yearning that comes from the ideas of home that we've been sold and conditioned to desire and consume. *Is home a place, a group of people, a person? Is home imprinted in us, in our minds, in our hearts, in our DNA?* Home might be an accident of birth, one specific place imprinted upon us the day we were born, or it could be almost boundless—the open ocean or sky, never fixed, in perpetual motion like a shark who is always swimming, or a swift who is almost always soaring. Even when we are able to stay in one place we might take it for granted. Being rooted in one place is not always synonymous with treating the environment well, let alone being tolerant of other humans, wildlife, and ways of being.

It's also true that some animals don't have the luxury of leaving or the capacity to adjust to changing circumstances and landscapes the way humans, coyotes, and pigeons can. We have to be more sensitive to creatures that evolved to be where they are, within specific constraints, and learn how to coexist. Maybe home isn't a place as much as permission for an animal to be where they are or where they have to be without being harmed.

Settling can mean giving up: she settled for him, he settled for her. But it can also mean rooting down. And that is what I am ready for. I feel relief when plans are canceled; I just want to go deep inside. My mind might be restless but my body wants to stay.

Being with you, the right partner, feels like home. Let's see where we land.

Monarch Butterflies

Each fall, North American monarchs fly from their summer breeding sites to overwintering grounds they have never seen. Butterflies who emerge after mid-August in the northeast begin migrating south, traveling up to 3,000 miles to central Mexico. Decreasing day length and temperatures, along with aging milkweed and fewer nectar sources, trigger this instinct in monarchs. Unlike summer generations, which live for two to six weeks as adults, adults in the migratory generation can live for up to nine months. After five months in Mexico, they begin the long voyage back north in spring. It takes three generations to complete the journey. No butterfly making the return journey has flown the entire route before.

It turns out, if you want to save a species, you don't spend your time staring at the bird you want to save. You look at the things it relies on to live instead. You ask if there is enough to eat and drink. You ask if there is a safe place to sleep. Is there enough here to survive?

—C. J. HAUSER, *The Crane Wife*

19

Genetic Memory

A woolly bear caterpillar folds, stretches, and feels her way through dead wood on the hiking trail. She seems indifferent, unafraid even though she is tiny, about the size of a daisy petal. I hold out a leaf to make her travel easier, to get her off the footpath, but she is determined, her route worked out, her destination clear. I wait for her to complete the journey across the trail. Soon, she will tuck herself into a pile of leaves for protection from cold weather and predators.

The crisp autumn air has arrived. Flower blooms are at their peak and goldenrod is alight with monarch butterflies. A weed to many, goldenrod, whose botanical name is solidago, "to make whole," is native to the monarch's range and supports the most species of butterflies and moths year-round. While milkweed is necessary for a monarch caterpillar's development, goldenrod is a vital late bloomer that supplies nectar for the long migration to their overwintering site in Mexico.

As monarchs from the eastern United States and southern Canada travel to Mexico, they search for refuge in stopover sites with nectar-rich wildflowers and shelter from harsh weather. But finding food and refuge on their multigenerational journey is not always easy. The decline of monarch butterfly populations in North America since the mid-1990s has been linked to the use of glyphosate-containing herbicides on genetically modified corn and soy crops. Monsanto's guidance for farmers specifically mentioned that their glyphosate-containing herbicide Roundup WeatherMAX "will provide suppression and/or control of . . . milkweed, quackgrass, etc." Milkweed is where monarchs lay their eggs. The young caterpillars are dependent on milkweed as their primary food source. Common "weeds" and native wildflowers are irreplaceable food sources for countless insect, bird, and animal species, especially in agricultural areas. Monarch butterflies were added to the IUCN's Red List in July 2022 following an estimated population decline of nearly 80 percent since the mid-1990s. Still, the U.S. Fish and Wildlife Service (FWS), responsible for managing endangered species, announced that they "did not have the resources to conserve the species." Really? A species that relies on wildflowers?

The United States Department of Agriculture (USDA) played a role in the decision not to list the monarch butterfly as an endangered species because of its involvement in managing agricultural lands, which are a crucial habitat for the monarch. While the FWS has the primary authority for listing endangered species under the Endangered Species Act, the USDA's power in agriculture and land management made it an unfortunate stakeholder in the decision-making process. Both Monsanto and Bayer (who acquired Monsanto in 2018) have actively lobbied the USDA, seeking to influence the agency's policies and regulations that impact their GMO and pesticide businesses. The company has spent millions of dollars to sway regulations on pesticide use, GMO crop approvals, and labeling requirements.

The decision not to list the monarch butterfly as an endangered species has been met with outrage from conservationists, who argue that the agencies are ignoring the scientific evidence that the butterfly is in decline. They point out that the monarch population has been in decline for decades, and that this decline is likely to continue due to habitat loss, climate change, and the use of pesticides. They also argue that the butterfly's range is shrinking, and it is now only a small fraction of their historic range.

If we want to help butterflies, we can encourage our communities to ban herbicides like Roundup, advocate for corporate transparency and accountability, promote legislative action, and educate neighbors about the harmful effects of pesticides. We can let wildflowers like goldenrod and milkweed thrive, and if possible, plant milkweed in our yards or community spaces, protect existing habitats, raise awareness, support conservation organizations, support sustainable agriculture, and spread the word.

If the butterflies find their plant partners and make it to their destination in central Mexico in early November, they will congregate on pine and oyamel fir trees there. Millions fly into the forest, clustering in such densities that the weight of these seemingly weightless insects bends the trees' branches. Thankfully, much of the monarch's wintering grounds are protected by the Monarch Butterfly Biosphere Reserve (Reserva de Biosfera de la Mariposa Monarca), a UNESCO World Heritage Site whose mission is to protect the butterfly species and their habitat. The south-southwest-facing mountain slopes of the reserve provide just the right weather conditions and shelter, allowing the butterflies to conserve enough energy to survive winter.

I've seen the congregation of monarchs only in videos and pictures and yet it is absolutely stunning. I can only imagine witnessing this miraculous event for the first time. According to the lore of the Indigenous Purépecha of Michoacán and the Mazahua of Estado de México, the migrating butterflies carry the souls of their ancestors visiting from the afterlife. For pre-Hispanic cultures, death is seen as a natural phase in the long, mysterious drama of life, much like the multigenerational journey of the monarch. The annual butterfly

migration coincides with Día de Muertos celebrations that origi-
nated centuries ago with the Aztec, Toltec, and Nahua people. Incredibly, the overwintering generation of butterflies can survive for
five months amid the evergreens of Mexico—from late autumn to
early spring—with little or no food.

In March, when winter is over and they take to the skies, the butterflies journey north into Texas and southern states. Searching for
wildflowers so they can refuel, they also seek the one and only milkweed so they can lay their eggs. If milkweed is found and the eggs and
caterpillars survive, their offspring will continue the journey from
the southern United States, migrating north through the central
states in late April through May. Second and third generations will
populate eastern breeding grounds throughout the summer, and it is
usually the fourth generation of butterflies that begin the cycle again,
migrating through central and southern states to oyamel trees in
Mexico they have never seen.

   The fact that species like monarch butterflies continue on without
a parent teaching them demonstrates that many animals are hardwired to learn how to live. While it is a mystery, genetic memory exists to some degree in all of us. Somewhere inside, we know where
to go.

Back in Massachusetts, when driving along the winding roads of
Route 116 to our temporary sublet in Ashfield, we saw BLACK LIVES
MATTER and LOVE IS LOVE signs and pride flags in front yards along
the beautiful landscape. While you joked about the potentially per-
formative nature of those signs and flags, they were incredibly com-
forting to see in rural, so-called United States. When we settled in for
the night amid the sound of tree frogs, reminiscent of the beloved

coqui in Puerto Rico, we looked at land for sale and sure enough, there was a mountain, Mount Owen, within 268-plus acres for sale along that same road. Portions of the land were once used for logging but hadn't been touched in over fifty years. The price was out of reach but we arranged to hike it anyway. *Anything is possible*, you said, but I was doubtful.

I don't believe in the concept of owning land—*How can something alive, home to so many creatures, ever be owned?*—yet it has been a dream to "own" as much land as possible to protect, rewild, and restore depleted places if necessary, and provide access for people who have been left out or pushed out. You have always held on to a romantic idea of living off the land, too. *Maybe I got the idea from my parents, my grandparents, and generations of family who lived off the land in Puerto Rico*, you tell me. *But growing up in Chicago, living in big cities, and being puertorriqueño, it seemed like living in a rural environment in the United States was not only financially inaccessible but culturally uninviting.*

More than 1,500 feet in height, Mount Owen is located on the traditional homeland of the Nipmuc Tribal Nation, the original stewards of the land for over 12,000 years. Before the region around Ashfield, Massachusetts, was forcibly colonized, the Nipmuc homeland stretched over 2,000 square miles, encompassing central Massachusetts, northern Connecticut, northern Rhode Island, and southern New Hampshire. Part of the Algonquin language group, there are roughly 3,000 family clan members living throughout southern New England today. This area is their ancestral home.

Thanks to the gift of flight, monarchs are able to migrate from Mexico naturally, but they face obstacles. Prostrate milkweed, a rare species of milkweed that monarchs depend on after their long winter fast, is threatened in part by border security activities disturbing land. Lawyers at the Center for Biological Diversity said that an endangered species designation for the plant is important but wouldn't prevent border construction by the federal government. The law only requires that federal agencies take additional steps for the plant's protection, like setting aside nearby habitats for species at risk. And because most of Texas's land is privately owned, the future of the prostrate milkweed will largely depend on the actions of landowners along the border. In Texas, private landowners can remove endangered plants on their land without consequence.

Land-bound animals on the border of the United States and Mexico have it even worse than monarchs. The construction of 458 miles of wall during the ecologically and culturally disastrous Trump era was enabled only by multiple waivers of the Endangered Species Act. The wall destroyed decades-old saguaro cacti growing in national parks, drained scarce freshwater sources like the Quitobaquito oasis in Arizona's Organ Pipe Cactus National Monument (home to unique species of turtles and fish), and eliminated critical wildlife migration corridors, making it difficult for animals to move as they naturally would to find food and mates and to travel along necessary routes for survival. A recent report by the Center for Biological Diversity speculates that the wall could lead to the extinction of up to twenty-four animals, including the ocelot, the jaguarundi, jaguar, Sonoran pronghorn, and Mexican gray wolf.

The wall also desecrated sacred sites of the Indigenous Tohono O'odham and Kumeyaay, whose tribal lands are on the wall's path, meaning that the Department of Homeland Security waived laws protecting Indigenous lands. In a 2020 article in *High Country News*, the Tohono O'odham chairman, Ned Norris Jr., states, "The O'odham have always been compassionate and welcoming. We have a long history of helping travelers passing through our lands. These values are part of who we are. These values are so ingrained in our worldview that it is reflected in our language, which has no word for 'wall.'"

The "We Are All Immigrants" hats and T-shirts made in solidarity with people attempting to cross the man-made border—who ended up jailed while their children were forcibly torn away from them—were well meaning but seemed tone-deaf to me. People from Mexico and Central and South America fleeing violence and persecution who are inhumanely blocked from natural migration are Native Americans. They naturally migrate as all humans have, but are not immigrants.

NAVIGATION

We received permission from the current landowner's real estate agent and arranged to hike Mount Owen the weekend after we saw the listing. It was early May 2022 when we pulled into a meadow covered in fledgling goldenrod, milkweed, and countless wildflowers. A butterfly oasis.

As we entered the forest through overgrown logging trails, I felt uneasy, as though somehow, we were trespassing. Plus, I didn't like the fact that we could still hear the road. But as we hiked farther into the forest, the cars and the chatter of my mind quieted. I began to lose myself in the swells of the land, in the undulating ebb and flow of her mounds and waterways, in the dramatic depth of her rock ledges, and ravines populated with birch, pine, beech, hickory, hemlock, and old maple trees. As we hiked, no one could see me, not even you, my beloved. Just the trees, the quiet animals. The porcupine in the tree was so still, he looked like a fungal growth. You waited for me when I got too far behind.

We began hiking on Mount Owen a few times a week and as we became more intimate with the forest, we noticed who was there—at-risk species like chaga, trillium, ramps, and bloodroot—and I kept an eye out for who might be missing. We researched the land's name and story. It turns out that Mount Owen was named after Daniel Owen, a surveyor who got lost and had to spend a few nights on the mountain in the early 1700s. We imagine that his friends must have given him shit for getting lost and called the mountain Mount Owen to make fun of him. For this reason, you liked the name, but I wasn't so sure.

You download GPS apps, but with no internet or phone signal on the land we pay more attention to natural cues. In summer, reishi mushrooms illuminate our path. You give directions in cryptic, Yoda-like ways. *Keep the sun on your left* or *Move in the direction of your shadow.* I get lost easily—looking down at mosses, fungi, and tiny medicinal plants—so I follow you, trusting you to navigate east, south, west, and north, and lead me through this living land.

Since monarchs migrate during the day, the sun is the celestial cue most likely used in pointing the way to their overwintering sites. It is thought that monarchs use the angle of the sun along the horizon in combination with an internal body clock to maintain their south-westerly path. For example, if a monarch's internal clock reads 10:00 a.m., then they will fly west of the sun to maintain a southern flight direction, but if their internal clock reads noon, then their instincts tell them to fly toward the sun. Later in the day the monarchs will fly to the east of the sun.

On cloudy days when the sun is obscured, scientists speculate that monarchs use a magnetic compass—requiring short-wave UV light—as a backup to navigate. The incredible light-sensitive magnetic sensors reside in the adult monarch's antennae to consistently orient themselves south. When eastern monarchs encounter a mountain range, their instincts might tell them to turn south and follow the mountains.

MIGRATION

We have been hiking all summer and now it is fall. Throughout the seasons we've identified more at-risk species and areas where land is depleted. The more we hike and learn from the land, the more we want to protect the species that live there and restore areas that are struggling.

After getting some outdoor gear at Eastern Mountain Sports, I turned on my GPS to get to where I was going and looked at Google instead of the sky to find out what the weather would be. That's when a beautiful flock of geese flew over the parking lot. They were leaving us, flying south. I looked up to notice the beauty of the sunset while people around me looked down at their phones in a holiday-shopping daze. It was a strange and sad juxtaposition. The geese, like the monarchs, still know how to read the skies, feel the magnetic pull of Earth. Other animals use the sun, moon, or stars, the Earth's magnetic field, mountain ranges or bodies of water, polarized light, infrared energy perception, or some combination of these cues to navigate. With reliance and increasing dependence on technology, we are losing our innate sense of direction.

Like the monarch caterpillar's relationship to milkweed, we are increasingly vulnerable and dependent on this one thing: our "smart" phones. So many of us rely on our phones to see where we're going these days instead of trusting our instinct and really noticing where we are. We might look down at the screen and know what's happening on another continent but may not know loved ones' phone numbers, how to identify or care for plants or animals on the landscape we're standing on, or how to get to where we're going.

The day after seeing the geese and reflecting on my own poor navigation skills, I took *Wild Signs and Star Paths* by Tristan Gooley off my bookshelf. Gooley explains how we can use trees to find our way: "We can look for how the tree's growth is influenced by the sun and how their shape is altered by the wind," or "use a tree's preferences to work out the nature of the terrain ahead of us." I tried to notice but with too much time looking down at the plants, I still rely on you and your app to help us navigate. But the land is getting more familiar. Certain trees, like the one we call Grandmother Maple, have become landmarks. We're getting to know them, and I imagine they're getting to know us, too.

Every time we hike through the unmarked trails, we build intimacy with the trees, mosses, countless plants, and fungi and imagine what we would do if the vast expanse of life were under our care. We don't know what will come next, or if we can even afford to be there yet, but the process is hopeful and exciting. If we are able to make it happen, I will be circling back, a third-generation daughter in Western Massachusetts, migrating toward the place where I was born. And you on your generational cycle of finding home wherever we are.

Black Bears

Bears like a certain degree of personal space, but several animals often overlap living areas at different times. A bear's living space—providing food, water, and adequate cover—is called a home range. Black bears are solitary by nature, except when in family groups of mothers and cubs or in pairs during the mating season. They may congregate in areas of high food density, such as oak stands, berry patches, or farm fields. When abundant food sources are found across large areas, black bears tend to tolerate each other more than usual. They may defend a food resource or mate while they are present, but they are not territorial nor do they defend a specific area from intrusion by other bears.

*I have waked deep in the woods
in the early morning, sure
that while I slept
your gaze passed over me.
That we do not know you
is your perfection
and our hope. The darkness
keeps us near you.*

—WENDELL BERRY, "TO THE UNSEEABLE ANIMAL"

20

Home Range

We are taking a huge leap and have made an offer on the land. *It's a reclamation,* you tell me. *But more than that, I've realized that stewards need the land as much as the land needs stewards.*

Last night, I received an email from you with a draft of the deed. A modern, legal document imposed on the land; the clearest way to link ourselves to the genocide that preceded us. This document of stolen land also makes it possible to begin the work of giving the land back to herself. "The only repentance available," you write, "is to aspire to live an indigenous life. Not devoid of technology but full of love, conservation and compassion for human, plant, beast and earth."

Just a few words on a page and soon the land will be ours. While I'm deeply grateful to become a steward of the land, the fact that a piece of paper—or for that matter, your electronic signature on a computer screen—allows us to do what we will with the living, breathing landscape that is home to so many creatures isn't right.

We continue to hike and are quietly discovering our new neighbors. Red oak and red maple populate the living landscape along with black birch, paper birch and yellow birch, shagbark hickory, hemlock, white pine, beautiful old sugar maples, and more. Understory plants include native medicinals—common plants like violet and rare ones like blue cohosh. Spicebush grows around the vernal pool while goldenrod flourishes around the forest edge. Flushes of reishi, oyster, and turkey tail mushrooms grow throughout the woods amid dramatic moss-covered ledges, often cascading with seasonal streams. We hear songbirds like the veery, hermit thrush, black-throated blue warbler, scarlet tanager, and the beloved wood thrush. We catch glimpses of white-tailed deer and find animal tracks and scat. Evidence of red foxes, bobcats, and black bears.

We encountered a black bear as we were hiking one day. I knew that black bears have acute hearing, about twice as sensitive as humans, and often move away before they are noticed, but this bear seemed young and too absorbed in foraging to care that we were close. It was autumn, so he was likely harvesting nuts and berries. In spring he would forage mostly plants; in summer, he would feast on berries and insects, and if necessary, he might eat carrion, small mammals, birds, and amphibians. His strong, stocky legs would allow him to move rocks, tree trunks, and tree limbs that get in the way of his food. His large, padded feet and curved claws would allow him to climb trees to pick fruit and nuts and find honey, while his long, sticky tongue would help him reach insects.

Shy and peaceful, black bears are relatively quiet creatures but will occasionally make sounds to communicate. A bear that feels threatened doesn't roar or growl. They may slap the ground, "huff" or blow air forcefully through their nose or mouth, and snap or "pop" their teeth together. If these behaviors don't scare off the source of their unease, the bear may bluff charge, running toward the perceived threat and then veering away. A bear that is truly aggressive toward humans does not make a sound. Instead, they stare, protrude their lower lip, and flatten their ears. Typically, they become aggressive only when people or other animals threaten them or their cubs.

Since bears are notoriously great moms, the youngster's mom was likely nearby, waiting anxiously for us to disappear. The longer humans linger, the longer a mother bear will be separated from her cubs. Typically, a mom will return to gather her family when no people are around, usually after dark. As the cubs get older and more mobile, mother bears often leave their cubs to forage for food as far as two miles away. This big cub seemed like a bit of a teenager, and we soon left him alone.

MARKING TERRITORY

We all mark territory and claim personal space in different ways, some more benign than others. We might drape our coat over the back of a chair in a restaurant, spread books across a table in a library, or build a fence around our yard. But when marking territory goes too far, people claim forests, continents, even bodies.

Personal space is important, and I have a palpable fear of being intruded upon. But I wrestle with the idea of marking territory, especially land, as my own.

It is October 24, 2022, and we are closing on the land today. You've traded your dream of a forest in Puerto Rico for a forest in Western Massachusetts. Now we are claiming our space, marking our territory in ways I never imagined I ever would. PRIVATE PROPERTY signs that used to irk me are the same ones I have in my backpack now. In Massachusetts, it is legal to hunt on land without posted NO HUNTING signs, so we must put them up to prevent it. We want who we want there, no surprises and no weapons. We want to provide access for the Indigenous people of this land that was stolen. But others, well, we'll have to see. With the money from the heart-wrenching sale of your art collection and part of your business, along with a little paperwork, the responsibility of stewardship now transfers to us. Boundaries are now a critical part of protecting the plants, the animals, and the land.

Black bears of all ages and sexes rub their scent on marking trees, including wooden signposts and utility poles. But the majority of the scratch, claw, bite, and scent marks are crafted by mature males during the mating season. Claw marks are usually superficial, but incisor bites are deep enough that pieces of bark and wood are sometimes pulled out. Marks communicate breeding status to ensure males and females are synchronized successfully for breeding. Marking home range boundaries among females may mimic territorial behavior. Marks may serve to help orient bears in new or little-used areas, as markings increase when a bear enters a new area.

The size of a home range may vary each season and year depending on food availability, the bear's sex or age, reproductive status and density of the area's bear population. Males have larger home ranges—up to 300 square miles—than females, who roam up to 50 square miles. Bears travel farthest when food is hard to find, especially in early spring. During major droughts and famine, bears will range much further than normal to search for food. Black bears have the ability to navigate homeward from unfamiliar areas, which often brings them across dangerous roads.

Under normal circumstances, black bears are awake from spring through fall and mostly asleep in winter, curled up in their dens, which may be hollow trees, fallen trees, or excavated mounds, or in "nests" under briar patches. During hibernation, bears don't eat at all, nor do they go to the bathroom; bears' dens are remarkably clean and odor-free. A bear's body is a model of recycling. While they're hibernating, they recycle all their waste products and, incredibly, heal any injuries they may have suffered before they went to sleep. Many scientists now call bears super hibernators because they can fall into a deep sleep for four to six months without eating or drinking, wake up in the spring, and head back out into the world.

———

You downloaded a hunting app not to hunt but to determine where our boundary lines are. Right outside our bounds, on land that belongs to our neighbor—also a New York City transplant, but also, unfortunately, a member of the Rod & Gun Club—you found black bear scat. A lot of it. You mentioned it to him and he jokingly said he should mention it to the hunters. Then he proceeded to talk about how many bears there are, and that they are a potential nuisance. I was pissed. Now I want to buy and protect that land, too. If only there were a way to warn the animals.

PROTECTED FOREVER

Development is increasing in the surrounding towns of Amherst, Hadley, and Belchertown, but in the hill towns where we are, much of the land is "protected forever" thanks to a local land trust. But it's a "sticky wicket," as you say, since conservation restrictions like the "forever wild" CR (in which no alteration is allowed whatsoever) assume people can't be trusted with the land. As stewards, we have the potential to make a positive impact where land was logged and grazed, but since humans haven't shown that they are listening to the land, land is protected—left untouched—which may not always be the best thing for the soil, flora, or wildlife.

With dwindling populations in these areas, conservation restrictions relegate some people to cities, while others are forced to explore increasingly expensive rural areas that may be out of reach financially or unappealing culturally. And what about the Nipmuc indigenous to this area? How do they feel about the fact that their unceded land is now protected from them?

Since mass suburbanization in the middle of the twentieth century, the racial geography of most metropolitan areas has followed a pattern: Black and Latinx households reside in neighborhoods proximate to the dense urban core, with each subsequent ring of suburbs becoming whiter and more sparsely populated. You talk about how local zoning regulations of a two-acre minimum and single-family zoning—meaning it's illegal to build anything other than single-family homes—have played a role. Single-family zoning and two-acre minimums are prevalent in rural areas. A White House blog from June 2021 states that research "connected exclusionary zoning to racial segregation, creating greater disparities in measurable outcomes . . . For instance, many lower-income, predominantly minority neighborhoods in cities have become 'heat islands'—experiencing significantly higher temperatures than other neighborhoods in the same metropolitan area because of factors such as fewer trees and more concrete buildings and parking lots."

We talk about ideal scenarios. *People should have to go through incentivized, mandatory land stewardship education programs in order to buy land.* While we debate solutions, one thing remains clear: the wild animals belong here in their homes and we are pushing them out, and as a result, they have no choice but to alter their normal behavior. We humans are pushing each other to the margins, too.

Luckily, it isn't necessary to buy land in order to steward land. In New York City parks, and many city parks around the world, people can volunteer to learn how to help with forest and wetland restoration, plant and prune street trees, propagate native seeds, and monitor local wildlife. In Scotland, where everyone has the right to roam (often called freedom to roam), wild camping is a right and anyone can make overland journeys anywhere. While many of the hills, valleys, moors, and waterways of the country are privately owned, fences can be crossed. This brings forth a feeling of continuity in rural Scotland, as well as a sense of trust and belonging. Though some areas of land are depleted, they are cared for as they are, and I've never seen litter. *Everyone knows there are eyes on the land; we take notice if someone isn't treating her well*, friends have told me. And it shows. Legally the land belongs to someone, but in practice it belongs to everyone and no one.

It is rainy today. I've always loved the sound of the rain. When I'm safe and cozy inside, the rain on the windowpanes soothes me. I know the plants outside are getting a good drink, and depending on the season, mushrooms may appear. But the sound of rain keeps you up at night. Your factory—an art-fabrication studio you are peeling away from—has a leaking roof that you worry will be further ruined. Buckets will be overflowing. The sound of the rain is stressful. We are lying next to each other but our minds are worlds apart. There are stresses that we can no longer put off, forget, or avoid. There is life outside our cave.

It is spring 2023, and we steward a beautiful area of land but are living a life in limbo—still straddling two towns—because you, my chosen partner, are still removing yourself from your past life. Responsibilities and your business, though winding down, are still stuck to you. The things we've ignored will not go away and they are haunting us now. They are like swampy bogs we are trying to get out of but we sink and sink, only occasionally stepping onto solid ground. Today, we are visiting the house, the cave in New Haven, where we first descended into love. Where we fell hard and neglected everything else. Now we're back and it is different. Our relationship is deeper. This unsettling time has put our relationship and our communication to the test and though we're stressed, we've grown closer. Now that we've gone through stress and struggle, I love you more and I feel even more loved. You know I'm not perfect, not by any means, and you have not abandoned me.

Spring is the time when bears come out of their caves, too. But for some reason, like us, they've been restless. I imagine it is because of us humans. A bear and her cubs were seen walking down Route 9, a busy highway of strip malls—Walgreens, Barnes and Noble, Target, and Whole Foods. The person who told me said, *There are so many bears!* and it irked me. It's not that there are so many bears, it's that we are destroying their habitat, their food sources, so they must interrupt their sleep and come out of hibernation hungry, in search of nourishment amid our wasteland. They are not everywhere, they are simply trying to hang on to the homes they've had. As more people destroy habitat or live close to their woodland homes, the chances of seeing black bears rise.

In areas where land is fractured, bears may overcome the necessary fear of humans if their exploration is rewarded with birdseed, high-calorie dog food, or greasy barbecue grills. With the best sense of smell of any land mammal, they can pick up a scent from over a mile away.

Wild animals around the world are increasingly disconnected from their natural habitats, trapped in islands of wilderness amid a growing sea of people. At least we can protect the bears who sleep and forage on the land we steward. We might be wandering souls with a shape-shifting home range, but we have the honor of stewarding land.

Land, you belong to yourself, but we now have the privilege of protecting you.

Red Fox

Of the many species of fox around the world—from scorching deserts to the Arctic—the red fox is thought to be the most common non-domesticated carnivore. Most of the year, red foxes are solitary, often found sleeping out in the open with their fluffy tails curled around themselves for warmth. But during midwinter mating season, it is common to find tracks of pairs trotting together, searching for denning sites. The pair may prepare and clean several fresh dens or modify existing burrows in their territory, one of which they'll select for their litter. Foxes dig out dens, creating several entrances to provide safe underground passages and spaces that are mostly used for raising fox kits. In urban areas, the dens—known as earths—are commonly located under sheds, but they can also be among tree roots, in bushes, or on railway embankments. If all goes well, the same den may be used for generations.

Few tasks are more like the torture of Sisyphus than housework, with its endless repetition: the clean becomes soiled, the soiled is made clean, over and over, day after day.

—SIMONE DE BEAUVOIR, *The Second Sex*

21

Domestication Syndrome

Our first cry is a cry of shock, fear, and intense hunger. We have fallen from our mothers, from the ocean, and learn that if we don't speak up, we may never get what we need. We scream, almost involuntarily, when we feel unsafe. We wail, howl when we feel grief. But for many of us, it doesn't take long to learn to quiet down, become "tame," and suppress our needs. And if we're tamed for too long, we may question our instincts. Somewhere along the way, most of us learn that life in the wild is too hungry, lurking with danger, and lacking the comforts of human civilization that keep us safe. Our bodies and behaviors change through the rules and routines of civilization, which eventually seem natural in and of themselves. And women—capable of giving birth and feeding babies from our bodies, while waxing and waning with the cycles of the moon—are often accused of being more body than mind. It is the unruly, sensual animal in us that is often blamed for the sins of men.

Today, February 2, is a turning point known in Gaelic tradition as Imbolc, an agrarian festival of fire that symbolizes the awakening of the Goddess and life trying to shed winter. Here in Western Massachusetts and in many temperate regions it is mating season for foxes, known as *sionnach*, "the old ones," in Gaelic. Outside, we hear high-pitched wails of vixens in the middle of the night. It was once thought that their screams were sounds of pain when locked together during mating, but the screams are actually vixens trying to summon a mate. In her book *The Blood Is Wild*, the nature writer Bridget MacCaskill describes the behavior of a vixen she rescued and hand-reared in the Scottish Highlands. When she took the fox for a walk during her first breeding season, Bridget writes, "She pulled me along as if we could not get anywhere fast enough, leaving her mark everywhere, on pathways, patches of moss, flat-topped boulders, and generally making sure the fox world knew she wanted a mate."

Using barks, whines, and throaty noises for conversations with their young, alarm calls, and loud aggressive "gekkering," or mating calls, red foxes are incredibly vocal compared to other fox species. But I hold back when we make love. We have to be quiet. I worry about talking too loud, screaming too enthusiastically, having too much fun. Even in our sublet there are noise constraints. I feel like a teenager with all the rules and regulations, as though I have to sneak around.

In the morning, I want to stay curled up next to your warm body, but there are chores to do: I have to go to the post office and send packages, pay bills, do administrative work. I resist, in part, because life is heartbreakingly precious and tomorrow isn't promised to either of us. I also know (and learn over and over again) that avoiding mundane tasks takes away from the present, eventually. An ongoing conundrum. So I peel away, reluctantly, and get up and do my work.

Moving from place to place, it hasn't been easy to do basic things like wash our clothes. Some places have a washer and dryer, and others, like our current rental, don't. You hate doing dishes, so the laundry is your department now, and you've tried to get a card for the laundry machine across the street, calling their office to no avail. We've successfully divided tasks and work well together, but I've let things pile up lately and have a list of things to do: the people I haven't called back, those I miss, and those I wish to avoid. I will clean today. Our space, my mind.

In 1973, the year I was born, *Roe v. Wade* and the Endangered Species Act both passed and, oddly, *The Total Woman*, a scary book of garbage by Maribel Morgan, sold millions of copies. Urging women to be submissive to their husbands, she writes, "The biblical remedy for marital conflict is stated, 'You wives must submit to your husbands' leadership in the same way you submit to the Lord' . . . God planned for women to be under their husbands rule." Apparently, "it is only when a woman surrenders her life to her husband, reveres and worships him, and is willing to serve him, that she becomes really beautiful to him." Truly a scary book of garbage.

I have been told I'm beautiful because I'm strong and also that I'm bad at cleaning (an important aspect of "domesticated bliss," according to Morgan and many others). I think my cleaning is adequate, but my mom—resisting the idea that women are supposed to obsess over a tidy home—admits she passed traits of messiness down to me. My asthma and allergies gave me a bit of a pass growing up too. My mom was worried I might stir up allergens and start wheezing if I swept, vacuumed, or dusted. So apart from my tendency to organize and avoid clutter, I had strange, inconsistent ways of cleaning. My mom reminded me that highly creative people tend to have bigger and better things to think about.

Her mom, on the other hand, was fastidious. A nurse in New York City during World War II, Grandma became the quintessential 1950s housewife when my grandpa came back from battle. Instead of finding fulfillment from careers, women of the era were suddenly supposed to leave their jobs behind, as she did, when the men came home, and find joy and fulfillment in polishing floors and seeing their reflection in sparkling dishes. Rosie the Riveter was no longer

needed, and new messaging told women what to buy to become better, happier, more desirable wives. A glamorous woman at home, my
grandmother scrubbed, dusted, ironed, and cooked without a hair
out of place and with a little help from copious amounts of coffee and
diet pills.

I adored my grandmother but didn't inherit the cleaning genes
and didn't choose men (like the doctors she hoped I'd meet) I would
submit to or even who could take care of me financially. I don't know
if it was rebellion or if these just happened to be the men I was attracted to. In my twenties, I lived in the Bronx with my first true love.
We "played house," and at first, it was thrilling. I loved the intimacy
of cooking our meals, even ironing his shirts, because he didn't expect it. It was out of love, part of our role-play. But soon, the role-play
became real, even expected, and the pile of chores never seemed to
diminish. I didn't see it when he told me the counter was a mess, so I
scrubbed the floor instead. Then he told me to get off my hands and
knees because he liked his women strong (I was working as a personal trainer, after all), but he never ceased to complain about how
messy I was.

He wanted to have a child, but I wasn't ready. I didn't have an intense urge to procreate. I was constrained for so long due to health
limitations, I didn't want my body held captive anymore. Not to a
child or even a home, not yet. I was living with him when I began boxing. Unlike domesticated animals who might be more docile or lose
the ability to respond to threats, I knew I needed to learn how to defend myself after being sexually assaulted as a teenager. I was full of
pent-up rage and I wanted to revive my dulled instincts. I wanted to
be in charge of my own needs and desires in a culture that wished to
tame me.

Now that I'm beyond my ideal procreation years, people have
said, *It's a shame you never had kids. We need more Earth warriors in
the world!* But I've felt more compelled to care for plants, other

animals, and humans who are already here. And there is no guarantee that a child would have the same convictions as I do, and I would never want to force them to conform to my expectations. I've been grateful to have had the choice. Choice should be an obvious inalienable right, but not all women or creatures are so fortunate.

WELL BEHAVED

While taming can happen to one wild animal, *domestication* generally refers to generations of changes in an animal's behavior and appearance. Tamed animals can often become wild again, but the danger for many domesticated animals—like pugs and Boston terriers, bred into bodies that have a hard time breathing and birthing—is that they become dependent on those who domesticated them. Unable to fend for themselves anymore, most dogs are kept indoors and yelled at when they act like animals.

When training dogs, domesticated ancestors of wolves, we are told that what we say is less important than how we say it. When we approve of their behavior, when they are well behaved, we excite them with our voice, give them treats, and call them good. A good dog? Comes when they're called, knows their boundaries, doesn't beg for food, is grateful for what they're given, and is unconditionally, heartbreakingly loving. Domesticated dogs are at the mercy of humans and the mess we've made of the world.

In 1958, a now-famous project called the farm fox experiment began at the Institute of Cytology and Genetics in Novosibirsk, Russia, by the scientists Dmitri Belyaev and Lyudmila Trut. The purpose was to breed wild silver foxes in an attempt to make them tame. The scientists wanted to explore whether selection for behavior rather than morphology (size, shape, and structure of an animal's body and relationship between constituent parts) may be the reason wolves became dogs. The scientists recorded the changes in foxes when in each generation only the most tame foxes were allowed to breed. The story goes that in just ten generations of selection in wild foxes, they produced foxes who looked and acted like domesticated dogs. But the experiment has been criticized because it didn't begin by taming wild foxes. The caged foxes they bred were descendants of foxes born in inhumane Canadian fur farms who already showed symptoms of domestication syndrome. Something we humans suffer from, too.

Symptoms of domestication syndrome in animals include floppy ears, curly tails, reduced brain size and body mass, smaller teeth, docile behavior, and hormonal changes, including the ability of females to reproduce year-round instead of seasonally. Brain size diminishes due to decreased neural crest cells, the brain cells involved in processing and responding to threats. Competition for mating partners is often reduced, so wild reproductive features and behaviors often decline, or disappear. Domestication becomes part of animals' DNA.

The term *domestication syndrome* was first used by botanists to describe the genetic modification of plants in the early 1900s; Charles Darwin was the first to describe the syndrome (although he didn't coin the term we use today) in his book *The Variation of Animals and Plants under Domestication,* published in 1868. While debating whether or not to include humans in his book, Darwin wrote a letter to his publisher, stating, "I feel a full conviction that my Chapter on man will excite attention & plenty of abuse & I suppose abuse is as good as praise for selling a Book." He eventually decided against using humans as an example of a domesticated species, though he did, of course, include controversial theories in his later book *The Descent of Man,* by asserting that humans evolved through both natural and sexual selection, as did every animal species.

Typically, qualities of a domesticated species include (among other things) increased socialization and an eagerness to please, attentive and anxious behaviors, and decreased risk-taking and exploration. Not to mention impaired vision, poor reflexes, a confused survival instinct, and, of course, a disconnection from nature. We learn that the animal part of us, our body, can't be trusted. It needs to be kept in check, subdued. The human part, we learn, is our coveted intellect or maybe in some cases the pious or spiritual part. But there is serious dissonance between the head and heart. The "smartest" creature on the planet has caused the most harm.

Like many animals, sexual selection for foxes appears to be the females' choice. Male foxes produce sperm only during their mating season (if only that were the case for humans), and female foxes get their estrous cycle only for about one week per mating season, when their hormones alert them to breed. Monogamous animals, the pair usually stay together for life, having multiple litters until their dying days.

Red foxes help control populations of prey animals such as rats, mice, and squirrels, and by eating fruit, they are also seed dispersers. In rural areas where foxes were intentionally killed, rodents increased so much that farmers regretted the decision to murder them and wound up bringing in other foxes. Urban foxes primarily scavenge for food, but when they hunt they also help to keep rodent numbers under control.

Like me, my mom loves animals. Family lore has it that as a child, when she walked home from school, she would be followed by a parade of the neighborhood dogs. Now a family of bears live in her yard and she swears that the squirrels who have taken over her bird feeder wave to her. She wants everyone to get along and, unfortunately, chases the foxes from her yard so they don't eat the fat squirrels. *The fox needs to eat too, Mom,* I remind her. It's more difficult for wild predators; kills are successful only about 10 percent of the time.

Human activity is the most common cause of fox deaths, of course. Road accidents are all too frequent for males and young foxes as they start exploring and disperse from breeding sites from August to December. Wild foxes also suffer from mange, known as canine scabies, caused by the parasitic mite *Sarcoptes scabei canis*. A widely accepted hypothesis suggests that humans were the initial source of contamination in both wild and domesticated animals. Whatever the cause, mange is highly contagious between foxes and dogs but also treatable. The mites can be passed to humans, too, but they can't complete their life cycle on a non-canine host. In the case of foxes, the mite burrows into their skin, causing lesions and fur to fall out. Without treatment, mange lesions can lead to secondary infections that can be fatal.

While reading in the early afternoon recently, I looked out the window and saw a fox. She was on the ground writhing, scratching her body against brown, dried spring grasses. When the fox stood, I noticed her fur was patchy and her iconic bushy tail was not so bushy. It looked like the poor fox had mange. Incidences of mange are increasing because of human activity and climate change, so I feel that since we (humans) play a hand in making things harder for wildlife, it's only right to help and alleviate suffering when and where we can.

That night, I dreamed I was talking to the fox about treatments. One of the herbal treatments for humans is a mixture of wormwood, clove, and black walnut hulls (and of course some topical treatment). I explained this to the fox in my dream (we were in a tree hollow together—pretty magical), who let me administer some herbs. *Poke root tincture is helpful, too*, she told me. I had to look that one up. It turns out she was right. I may not see the fox again, but I'd like to have a treatment plan ready if I do.

In the morning, I look through my apothecary and pull out my wormwood tincture, made in alcohol, but wonder if a strong decoction in water would be best. In the past when I've made formulas for animals, I've made strong decoctions instead of using alcohol tinctures. I looked online and even asked a couple of holistic veterinarians and got mixed replies about helping. Some say it makes things worse to feed or help wild animals who are suffering because they'll lose their instincts and become dependent. *But what about the fact that they are often suffering because of us?* I remember watching a documentary about seals who were starving and suffering amid human encroachment, clearly asking for help. The filmmaker said it broke his heart, but he "couldn't do anything." The problem is, he and other humans already had. The seals were struggling because of people. After ruining their environment and home, now we worry about harming or domesticating them through help? Wildlife rehabilitators know that this is not true. As Encar, wildlife rehabilitator and founder of the Jaguar Rescue Center, said, "The wild will always want to remain wild and free."

KEEPING THE WILD WILD

In 2018, I guided a retreat in the Scottish Highlands called Magic, Medicine and Myth with my friend Ancel, who grew up outside Glasgow. On day three of the retreat, after hiking, clearing debris from a sacred well, and exploring wild medicine, I was dirty, sweaty, and covered in mud, and I felt alive. That night, following a long, satisfying day outdoors, our group of eight shared a delicious meal and sat around the table telling stories. It was our evening ritual and Ancel is an amazing storyteller. One of my favorite stories she shared is "The Fox Wife," an Inuit story. This is my version of the story she told:

There was a hunter who lived alone in the woods. He was a good man. He respected the animals and hunted only the deer or rabbits he needed to survive. He foraged fungi and wild greens and came to know the woods intimately. He left offerings and always asked permission before harvesting. The animals took note; they were always watching. He loved the land but he was lonely. He wanted a companion. He always came back to his cottage alone.

One day upon his return, he noticed smoke rising from his chimney. *An intruder!* he thought. He braced himself and slowly, stealthily moved closer to his cottage. As he did, the smell of delicious food emanated from inside. It was intoxicating, and he was so hungry. But he quickly shook himself free of its spell and remembered, *No, this is not right!* Ready to defend himself, he entered cautiously. He found an empty, orderly house, and a beautiful meal set for him. He was wary but his fatigue and incredible hunger overcame him. He sat down to eat and the meal was delicious. He also detected the faint scent of a fox.

He went out again the next day, and the same thing happened. Gradually, he became a little more trusting, able to enjoy the meal and the fire before going to sleep. But on the third day, he left his cottage and stayed close, hiding in the woods to reveal the mystery. After a few hours, he saw a fox slip into his cottage. Suspecting the fox was after the food, he snuck in, but upon entering, he saw the most beautiful woman with long red hair at the stove. Inside the door hung the musky, furry pelt of a fox. The man inquired if it was she who had done these things. She replied, "Yes, I am your wife, and it is my pleasure. For you are a good man."

And so it was, and for weeks they lived happily. He did not know how she spent her days sometimes; like him, she disappeared. She assured him she was loyal but that she, too, was a hunter for herbs, medicine, and wild game. She warned him not to ask too many questions, for if he did, he would spoil the romance. He abided but was becoming increasingly restless.

After they lived together awhile, the husband noticed that the wild odor about the house had grown stronger. He sniffed around and realized that it came from her fox pelt. He asked her to get rid of it. "The pelt is a precious part of me, you must let it be," she said. But the scent bothered him more and more. He began demanding that she throw it away. "Get rid of it! Clean the place of this stench!" He became irritable, expecting his meals, less and less in awe of her generosity.

One day he had enough of the musky odor, he was angry. "Get rid of that fox pelt, or else!" He had forgotten his loneliness and grown distant from the forest. He had become spoiled, too domesticated. She knew it was time to leave.

The next morning the fox pelt and the fox wife were gone.

Beavers

Beavers are one of the few animals, like humans, that modify their habitat to be more comfortable. In order to protect their families, they build their homes—lodges made out of tree branches—in the middle of ponds, with entrances underwater. This keeps predators out and also regulates the temperature inside the lodge when it is too hot or too cold outside. Each lodge contains at least two water-filled tunnels leading from the chamber to the pond so the beavers can enter and exit the lodge underwater without being seen.

The whole beaver family helps in building both the lodge and the dam, with the younger ones learning from the older beavers. First, they fell a tree by gnawing through it. Then they carry or push the branches to the water and float them to use in dam building. Stones might be gathered with their front paws to reinforce the dam, and they use mud and grasses to pack their dams into place. In making their home to protect themselves, they create and heal ecosystems. But ecological healing can, at first, look like destruction.

Land and water are not really separate things, but they are separate words, and we perceive through words.

—DAVID RAINS WALLACE,
Untamed Garden and Other Personal Essays

22

Engineering

The more time I spend on Mount Owen, the less I want to build anything there. Not because it isn't beautiful but because I don't want to disturb the plants, the fungi, the animals, or the trees. Yet there are some areas and animals that may benefit from mindful disturbance. We are taking baby steps and have so much to learn.

When I first started practicing herbalism, I was afraid of hurting plants when I harvested them. All of my teachers imparted the rule: ask permission from the plant and the environment they grow in if you are taking them from the wild. For some, this sounds like a crazy thing. *Ask a plant?* But even if it seems strange, the practice makes me pause, survey the environment, and think about whether or not I really need the plants, why I am harvesting them, and what I intend to use them for. A valuable lesson in this day and age of consumption.

There has never been a house on Mount Owen, so if we are going to live on the land, we have a lot to do: dig a well, install solar panels, build a dwelling. While we can't afford to do it yet, we talk about methods of building that are least harmful to the forest—maybe even helpful if at all possible. While there are areas of biodiverse landscape that seem to be thriving, many sections of the forest have been pastured, logged, and shaped by historic overharvesting and non-native species that have been introduced. Forests may appear natural to the casual observer, but the way something looks is not always an indicator of well-being. We imagine building on areas that are already depleted, using reclaimed wood or trees that have fallen in winter. We want the home to be compostable, with no plastics.

As we are talking about it all and looking through books on traditional timber frame homes we stumble upon *How to Manage Your Woods*, a disappointing human-centric book that talks about the land solely as a resource for people, with little mention of the animals that already live there. The author suggests getting rid of beavers—"a nuisance animal"—if we have them. *A nuisance animal?* We wish we had a beaver family and their lodge to prevent drought, filter water from nearby farms, and keep the overflowing and erosive water in. In Massachusetts, the state law prohibits capturing beavers in one area and simply releasing them in another. Which means that people who reach out for assistance concerning beaver problems (and likely assume the "troublesome" beavers will be peacefully relocated) aren't aware that those captured beavers are most often euthanized. In other words, "nuisance" beavers that are trapped are not relocated, but are mandated by law to be killed.

There was an adorable beaver family near my mom's house that created a small pond teeming with plants and wildlife—until a nearby neighbor worried that their basement might flood. Instead of "relocating" the beaver family, a solution might have been an over-under pipe that lets the beaver family build the dam as tall as they want while leaving the water level where the humans wanted it. But no solution was explored, and when the beavers disappeared, so did the pond, the frogs, and the wildlife. Now the area is a depressed boggy field.

As we look through more anthropocentric books and imagine our home, it is winter and my feet are cold. They need warm fuzzy socks.

In early spring, I'll want to walk barefoot as the ground warms, but there are ticks to consider. In summer, I'll need my flip-flops because the pavement is too hot. I need to bring sweaters to the beach and also my raincoat just in case. My hat to shield me from the sun. My bathing suit, my towel. As wild as I want to be, I am still naked in this world. *Why have we humans evolved or devolved to be so ill-equipped to handle the weather, while animals shed, burrow, or grow more fur?* I wonder out loud. You remind me we weren't meant to live in this latitude.

You are also schooling me on building codes that in some areas mandate vapor or moisture barriers for new housing. Plastic or Tyvek wraps are the cheapest and most utilized solutions. Plastic-wrapped houses are everywhere but it's something I hardly noticed before. In the 1960s, wraps like Tyvek were introduced as a new and "innovative" way to protect houses from the elements. The commodity's proponents aggressively marketed the virtues, painting a picture of a future where homes stood impervious to the forces of nature. As homeowners were convinced and the demand for house wrap soared, so did the influence of its manufacturers. Driven by an unquenchable thirst for profit, corporations wielded their considerable power to sway the course of building codes and regulations. Marketed as a way to prevent moisture from penetrating the walls of homes, which could lead to mold growth, rot, and structural damage, the wraps are made most cheaply from nonrenewable resources such as petroleum or natural gas, and they can take hundreds of years to decompose in landfills. And the truth is, these wraps can release harmful chemicals into the air, as well as trap moisture between the siding and the sheathing of a house. This can lead to mold growth that is far worse than moisture trapped by houses like the traditional timber frame home we want to build, one that can breathe.

Misguided plastic wrap and all, humans manipulate their environment to be more comfortable. We turn on the heat when it's cold, use air-conditioning when it's hot, and build shelters to stay dry during rain. Beavers are one of the few wild animals that manipulate their surroundings to stay safe and warm, too. Like civil engineers who build dams that create ponds and wetlands, beavers build and maintain two primary home designs—the conical lodge and the bank lodge. In building their lodges, beavers help filter water by trapping sediment and pollutants, prevent flooding by slowing the flow of water and storing runoff, and alleviate droughts by creating essential carbon-storing wetlands. The presence of beavers, a keystone species, increases biodiversity, creating habitat for a variety of plants and animals, including fish, amphibians, reptiles, birds, and mammals, and makes ecosystems more resilient to ever-present change. Nearly half of all endangered and threatened species need wetlands to survive. In the western United States wetland habitats cover only about 2 percent of land area yet support about 80 percent of species.

The most recognized beaver lodge is the conical-shaped dwelling surrounded by water, made from sticks and layers of mud and rocks. When the family works together to build the lodge, beavers tasked with securing it with piles of mud walk upright, on their hind legs, and carry the mud in their hands. It's adorable to see, and no wonder Native Americans like the Blackfeet call beavers the Little People. While some tribes hunted beavers for their meat and their fur, they also understood the balance of nature and maintained taboos against overhunting. The Blackfeet—whose territory ranged from the northwestern part of the Great Plains to northern reaches of the Saskatchewan River in Alberta, Canada, and the southernmost headwaters of the Missouri River in Montana in the United States—considered beavers to be sacred animals that must never be harmed. Old stories give accounts of how they once lived in domed stick lodges, modeled after the beaver lodge.

The second type of structure—the bank lodge—is usually built by excavating into the bank of a large stream, river, or lake where water is too deep or fast-moving to construct the more common

conical lodge. Within each type of lodge beavers hollow out a chamber where they sleep, eat, and groom each other, and where the kits
are born. Beds of grasses, reeds, and wood chips are changed regularly. Their efficient homes will not drop below freezing even with
subzero temperatures outside due to well-insulated architecture that
can retain body heat from the family of beavers. Generally, two to
eight beavers live in one lodge: the adult mating pair, and three years
of offspring. In order for the family to breathe fresh air, they don't
apply mud to the peak of the lodge, creating a sort of chimney. In the
winter, they stay inside their lodge, only leaving to gather cached food
from the bottom of the pond. On cold winter days, we might be lucky
enough to see breath escaping from their chimney. And if we're quiet
and still enough, we might even hear the sounds of the adorable beaver family, sometimes all three generations, living inside.

Beavers mate for life and are fiercely loyal to their families. Only if
their partner dies do they find new love. Older siblings frequently
pitch in to groom or babysit the kits. If danger approaches, they slap
the water with their tail to warn their family to take cover. Sadly, that
signal wasn't enough when the cold Europeans arrived to the so-
called New World.

In *Beaverland: How One Weird Rodent Made America*, the author
Leila Philip explores the history of humans' relationship to beavers
and explains how the global fur trade and near extinction of beavers
coincided with what American geomorphologists call the great drying; the three centuries between 1600 and 1900 during which the
country's rivers and wetlands shrank, and in some cases disappeared.

Beaver fur consists of short fine hairs for warmth and longer hairs
for waterproofing, and Europeans knew that wealthy acquaintances
from across the pond were willing to pay huge sums of money for
warm, waterproof beaver pelts. So upon their arrival in the New
World, the fur trade exploded and beaver populations plummeted
along with the wetlands they created. It is estimated that between 60

million and 400 million beavers populated North America prior to the 1500s. By the 1900s, there were roughly 100,000 beavers left. Though beavers also lived in Eurasia, they were hunted to near extinction throughout their native land for their fur, meat, and, weirdly, for their castoreum secretions—an oily substance from the underside of a beaver's abdomen they use in their grooming and to mark their territory. Humans have used these beaver secretions in perfumes and medicines and to create strawberry and raspberry flavorings or enhance vanilla substitutes. Though related, the Eurasian beaver is a different species, whose scientific name is *Castor fiber*. The North American beaver's scientific name is *Castor canadensis*.

Beavers became the first endangered species in North America. These essential ecosystem engineers almost went extinct on the continent because humans, with their cold heads and thirst for so-called fashion, liked beaver hats and pelts. Eradicating beavers as a resource was a cruel and harmful undertaking that cascaded through living systems. But thankfully, beaver populations are increasing and many (but still not enough) of the descendants of those European colonizers are beginning to realize how little they knew. Bringing back the beaver to depleted lands can be deeply restorative. An abundance of wildlife accompanies beavers, wherever they make their homes. Leila Philip writes, "In beavers, we have millions of highly trained engineers ready to work for us for free if we're willing to coexist with them."

LAND STEWARDSHIP

We have been hiking through the seasons and are slowly learning to steward the land while making sure we pay attention to the trees— both dead and alive—where animals live. We must cull a few individuals like saplings that are choking healthy, mature trees for biodiversity, just as wolves help to strengthen deer herds by culling weak and sick prey. We've learned that forests that grow too dense can lose structure, affecting wildlife habitat, and slowed tree growth may indicate a forest under stress. *But is it right to take the lives of these trees?* All that I learn and study says yes, this is the right thing to do in order to care for areas of land that have been logged and pastured for decades, to bring the ecosystem to a place of health and vitality. In the city, I worshipped every weed; now in the forest, I am coming to terms with cutting down trees.

Known for their ability to topple large trees, beaver teeth never stop growing, and therefore don't become too worn despite years of chiseling hardwoods. Their four front teeth are self-sharpening due to hard orange enamel on the front of each tooth and a softer dentin on the back. As beavers chew wood the softer backside of the tooth wears faster, creating a sawlike cutting surface. In the fall, they anchor branches in the mud at the bottom of the pond near the entrance to their lodge, which then become new trees. Willow trees can be grown by simply taking a stem and sticking it in moist soil. The beavers essentially cut vegetation in one area while cultivating their next crop in another. Not only are they builders but it appears they are farmers, too.

"Yes, beavers cut down the trees, but then they bring in all this other plant life," the environmental engineer Jordan Kennedy said in a recent interview with Harvard Kenneth C. Griffin Graduate School of Arts and Sciences News. Raised on a cattle ranch in northwestern Montana on the Blackfeet Indian Reservation, Jordan is a first-generation descendant of the Blackfeet tribe. "A number of papers demonstrate that plants start to flourish and invertebrates start to populate the areas beavers inhabit," she said. "Even if you don't think that beavers are sacred, it's coming more and more to the forefront how important they are to the health of our waterways and everything that lives there."

Herbivores, beavers feed on numerous plants and trees like willow, whose inner bark is filled with a constituent called salicylic acid, which we use to create aspirin. I wonder if this has anything to do with the fact that this seems to be their favorite plant. It must help to have some pain relief amid all that building.

I love the dappled light of spring. The veins of deciduous leaves look like the veins in my hand. There were a maple and a black birch tree that you had to take down. Both were cracked and tangled with vines. Crowded, yes. Suffering? Maybe. But still, the trees were striving, almost there, buds unfurling. We count the rings on the maple and discover that the tree was about fifty years old, born around the same time I was. It feels tragic: fifty years of growth and less than five minutes to fall. Like me, the tree strived for sun, had relationships, and saw so many things I'll never know. I feel a deep ache. You assure me, *The tree was suffering and unhealthy. If I have to cut down a tree, I'm going to honor the tree and use every part.* You also remind me, *We need solar, there may be a million trees on the land we steward, we need meadows for pollinators.* These things are all true, but still, I don't want to become cold or desensitized; I want to honor the trees and creatures of this land. We have a responsibility to be mindful of the impact we have on this forest and the world around us.

I look at the black birch now on the ground and think about the trees' wind-dispersed seeds. The seeds are too small to germinate successfully underneath piles of leaves, so they seek out raw, exposed places. I think about this as I grieve the birch, grateful for the ways in which the tree healed the land. Birch trees respond swiftly to logging and other canopy disturbances and heal gaps in contiguous forest. Known among permaculturists as a dynamic accumulator, black birch pulls minerals from the subsoil and retains them. Their edible leaves are rich in potassium, phosphorus, and calcium. In some cases, black birch halts erosion of newly disturbed soils and also enriches them with nutrients critical to the growth of other plants. The rapid life cycle of birch pushes them upward fast, causing them to fall and rot and break easily, and in collaboration with the fungi, their rotting creates more fertile ground for generations to come.

I gather branches of black birch to bring home, intending to drink the tree's healing wintergreen tea. Medicine of the forest. Change can be disruptive, but it can also lead to healing.

Humans

Humans are primates, originally from Africa, who usually live in groups. It has been more than 30,000 years since there was more than one species of human; brief in an evolutionary timescale. About 1 million years ago, a group of these early primates left Africa and moved into what we now call Europe. Over the course of thousands of years, they evolved into Neanderthals, while the population in Africa evolved into modern humans. Archaeological findings show that Neanderthals were present and active in Europe until approximately 30,000 years ago, but then something happened. We don't know how or why, but they vanished.

These animals walked on two legs and had complex systems of communication that have evolved into language, writing, art, and story. Through the development of agriculture and technology, the lives of most humans now depend less on instinct than other animals, and more on education. Many have forgotten that they *are* in fact animals, and are not clear about their role in the ecosystem like other wild creatures are. Because of this, humans seek stories, guidance, meaning, and belonging, and they are often led astray. These animals live on every continent. There are an estimated 8 billion humans now living on Earth.

Man in his arrogance thinks himself a great work, worthy of the interposition of a deity. More humble, and I believe truer, to consider him created from animals.

—CHARLES DARWIN, *The Origin of Species*

You are not Atlas carrying the world on your shoulder. It is good to remember that the planet is carrying you.

—VANDANA SHIVA

23

Animal Nature

It is spring, and I have been busy building a nest; a boundary. A quarter-acre garden fence of fallen trees. Many trees fell in winter and after a heavy, early spring snow. Now I am weaving their crowns and branches together to protect fledgling plants from deer. We have decided to plant a garden on one of the few relatively flat open areas of Mount Owen and if I don't build an enclosure, the deer might eat all the vegetables and herbs we started in early spring, now barely emerging from the ground. Transitional life needs enclosures and spring is the most vulnerable time for plants. From afar, the experimental fence looks like a huge nest for a dragon's egg.

From what I've learned, deer are highly visual animals and need a bit of a running start to clear serious heights. Selective browsers, they eat many of the native endangered medicines like ginseng and goldenseal we are reintroducing and trying to protect. *I want to create a massive fence on the land to see what happens when the understory and all the native plants are relieved of deer,* you tell me. We have become part of United Plant Savers' Botanical Sanctuary Network. But I don't just want to offer sanctuary to the plants, I want to offer sanctuary to the animals, too.

In the evening, we build a fire in the middle of our dragon's nest to cook a modest meal. We are exhausted from planting and clearing trees from the former logging trail, and my hands ache from weaving the fence. We sit by the fire and tell stories. We imagine the future of this land where wolves would roam. We talk about having a wolf sanctuary one day, helping people to get used to their presence.

Without wolves here in their native land, the whole forest ecosystem is suffering. *In the absence of wolves*, you say, *I may have to assume the role of the Wolf and hunt, become the thing that we fear.* There are too many deer. A forest suffers without natural predators.

Agriculture, language, and fire. These are among the things that some say separate humans from other animals. Although various insects, birds, and small rodents use some form of agriculture or harvesting, many use tools and have their own languages to communicate. But no other animal that we know of works with fire. The British primatologist Richard Wrangham believes cooking may have played a role in our evolution and the expansion of human brains. Cooked foods tend to be softer and easier to digest than raw foods, and interestingly enough, fossils have shown that the teeth and digestive tracts of our early ancestors decreased in size around the same time our brain size increased. Since cooking is generally a communal process for humans, Wranghan, like other scholars and historians, speculates that circling around fire formed a social focus, helping the development of human language.

It's possible we first told stories around the fire. This makes sense to me. The nourishment of a kitchen is the heart of a home. Humans have told stories and shared around fires and over meals for eons, and neuroscientists have demonstrated that we internalize knowledge much more thoroughly through story than we do through lists and litanies of facts. Stories create neural pathways; they become us. Some stories we believe so strongly that we kill for them, unlike other animals. Or do they worship invisible gods and kill because of stories, too?

I recently went to a poetry reading by Larry Spotted Crow Mann, a member of the Nipmuc nation, whose people live here in Western Massachusetts, their ancestral land. He opened the talk with a warm welcome and song in his native language. Sounds, words, and vibrations born from the land, rarely heard here anymore. As he spoke and sang, my body stirred, and tears welled in my eyes. It felt like I could almost sense the land's sorrow, the yearning of the trees reaching in from outside. After his talk an audience member asked: "What is the difference between your language and the English that was forced upon you?" Larry Spotted Crow Mann thought for a while, then responded, "Well, the easiest way to put it is that my language is verb based, everything is alive. English is a noun-based language in which everything is separate, and dead."

Language has helped us evolve and devolve. Books exalted, books banned, books burned. Language, writing, and foreign legal documents helped humans steal land and suppress oral traditions, Indigenous languages, and cultures, including local cosmologies that protected ecosystems. My ancestral Gaelic, born of the land, reflects this bond. Its very form, with an alphabet inspired by trees, and its lack of a direct word for "ownership," suggests a different worldview. Languages define how we perceive ourselves, our communities, and concepts of possession. Most of the stories that have been written down up to this point have been skewed toward the white European male perspective, in which nature is othered and, as Larry Spotted Crow Mann said, often deemed dead. The land needs her stories. Not just stories about how the grass grows or why monarchs migrate but stories that restore our emotional connection to land. We need to get quiet and listen to the land and other animals. We need to let them speak to us. Language is communication and it also means listening.

I still revel in the strangeness of language. As a child, I said words over and over until they felt like strange hollow grunts and made me giggle. I have always had conversations in my head. Rehearsals to find the right words. But now I realize I wasn't just talking to myself, I'm a writer. I have been chewing over ideas to write down. To share with readers who may be feeling the same things as me, and to speak for those, like plants and more-than-human animals, who can't speak for themselves. To share the depth that gets lost, as Neruda puts it, "between the lips and the voice" and share my version of the human experience.

Just as we need to reclaim and steward land, we need to reclaim language, writing, and laws, too. We need to use language to tell our stories and learn from voices that have been silenced, while continuing to rewrite harmful stories, like colonial, misogynist, and anthropocentric histories that are untrue. For the past 2,000 years Western law has been set up for the rights of "persons" while diminishing all other living beings to the realm of "things," with no legal recourse. And while we might think of *persons* as referring solely to humans, companies and corporations are considered persons, but primates, elephants, wolves, and the rest of sentient nature are deemed things. But thanks to people using the legal system for common ground, the Rights of Nature movement is beginning to give nature back to herself. It seems absurd to have to use static words to enforce protection of flowing rivers and diverse living ecosystems, but that is where we are. We might as well use our current system for healing instead of harm. On Mount Owen, we're talking about creative ways to protect the land even when we're gone, such as how to leave the land to the grandmother maple tree and her kin, who are vast and include us, of course. We have to start somewhere.

If I look at evolution, I share a common ancestor with the weeds, wildflowers, and every other plant, animal, fish, alga, and invertebrate. It is incredible to have such a large extended family and a comfort to know I am nature, that I belong here. But many people want to be something else, something "better" than an animal, something divine beyond the boundaries of death. I don't know what is more spectacular than nature, and if this is it, if this is all we have, why consume, extract, and destroy—or pretend there is something beyond this earthly life?

We need the same things as a wood thrush or a coyote on hot dry days—water, cooling, shelter from the sun. We need love, caring, patience, nourishment from the land, and protection. Are we not related? A maple tree is a maple tree, and a wolf is a wolf. They know who they are and cannot be anything else. We humans, on the other hand, can choose or pretend to be something other than ourselves. We are traumatized domesticated animals, we humans. When our basic needs for food, clothing, and shelter are met, our minds continue working, problem-solving and creating problems where there are none. But if we remembered we are nature, that we *are* animals, I believe we would be more content, less destructive, more humble. Our aversion to being animals is truly strange.

But what makes us human? How about the mirror self-recognition test? Chimps, dolphins, elephants, magpies, orangutans, and gorillas recognize themselves in a mirror and so pass this test. The so-called rich interpretation says that those who pass the test are self-aware. But any animal who avoids bumping into things, biting themselves in a fight, or even surviving and thriving in their environment has the ability to distinguish the self from nonself. What about the pleasure of reflection? Do other animals take time to pause and revel in wonder? I've seen chipmunks sitting in the sun, gazing out into the forest, and seen pigeons gazing out to sea, seeming to revel in wonder. But sadly, like any response to a reflection, sometimes we can be cruel, like we are to our own bodies. We are nature, after all.

Our miraculous bodies work hard, all day, every day, doing their best to help us thrive with what we give or deny them. They love us even if we don't love them back. But how do we fall in love with our earthly, animal bodies? We might start by peeling away the incessant noise of social conditioning and ask ourselves: *Is my emotional body at odds with my instinctual body? Are "gratitude lists" standing in for instinctual needs or feelings? Am I contorting myself to fit into others' ideas of who I am, or confused about my own needs and the needs of a beloved? Do I feel trapped by shame, believing that the animal body I was gifted with isn't good enough?* In my experience, the animal body—the gut instinct—is the one with the answer. The body never lies.

After two decades of being in conflict with my animal body, more and more, we are at peace. Now I ask my body what she would like to eat, how she would like to move, where she would like to live, who she would like to love. I stretch, breathe, walk in the woods, swim in freshwater, and bring my limbs, soft belly, and legs out into the sun. When my body wants to be still, I try to rest and I abide. Although like all loving relationships, we still have occasional conflicts. Sometimes I'm critical, am still prone to judge her appearance, and when I've gone too far and haven't listened, she whispers with pain. She has always worked hard for me, and I know she always will.

Today, I wrote a love letter to my body:

> *Thank you for all you have seen me through, and for all you continue to teach me. When we were sick as a child, you figured out how to help me breathe through constricted lungs. All the while, continuing to offer joy through the love and care of my mother, the sound of songbirds in the morning and crickets at night. Through the feeling of soil in my hands and the miracle of planting pumpkins and witnessing the community—the bees, the sun, the rain—that helped them*

*grow. Through sensations of warming sun and cleansing rain
on my skin, and cold snow on my tongue.*

*As I grew older, you showed me how to heal from pain and
sorrow. How strange that I and You are both me but I, this
consciousness, is so much more ignorant.*

*You are ancient. You are the blood of my ancestors,
creatures of the Earth, water, fire, organisms that have been
around for billions of years. And I, a new body experiencing it
all, stumbling along the way. Completing my leg of life's relay,
much like the monarch, often ignorant of where I've come from
and where I'm going. I'm learning to let go, to let you guide
me. It is a lesson that takes a long time to learn in a world with
so much useless noise. You guide me silently with sensation,
with feeling, with knowing, with magnetic pulls of attraction
more powerful than any word, more powerful than anything I
can touch. Thank you. I love you.*

A NEW STORY

A recent article in *The New York Times* inspired you, my beloved, to
tell me a story, a new vision of the future: *It will be a matriarchy, a
chance for a humane culture and a chance for Earth to breathe.* The article illustrated and explained why a human population slowdown in
the next sixty years is anticipated due to lower and lower birth rates.
In part because in many places around the world, women now have
the freedom to choose. Demographers at the U.N. expect the size of
humanity to peak at 10 billion in the 2080s, and rapidly decline to
less than 2 billion in less than 300 years. Just as our extractive so-
called civilization is but a blip in human history, it seems our domesticated population explosion will be, too. The article speculates that
"children born today will very likely live to see the end of global

population growth." This may seem like a welcome breath for the environment, but a lot of harm can still happen in sixty years. We don't have time to sit back and wait to become loving stewards of our home, we have to start now. While the population decline is expected to happen quickly, as the article states, it will happen "far too slowly to be more than a sideshow in the effort to save the planet. Work to decarbonize our economies and reform our land use and food systems must accelerate in this decade and the next, not start in the next century." Yes. We have work to do. Or more accurately in most cases, work to eliminate.

For you and me, the predicted population decline feels like a relief, a juxtaposition to the doomsday messaging we are currently overwhelmed with. But ultimately, the future is unknown and will be shaped by us and those who follow us. While scientists and demographers may be able to predict the future based on current trajectories, it's up to us to create, live, and embody new stories. We can learn from animals—human and more-than-human alike—who have always known how to live in harmony with nature and remember how to coexist with our wild kin. I want a different world. One that is much more kind.

I've never been one to turn to the back of a book, and I don't want to ruin this story. But if I enjoy a story, I always want to read to the end. And so far, despite all of the trauma and pain on this beautiful blue planet, there is also incredible beauty and joy. I want to know what will happen next, but I don't even know what tomorrow will bring. I'll never know how this story ends. But I can imagine the stories the humans of the future, sitting around a fire, will tell about us, the Forgetters:

Once upon a time, a two-legged animal took over the world and their population exploded, causing incredible pain and suffering amid incredible greed and decadence. They believed they were gods or descendants of a god, forgetting they emerged from the living Earth like all of our animal relatives. There was a vacuum inside them, and incredible sorrow. They believed our green and blue planet was a resource to use to fill their voids. There was beauty and love among the Forgetters, too, of course, but also deep and tragic loss.

But the two-legged animal slowly learned. While the powers that be tried to manipulate them and separate them from each other, the females had fewer children, the civilians learned to care for Earth, and the people remembered they and all other animals are related. Slowly the population declined, and Earth could breathe again. And finally, the Remembering emerged. They no longer feared wolves—their brothers and sisters. They made homes for bats and let vultures eat carrion. They no longer poisoned land, and they learned to plant the way their Indigenous people had for thousands of years. They wrote and embodied new and ancient stories, remembering what was true.

I am content today, lying in the hammock in the woods, listening to you, my beloved, chop wood for our fire. I'm reading a guidebook on tree bark. The book is boring and dull but I am deeply relaxed. Finally, I am in a place in nature where we can just be, where I feel safe. Where I can let down my guard and be an animal—a mystery, a galaxy, an ecosystem, a loving partner. Where I can become land when I die. Like a flower, and every other living organism, I, too, am an ephemeral expression of nature, and my body will lie down in fertile ground when my energy is spent. Before that happens, maybe I'll carve a message for future stewards to stumble upon, somewhere in the mountain's stone:

Stewards of this land, tread gently, we are here. We watched seasons change, from the hopeful blooms of spring to the death and poignance of autumn. We cried until we felt hollow, put our hands, claws, talons, and hooves in living Earth and planted seeds that miraculously became food that became our bodies. We foraged sweet fruit in summer and found warmth in winter. We were grateful. We learned and unlearned, felt trapped and found release, and when broken, we forged paths to healing. We loved Earth, our home, and our fellow animals from a place so deep that our animal bodies felt both empty and endless.

The coiled baton of life that connects all of us, past and present, from the beginning to the end, passes to you now. Care for us, your wild kin.

We tried our best in our earthly bodies. We howled.

PART FIVE

Helping

24

Wildlife Organizations

Helping Us Help Other Animals

B e a voice for our wild kin. Help these organizations help them.

WOLVES

Wolf Conservation Center: nywolf.org
Defenders of Wildlife: defenders.org

BATS

Bat Conservation International: batcon.org
Bat World Sanctuary: batworld.org

HOWLER MONKEYS

Jaguar Rescue Center: jaguarrescue.foundation
Rainforest Action Network: ran.org/campaign/stop-deforestation

HYENAS

African Wildlife Foundation: awf.org/wildlife-conservation/hyena

CHEETAHS

Cheetah Conservation Fund: cheetah.org

VULTURES

The Peregrine Fund: peregrinefund.org/projects/asian-vultures

COYOTES

Project Coyote: projectcoyote.org

DEER

Aldo Leopold Foundation: aldoleopold.org

OCTOPUSES

The Ocean Conservancy: oceanconservancy.org

SPIDERS

Xerces Society: xerces.org

BUMBLEBEES

Xerces Society: xerces.org
Bee City USA: beecityusa.org

WOOD THRUSH

American Bird Conservancy: abcbirds.org/bird/wood-thrush
Center for Biological Diversity: biologicaldiversity.org

SEAHORSES

Project Seahorse: projectseahorse.org

SEA LIONS

Pacific Marine Mammal Center: pacificmmc.org
The Galápagos Conservancy: galapagos.org

HAWKS

Hawk Mountain Global Raptor Conservation: hawkmountain.org

PIGEONS

Wild Bird Fund: wildbirdfund.org

MONARCH BUTTERFLIES

Monarch Butterfly Fund: monarchconservation.org
Monarch Joint Venture: monarchjointventure.org

BLACK BEARS

Natural Resource Defense Council: nrdc.org

RED FOX

Fox Guardians: foxguardians.co.uk
Four Paws Foundation: fourpawsusa.org

BEAVERS

The Lands Council/ The Beaver Solution: landscouncil.org/beaver
Beavers, Wetlands & Wildlife: beaversww.org

HUMANS

Amnesty International: amnesty.org
Earth Justice: earthjustice.org

Acknowledgments

To Terra Chalberg and Laura Tisdel, thank you for believing in my vision and work and for helping to make this book a reality. To Jenn Houghton, and again to Laura, for your keen editorial eye, notes, and guidance. To Raven Ross, Julia Falkner, and the whole team at Penguin Life for supporting this project. To Lisa Ericson for your stunning cover art and to Nayon Cho, who found it.

Thank you, Courtney Maum and The Cabins, and Jane LaFarge Hamill, Jason Bereswill, and Martha at the Martha MOCA residency. My time spent wandering in the woods and lying in the hammock at your residency allowed the framework for this book to arise. I did some of my best writing at that magical desk. Thank you, Amy Shearn, for your feedback and inspiration when I felt stuck. To Sy Montgomery, Dr. Marc Beckoff, Erica Berry, Camilla Fox, and Kristen J. Sollée, who were invited to read a final draft, your thrilling praise kept me going when I was on the last leg of this journey. I admire you all so much.

To Regan Downey, Maggie Howell, and all the staff at the Wolf Conservation Center, our years of collaboration continue to be deeply inspiring. To ambassador wolves Zephyr, Alawa, and Atka for teaching me how to howl and communicating something intangible that changed me. To every human who works on behalf of these misunderstood relatives, thank you.

Christine Webb, thank you for all you're doing to foster empathy for our wild relatives and to change the conversation and cruel experiments done in the name of science. Encar Vila, I'm in awe of you and your work. Thank you for your dedication to howler monkeys and all

Costa Rican wildlife. You have offered sanctuary, love, healing, and freedom to so many. You are a powerhouse and I am so happy to call you a dear friend.

To all my incredible Rewilding Through Writing students and mentees, it has been inspiring to facilitate our gatherings, hear you read, and see your writing evolve. Guiding our groups and sessions has made me a better writer. And to Libby, Jessica, Andrea, and Amanda, it has been an honor to hold space for your creative projects.

To my personal support network: The Brooklyn crew and friends in Western Massachusetts—Boyuan, Malik, Akilah, Keat, Katrina, and Jonah—so happy we're close. To Jahan and Natalia, who I don't see enough, and to Heidi for your friendship and writing comradery, to Peri for being an ever-present sister, to Morisha for our ongoing conversations (even if they're mostly in our heads), and to Mallory for being a collaborator and kindred spirit. To Vanessa A. for your friendship and the barn where much of this was written. And to Adam R. for good timing and the beautiful space Enrique and I needed when we were moving way too much. To Àdhamh and Nicola, my Scotland family, thank you for being an integral part of my life and work—here's to continued magic! To Joan for your continued support and wisdom. And to all those in the book whom I've loved and who have made me who I am.

To my beloved human family: My sister, Alecia; my brother, Alex; my sister-in-law, Megan; and their baby, Callie. To Mitch for the music and especially to my mom for your unconditional love and love of nature. Thank you for nurturing my creativity. And all the more-than-human animals I've been fortunate to call family, too: Daphne, Elsa, Ebony, Kobe, Mavis, Mickey, Milo, Tasha, and Mudcat. To Lizzie the cat, thank you for sitting with me, reading along, and keeping me company as I typed the final words. To Mount Owen and all your trees, plants, fungi, and creatures, thank you for teaching me to become a better steward and better human. I am still learning.

To Enrique, my beloved partner. Thank you for being my companion on this wild adventure of life. I cherish our deep conversations and long hikes, your wildness and sense of wonder, your poetic analogies and insights, your tenderness, and your love. Thank you for reading draft after draft and for supporting me when I turned inward to write. You are an incredible animal. I adore you.

Finally, to all my four-legged, feathered, clawed, and water-bound relatives. I hope this book helps humans understand you better and makes your life a little (or a lot) easier and freer. Ultimately, the energy spent writing this book and all my creative efforts are for you.

Bibliography

PART ONE: ENCLOSURES

Gray Wolves: Predators and Prey

Coleman, Jon T. *Vicious: Wolves and Men in America*. New Haven, CT: Yale University Press, 2004.

de Waal, Frans. *The Bonobo and the Atheist: In Search of Humanism among the Primates*. New York: W. W. Norton & Company, 2013.

Mech, David L., and Luigi Boitani. *Wolves: Behavior, Ecology, and Conservation*. Chicago: University of Chicago Press, 2003.

Musiani, Michel, et al. "Life History, Population Dynamics, and Human-Wolf Interactions of Wolves in the Canadian Arctic." *Journal of Wildlife Management* 68, no. 4 (2004): 1200–11.

Perrault, Charles. "Little Red Riding Hood." *The Complete Fairy Tales of Charles Perrault*. Translated by Lowell Bair. New York: Penguin Classics, 2003.

Strayed, Cheryl. *Wild: From Lost to Found on the Pacific Crest Trail*. New York: Alfred A. Knopf, 2012.

Bats: Seeing in the Dark

Bardi, Jason S., et al. "The Future of Bats in a Changing World." *Frontiers in Ecology and the Environment* 13, no. 1 (2015): 26–32.

Bat Conservation International. Accessed October 26, 2023. batcon.org.

Haddock, Joanna, et al. "Light pollution at the Urban Forest Edge Negatively Impacts Insectivorous Bats." *Biological Conservation* 236 (2019): 17–28. 10.1016/j.biocon.2019.05.016.

Haskell, David George. *Sounds Wild and Broken: Sonic Marvels, Evolution's Creativity, and the Crisis of Sensory Extinction*. New York: Viking, 2022.

Kunz, Thomas H., et al. *Bat Ecology*. Chicago: University of Chicago Press, 2005.

Wainwright, Mark. *The Mammals of Costa Rica: A Natural History and Field Guide.* Costa Rica: Zona Tropical Publications, 2002.

White-Nose Syndrome Response Team. Accessed October 26, 2023. whitenosesyndrome.org.

Howler Monkeys: Fitting In

Cain, Susan. *Quiet: The Power of Introverts in a World That Can't Stop Talking.* New York: Random House, 2012.

Hare, Brian, and Vanessa Woods. *Survival of the Friendliest: Understanding Our Origins and Rediscovering Our Common Humanity.* New York: W. W. Norton & Company, 2013.

Spotted Hyenas: Ravenous

Silk, Joan B. "Hyena Politics: The Dynamics of Dynasties." *Proceedings of the National Academy of Sciences* 116, no. 18 (2019): 8644–45. doi.org/10.1073/pnas.1903407116.

Vullioud, Colin, et al. "Social Support Drives Female Dominance in the Spotted Hyaena. *Nature Ecology & Evolution* 3, no. 1 (2019): 71–76. doi.org/10.1038/s41559-018-0718-9.

Cheetahs: Wanting to Be Wanted

Cheetah Conservation Fund. "About Cheetahs." Accessed October 27, 2023. cheetah.org/learn/about-cheetahs/.

Holekamp, K. E., et al. "Estrous Cycles in Cheetah (*Acinonyx jubatus*) Queens: Hormonal Changes and Behavioral Correlates." *Hormones and Behavior* 30, no. 4 (1996): 391–402.

Kaplan, Matt. "Male Cheetah Bark Triggers Female Ovulation." *National Geographic*, January 9, 2009. nationalgeographic.com/animals/article/cheetah-gender-hormones-animals.

Pittman, Arianna. "Pet Cheetahs Are Being Used as a Status Symbol—Why This Needs to Stop Now." One Green Planet. onegreenplanet.org/animalsandnature/pet-cheetahs-are-being-used-as-a-status-symbol.

Roth, Madeline. "Cardi B Says She Almost Got Attacked by a Cheetah While Filming 'Bodak Yellow' Music Video." MTV News, February

9, 2018. mtv.com/news/ql9q74/cardi-b-cheetah-attack-bodak-yellow
-video.

Vitale, Kristyn R., et al. "Attachment Bonds between Domestic Cats and
Humans." *Current Biology* 29, no. 18 (2019): R864–R865. doi.org
/10.1016/j.cub.2019.08.036.

PART TWO: REHABILITATION

Vultures: Quarantine

Cornell Lab of Ornithology. "Turkey Vulture." Accessed October 17,
2023. allaboutbirds.org/guide/Turkey_Vulture.

Frank, Eyal, and Anant Sudarshan. "The Social Costs of Keystone
Species Collapse: Evidence from the Decline of Vultures in India."
University of Chicago, Becker Friedman Institute for Economics Working Paper No. 2022-165, January 5, 2023. https://ssrn.com/abstract
=4318579.

Garson, Mort. *Mother Earth's Plantasia.* Warner Bros. Records, 1976.

Mandima, Jimmiel J. "Vultures Poisoned in India Recover and Take
Flight Back to the Wild." IFAW, March 30, 2023. ifaw.org/journal/poi
soned-vultures-recover-wild-india.

The Peregrine Fund. "Asian Vultures." Accessed October 17, 2023. pere
grinefund.org/projects/asian-vultures.

Coyotes: Between Two Worlds

Flores, Dan. *Coyote America: A Natural and Supernatural History.* New
York: W. W. Norton & Company, 2016.

Judson, Katharine Berry. *Myths and Legends of California and the Old
Southwest.* Chicago: A. C. McClurg & Co., 1912.

Kroeber, A. L. "The Yokuts and Miwok Languages of Central California."
*University of California Publications in American Archaeology and Eth-
nology* 5, no. 2 (1907): 113–368.

WildlifeNYC. "Eastern Coyote (*Canis latrans*)." Accessed September 24,
2023. nyc.gov/site/wildlifenyc/animals/coyotes.page.

White-Tailed Deer: Fight, Flight, Freeze, Fawn

Hand, David, dir. *Bambi*. 1942; Walt Disney Productions.

Lashley, M. A., et al. "White-Tailed Deer Vigilance: The Influence of Social and Environmental Factors." *PLoS One* 9, no. 3 (2014): e90652. doi:10.1371/journal.pone.0090652

Leopold, Aldo. *A Sand County Almanac: And Sketches Here and There.* United Kingdom: Oxford University Press, 2020.

Massachusetts Division of Fisheries and Wildlife. "Fishing & Hunting." Accessed February 24, 2023. mass.gov/topics/fishing-hunting.

Meine, Curt. *Aldo Leopold: His Life and Work.* Madison: University of Wisconsin Press, 2010.

Miller, Karl V., et al. "Signpost Communication by White-Tailed Deer: Research since Calgary, *Applied Animal Behaviour Science* 29, nos. 1–4 (1991): 195–204. doi.org/10.1016/0168-1591(91)90247-U.

Salten, Felix. *Bambi: A Life in the Forest.* Translated by Jack Zipes. Princeton, NJ: Princeton University Press, 2022.

Walker, Pete. *Complex PTSD: From Surviving to Thriving.* Lafayette, CA: Azure Coyote Publishing, 2013.

Octopuses: Too Sensitive

Ehrlich, Pippa, and James Reed, dir. *My Octopus Teacher*. 2020; Netflix.

Gumbs, Alexis Pauline. *Undrowned: Black Feminist Lessons from Marine Mammals.* Chico, CA: AK Press, 2020.

Le Page, Michael. "Female Octopuses Throw Things at Males That Are Harassing Them." *New Scientist*, August 21, 2021.

Mervosh, Sarah. "Carnival Cruises to Pay $20 Million in Pollution and Cover-Up Case." *New York Times*, June 4, 2019.

Montgomery, Sy. *The Soul of an Octopus: A Surprising Exploration into the Wonder of Consciousness.* New York: Atria Books, 2016.

Seagulls: Lost at Sea

Dalla Pria, Caitlin, et al. "City Living: Nest-Site Selection Preferences in Urban Herring Gulls, *Larus argentatus*." *Geographies* 2, no. 2 (2022): 161–72. doi.org/10.3390/geographies2020011.

Dantzker, Marc, et al. Cornell University Laboratory of Ornithology, Shoals Marine Laboratory, Cornell University, British Broadcasting

Corporation, and Sinauer Associates. *Signals for Survival*, directed by Hugh Falkus. Sunderland, MA: Sinauer Associates, 2009.

Stierwalt, Sabrina. "Why Do Smells Trigger Memories?" *Scientific American*, June 29, 2020, scientificamerican.com/article/why-do-smells-trigger-memories1/.

Spiders: Weaving My Web

Grierson, Elizabeth W. "The Scottish Fairy Book: Habetrot the Spinstress." 1918. Electric Scotland. Accessed February 27, 2024. electric scotland.com/history/fairy/fairybook11.htm.

Miceli, Courtney. "Spider Silk Five Times Stronger Than Steel—Now Scientists Know Why." *Science,* November 20, 2018. science.org/con tent/article/spider-silk-five-times-stronger-steel-now-scientists -know-why.

White, E. B. *Charlotte's Web.* New York: Harper & Brothers, 1952.

PART THREE: SOFT RELEASE

Yellowstone Wolves: Out of Bounds

Eisenberg, Cristina. *The Wolf's Tooth: Keystone Predators, Trophic Cascades, and Biodiversity.* Washington, DC: Island Press, 2013.

National Park Service. "Wolf Restoration." Accessed October 21, 2023. https://www.nps.gov/yell/learn/nature/wolf-restoration.htm.

"Newly Removed from the Endangered Species List: What's Next for America's Gray Wolves?" *On Point*, WBUR, January 26, 2022. https:// www.pbs.org/newshour/science/feds-wont-restore-protections-for -gray-wolves-propose-national-recovery-plan.

Niemeyer, Carter. *Wolfer: A Memoir.* Boise, ID: Bottlefly Press, 2010.

Smith, Douglas W., and Gary Ferguson. *Decade of the Wolf: Returning the Wild to Yellowstone.* Guilford, CT: Lyons Press, 2012.

Smith, Douglas W., David R. Stahler, and David R. MacNulty, eds. *Yellowstone Wolves: Science and Discovery in the World's First National Park.* Chicago: University of Chicago Press, 2020.

Rusty-Patched Bumblebees: Searching for Nectar

Statman-Weil, Zoe. "Rusty-Patched Bumblebee (Bombus affinis)." U.S. Forest Service. Accessed March 19, 2023. fs.usda.gov/wildflowers/pol linators/pollinator-of-the-month/Bombus-affinis.shtml.

Xerces Society for Invertebrate Conservation. "Rusty Patched Bumble-bee: *Bombus affinis*." Accessed February 27, 2024. xerces.org/endan gered-species/species-profiles/at-risk-invertebrates/bumble-bees /rusty-patched-bumble-bee.

Wood Thrush: Semantics

American Bird Conservancy. "Wood Thrush." Accessed March 12, 2023. https://www.audubon.org/field-guide/bird/wood-thrush.

Cornell Lab of Ornithology. "Wood Thrush Sounds." Accessed March 12, 2023. https://www.allaboutbirds.org/guide/Wood_Thrush/sounds? gad_source=1&gclid=CjoKCQjw-r-vBhC-ARIsAGgUO2BYNB guxRE4j2EUunDnzE2o3ArPBqTva1VJpIYuKYcO7MKwWkk7rs 4aAm5NEALw_wcB#.

"Dancing with Birds." Directed by Huw Cordey, narrated by Stephen Fry. Silverback Films, 2019. Distributed by Netflix.

Neruda, Pablo. *Twenty Love Poems and a Song of Despair*. New York: Penguin Books, 1993.

Partners in Flight. "Wood Thrush." Accessed March 30, 2023. https:// partnersinflight.org/species/wood-thrush/wood-thrush-breeding -habitat/.

Simard, Suzanne. *Finding the Mother Tree: Discovering the Wisdom of the Forest*. New York: Alfred A. Knopf, 2021.

Seahorses: Remember Me

Fortin, N. J., et al. "Critical Role of the Hippocampus in Memory for Sequences of Events. *Nature Neuroscience* 5, no. 5 (2002): 458–62. doi:10.1038/nn834.

Fromm, Erich. *The Art of Loving*. New York: Harper, 1956.

Harvard Medical School. "How a Seahorse-Shaped Brain Structure May Help Us Recognize Others." *Science Daily*. Accessed May 18, 2023. www.sciencedaily.com/releases/2017/12/171208085313.htm.

Kumaravel, K., et al. "Seahorses—a Source of Traditional Medicine."
    Natural Product Research 26, no. 24 (2012): 2330–34. doi:10.1080/147
    86419.2012.662650.
Moser, May-Britt, et al. "Place Cells, Grid Cells, and Memory." *Cold
    Spring Harbor Perspectives in Biology* 7, no. 2 (February 2015): a021808.
    doi:10.1101/cshperspect.a021808.

Sea Lions: Play and Pleasure

NOAA Fisheries. "Mammal Health and Stranding Response Program."
    Accessed May 20, 2023. https://www.fisheries.noaa.gov/national/ma
    rine-life-distress/marine-mammal-health-and-stranding-response
    -program.
Odell, Jenny. *How to Do Nothing: Resisting the Attention Economy.* New
    York: Melville House, 2019.
Pacific Marine Mammal Center. "A Patient's Journey." Accessed October
    2023. https://www.pacificmmc.org/a-patients-journey.
Pacific Marine Mammal Center. "Education Programs." Accessed May
    20, 2023, https://www.pacificmmc.org/education-programs.
ScienceDirect. "California Sea Lion." Accessed May 18, 2023. https://
    www.sciencedirect.com/topics/agricultural-and-biological-sciences
    /california-sea-lion.

Red-Tailed Hawks: Local Cosmology

BirdLife International. "It's Official: Birds Are Literally Dinosaurs—
    Here's How We Know." December 21, 2021.
    birdlife.org/news/2021/12/21/its-official-birds-are-literally-dinosaurs
    -heres-how-we-know/.
Miller, Madeline. *Circe.* London: Bloomsbury, 2018.
Singer, Emily. "How Dinosaurs Shrank and Became Birds." *Scientific
    American*, August 21, 2014. scientificamerican.com/article/how-dino
    saurs-shrank-and-became-birds/.

PART FOUR: HOMING

Pigeons: Finding Home

Blasco, Ruth, et al. "The Earliest Pigeon Fanciers." *Scientific Reports* 4, no. 1 (2014): 5971. doi.org/10.1038/srep05971.

Monarch Butterflies: Genetic Memory

Douglas, Erin. "Feds Seek to Protect Rare Texas Plant in the Path of Border Wall Construction." *Texas Tribune*, February 18, 2022. texastribune .org/2022/02/18/texas-border-wall-milkweed.

Furnival, Sophie. "A Surprising Threat to Monarch Butterfly Survival—Tropical Milkweed." *Mongabay*, October 23, 2015. https://news .mongabay.com/2015/10/a-surprising-threat-to-monarch-butterfly -survival-tropical-milkweed/.

Isacson, Adam. "400 Miles of Harm: Nothing to Celebrate about Border Wall Construction." Washington Office on Latin America, October 29, 2020. https://www.wola.org/analysis/400-miles-of-harm-nothing -to-celebrate-about-border-wall-construction/.

Norris, Ned, Jr. "Stop the Destruction of Tohono O'odham Lands." *High Country News*. October 30, 2020. https://www.hcn.org/issues/52-12 /indigenous-affairs-borderlands-stop-the-destruction-of-tohono -oodham-lands/

Perret, Meg. "Monarchs Become a Powerful Symbol for Justice at the U.S./Mexico Border." *Mongabay*, March 31, 2023. news.mongabay .com/2023/03/monarch-butterflies-become-a-powerful-symbol-for -justice-at-the-u-s-mexico-border-commentary/.

Unesco World Heratige Convention, White River Junction, VT. "Monarch Butterfly Biosphere Reserve." Accessed February 27, 2024. https://whc.unesco.org/en/list/1290/.

U.S. Fish and Wildlife Service. "Endangered and Threatened Wildlife and Plants; Determination of Threatened Status for Prostrate Milkweed." *Federal Register* 87, no. 152 (2022): 40564–95.

Black Bears: Home Range

Powell, R. A., J. W. Zimmerman, and D. E. Seaman. *Ecology and Behaviour of North American Black Bears: Home Ranges, Habitat and Social Organization.* London: Chapman & Hall, 1996.

Rouse, Cecilia, et al. "Exclusionary Zoning: Its Effect on Racial Discrimination in the Housing Market." White House, June 17, 2021. whitehouse.gov/cea/written-materials/2021/06/17/exclusionary-zoning-its-effect-on-racial-discrimination-in-the-housing-market/.

Stitz, Markus. "Freedom to Roam in Scotland: Everything You Need to Know." Apidura. Accessed February 27, 2024. apidura.com/journal/freedom-to-roam-in-scotland-everything-you-need-to-know/.

Zeller, Katherine A., et al. "Black Bears Alter Movements in Response to Anthropogenic Features with Time of Day and Season." *Movement Ecology* 7, no. 19 (2019).

Red Fox: Domestication Syndrome

Bednarik, Robert G. "The Domestication of Humans." *Encyclopedia* 3, no. 3 (2023): 947–55. doi.org/10.3390/encyclopedia3030067.

Darwin Correspondence Project. "Letter from Charles Darwin to John Lubbock, 11 July 1868." darwinproject.ac.uk/letter/?docId=letters/DCP-LETT-5384.xml.

MacCaskill, Bridget. *The Blood Is Wild.* London: Jonathan Cape, 1995.

Wilkins, A. S., et al., "The 'Domestication Syndrome' in Mammals: A Unified Explanation Based on Neural Crest Cell Behavior and Genetics. *Genetics* 197, no. 3 (2014): 795–808. doi: 10.1534/genetics.114.165423. Erratum in *Genetics* 198, no. 4 (2014): 1771. doi.org/10.1534/genetics.114.171975.

Beavers: Engineering

Grinnell, George Bird. "The Lodges of the Blackfeet." *American Anthropologist* 3, no. 4 (1901): 650–68.

Hansen, Anne Larkin, Mike Severson, and Dennis L. Waterman. *A Landowner's Guide to Managing Your Woods: How to Maintain a Small Acreage for Long-Term Health, Biodiversity, and High-Quality Timber Production.* White River Junction, VT: Chelsea Green Publishing, 2011.

Massari, Paul. "Dammed if They Do: Beavers in Academia." Harvard Kenneth C. Griffin Graduate School of Arts and Sciences, October 11, 2021. https://gsas.harvard.edu/news/dammed-if-they-do.

Philip, Leila. *Beaverland: How One Weird Rodent Made America*. New York: Grand Central Publishing, 2022.

Sherriff, Lucy. "Beavers Return to Native American Tribes in Washington and California." *Guardian*, February 23, 2021. theguardian.com/environment/2021/feb/23/beavers-native-american-tribes-washington-california.

Humans: Animal Nature

Dunbar, Robin I. M. "The Social Brain Hypothesis and Its Implications for Social Evolution." *Annals of Human Biology* 36 (2009): 562–72.

Montes Franceschini, M. "Traditional Conceptions of the Legal Person and Nonhuman Animals." *Animals* 12, no. 19 (2022): 2590. doi:10.3390/ani12192590.

Spears, Dean. "The World's Population May Peak in Your Lifetime. What Happens Next?" *New York Times*, September 18, 2023. nytimes.com/interactive/2023/09/18/opinion/human-population-global-growth.html.

Wrangham, Richard. *Catching Fire: How Cooking Made Us Human*. New York: Basic Books, 2009.

Awakening Artemis

Deepening Intimacy with the Living Earth and Reclaiming Our Wild Nature

For those seeking to recognize the power and omnipresence of the natural world, *Awakening Artemis* is an intimate, unforgettable resource capturing one woman's journey to reckon with her traumas that opens up a world of potential growth and remedy for us all. Using storytelling from her own life, Vanessa Chakour connects plants and their characteristics to issues we all grapple to heal from and even to understand.

life